Economic Reforms, Human Welfare and Sustainable Development in India

Economic Reforms, Human Welfare and Sustainable Development in India

Edited by

Narayan C Nayak
Kishor Goswami
Bani Chatterjee

Department of Humanities and Social Sciences
Indian Institute of Technology (IIT)
Kharagpur

in association with

New Century Publications
New Delhi, India

NEW CENTURY PUBLICATIONS
4800/24, Bharat Ram Road,
Ansari Road, Daryaganj,
New Delhi-110 002

Tel.: 23247798, 65396605
Telefax: 011- 41017798
E-mail: indiatax@vsnl.com
www.newcenturypublications.com

Editorial office:
34, Gujranwala Town, Part-2,
Delhi - 110 009
Tel.: 27247805, 27464774

First Published - June 2007

ISBN: 81-7708-146-2 (*10 digit*)
978-81-7708-146-6 (*13 digit*)

Published by New Century Publications and printed at Singhal Print Media, New Delhi -110 005

PRINTED IN INDIA

THE BOOK

Since the introduction of economic reforms in India in early 1990s, the major thrust of the country has been to achieve faster economic growth, higher export earnings, greater foreign exchange reserves, and enhanced foreign direct investment. Enormous efforts have been directed towards achieving the desired goals in all these macro-economic parameters.

While it is heartening to note the accomplishments at the macro-economic front, it is equally disturbing to note that the enhanced rate of economic growth has failed to address certain issues of vital importance. These issues and concerns include, *inter alia,* the dynamics of labour market, progress of the agriculture sector, gender equality, caste representations, cultural development and environmental protection.

Given the above, the present book, containing 16 articles authored by experts in the field, attempts to make a critical scrutiny of various strategic aspects of India's development efforts during the post-reforms period. The book is divided into three broad theme parts: (i) economic reforms and social sectors, (ii) women, labour and socio-cultural perspectives and (iii) management of natural resources and environmental protection.

The book will commend itself to academicians, researchers, policy makers, social activists, and students of economics, commerce and business management. It will also prove useful for all those who want to understand the nature and impact of economic reforms in India.

EDITORS' PROFILE

Narayan C Nayak is Associate Professor of Economics in the Department of Humanities and Social Sciences, Indian Institute of Technology, Kharagpur. He works in the field of Social Sector Development, Rural and Agricultural Economics, and Foreign Direct Investment.

Kishor Goswami is Assistant Professor of Economics in the Department of Humanities and Social Sciences, Indian Institute of Technology, Kharagpur. His areas of interest include Agricultural Economics, Food Security, Poverty, Gender Studies and Finance.

Bani Chatterjee is Professor of Economics and Head, Department of Humanities and Social Sciences, Indian Institute of Technology, Kharagpur. Her areas of research include Development Economics, Environmental Economics, Manpower Management and International Finance.

EDITORS' NOTE ON THE BOOK

Ever since the introduction of economic reforms in India, enormous efforts have been made to give reforms a human face. There has always been a concern to know whether development is becoming all pervasive transcending beyond the boundary of economic orthodoxy. A few well pertinent questions are often asked and analyzed in various circles including policy makers, researchers and governments. Does economic growth ensure equality? Does economic growth take care of poverty? Does social sector get enough attention? Are cultural perspectives addressed adequately? Does development ensure a sustainable environment?

Since the introduction of economic reforms in India in early 1990s, the major thrust of the country has been to achieve faster economic growth, higher export earnings, greater foreign exchange reserves, and more foreign direct investment and so on. Enormous efforts have been directed towards achieving desired success in all these macro-economic parameters.

While it is heartening to see successes at the macro-economic front, it is equally disturbing to face conspicuous failures in certain other aspects of vital importance. To illustrate a few, even after more than five decades of planned development, more than a quarter of the total population of the country remains under abject poverty (28.6 percent).

While the preceding discussions point to India's socio-economic characters at large, it may be worthwhile to mention here that given the extremely heterogeneous character of the Indian economy and society, India's achievements and failure may not be understood in composite terms. Rather, it is essential to examine the experiences in sufficiently disaggregative form and in adequate detail. India today remains a country of stark contrasts and striking disparities. Some districts and states perform so well that they are comparable even with the leading industrialized countries of the world, while there are some other regions, which even remain below the average of the poorest nations of the world.

While there has been serious concern and effort to ameliorate inadequacies in social sector development, there are other vital issues that have created worldwide debates and discussions including India. Amongst them, the most pertinent issue is the sustainability of our environment. While there is no denying the fact that growth of income is inevitable, no country can afford to ignore or pay scant attention to the sustainable use of our natural resources. While maximizing current human welfare, it is essential to honour natural resource constraint for the sustainability of the humanity. It is interesting to note that in India, where more than two third of the population lives in rural areas and are solely dependent upon agriculture, fishing, forestry and like, are faced with increasing degradation of the natural resource base. The overexploitation of the natural resources is believed to have resulted due to the absence of adequate and meaningful collective action or the persistence of abject poverty. On the contrary, it may also be attributed to the growth of income and concomitant consumption requirements, which are wasteful and unnecessary.

There is thus, a need for a type of development which would make the society not only materially sufficient but also environmentally sustainable and socially equitable. The management of natural resources through collective action and proper rules and regulations may act as a catalyst in finding remedies.

Other important facets of development *inter alia* are the dynamics of labour market, gender issues, caste representations, and cultural perspectives that may require special attention as they determine the social harmony, cohesion and sustainable social environment. In the first place, it is imperative to know the attributes of the labour market with regard to its composition, level of protection, the magnitude and types of migration and the like.

Further, in the neo-liberalized Indian economy, the status and role of women in the society appears to be decidedly mixed. On one hand, the gender stereotypes are getting redefined under the present structure of socio-cultural milieu; while on the other, women still remain an underprivileged class of people devoid of equal opportunities in various walks of life. To illustrate a few, the literacy rate amongst women in India is low and far below than men. There is greater dropout rate among girls and the enrolment of girls has declined in the ladder of successive education. Women's representation in organized employment market is also far from satisfactory.

Given the above backdrop, the present volume attempts to make a critical scrutiny of certain important facets of development in India, particularly in the post-reforms period. It aims to analyze whether development in India has been all pervasive signifying thereby that whether the crucial dimensions like education, health, gender equality, regional disparity, child labour, environmental sustainability, cultural perspectives, etc have been well taken care of in our endeavour towards attaining rapid economic development. Accordingly, this book presents a collection of papers thematically designed to cover almost all the above facets of development in a systematic way. While the papers individually focus on the issues that are independent of one another, they together form a common thread across various facets so that the development perspectives are understood as collective and interwoven dynamics.

The book is divided in three broad parts:

- Economic Reforms and Social Sectors;
- Women, Labour and Socio-cultural Perspectives; and
- Management of Natural Resources and Environmental Protection.

It may be mentioned here that these themes are not mutually exclusive. Rather, they provide a continuum of facts, observations and ideas on certain vital aspects of development in India. In doing so, while the issues centre round the broad themes as mentioned above, the studies have attempted to focus on India and its constituent parts on one hand and relative disparities across gender, castes and regions on the other.

***Part I - Economic Reforms and Social Sectors*:** As mentioned in the preceding section, development must be holistic that encompasses not only advancement in economic parameters but also noteworthy achievements in health, education, gender equality and empowerment, environmental sustainability, labour conditions, regional equality, etc. Amongst all, social sector development assumes the centre stage and is an integral part of the development process. It primarily includes education, health, and food and nutrition security.

It is, however, disturbing to note that the reforms process – both internal liberalization and privatization programmes, as well as globalization - as in force since 1991, does not seem to have benefited the poor and the underprivileged class of people in Indian society. The approach towards integrating social sector development with economic growth seems to be a mismatch. Consequently, desired targets have not been achieved in either of the dimensions. Analyzing the problems and identifying the key factors responsible for the same may thus provide some insight to this vital issue in the context of India.

Towards meeting this goal, chapter 1, authored by **Bhagabata Patro, Sarit Kumar Rout and Nilachala Acharya,** throws light on the extent and magnitude of inequalities that the non-special category states are faced with, regarding their performance in human development. The authors find wide differences in the achievements of various human development indicators across these states. States like Kerala, Gujarat, Maharashtra, Punjab and Haryana have achieved much faster progress than Orissa, Bihar, Madhya Pradesh, Rajasthan and Uttar Pradesh. Particularly, states like Orissa and Bihar lag far behind.

Chapter 2 authored by **Arabinda Mishra and Gopal Krishna Sarangi** examines the hypothesis in the wake of changes in sector-specific non-plan revenue expenditures of the Indian states during the reforms period as compared to their pre-reform spending. The study covers the period from 1980 to 2000 and identifies the reforms period specific to three groups of states (HIG, MIG and LIG) as well as the individual states from each group (Maharashtra, Karnataka and Orissa).

In line with the above, **Bimal K. Mohanty** attempts to ascertain whether growth causes social sector development proxied by expenditure on social services, or the latter causes the former. This state-specific study in chapter 3 proves that the structural reform measures on the one hand and increase in GSDP on the other have not been successful in displacing public expenditure on social services to a desirable extent to elevate the human development status of Orissa. The author maintains that over the last twenty-year period, Orissa has not shifted its position and remains almost stagnated at being a low human development state of the country.

In another study on Orissa in chapter 4, authors **Minati Mallick and Jagannath Lenka** reveal that according to UNDP standard, Orissa is treated as a low human development state. At the disaggregate level, none of the districts has yet attained the stage of high human development. The authors thus have made a deviation from the established norm of measuring the level of human development and categorized human development into high HDI as above 0.6, medium as between 0.4 and 0.6 and low as below 0.4. This deviation is in consonance with the need to measure the relative disparity across the districts.

Given the above backdrop, chapter 5 authored by **Himanshu Sekhar Rout** aims to find out the impact of household income and education of the head of the household on the pattern of health care expenditure based on primary data collected from four districts of Orissa during October, 1999. The author finds that *ceteris paribus* a rupee increase in household income brings eighty-two paise increase in household health care expenditure and if in addition, household's head is educated, the household health care expenditure increases by seven percent. This clearly indicates that there is a need for a concerted effort to take care of income and education level of the individuals. It may, however, be noted here that spending more on health services alone may not necessarily buy better health. It needs an efficient management and use of resources.

Needless to say, India is far behind the goal despite all the efforts made so far as pointed out by **Narayan C Nayak and Debabrata Samanta**. They argue in chapter 6 that higher income growth is not yet translated into greater educational attainment even at the primary level. India is lagging far behind many other developing countries in this regard. The other very disturbing aspect is that the gender disparity is more buoyant in India. India records one of the highest female-male literacy gaps in the world. Only 5 countries namely, Bhutan, Syria, Togo, Malawi, and Mozambique, have higher gaps than India. The state of Rajasthan alone has a population as large as that of all the five countries combined and no country in the world has a higher female-male literacy gap than Rajasthan, where the literacy rate for women is a mere 5 percent . The female-male literacy gap has widened over the decades from 1951 to 2001. Added to this, at the elementary level of education, the girls' enrollment ratio is very low. There also remains disparity in the attainment of literacy across states and union territories. Coupled with that, the gender disparity in this respect is more buoyant with those states which are already poor and have performed very badly in attaining overall literacy.

Part II - Women, Labour and Socio-cultural Perspectives: Development is required to be understood from various perspectives. Development may be associated with economic growth without compromising with key social sector parameters like health and education. Nevertheless, development efforts will be self-defeating if they do not go in conformity with the prevalence of social order and socio-cultural milieu. To be precise, development becomes sustainable *inter alia* if women are given equal share in all walks of life vis-à-vis men; socio-cultural perspectives, attempting to ensure an "overall social wellbeing", are respected; characteristics of labour is well defined within the boundary of set rules and regulations of a welfare government; and so on. This part is an attempt to address some of them in their own perspectives.

Venturing into gender equality alone, we are confronted with a host of issues that need our attention. Needless to say, gender equality needs to be pursued in all walks of life including health, education, human rights, socio-cultural status, etc. Taking the aspect of education only, in chapter 7, **Sharmita Dhar, Narayan C Nayak and Bani Chatterjee** attempt to analyze how women are represented in the hierarchical distribution of education in Indian scenario. The authors bring home the fact that women lag behind men in all aspects of educational attainment. According to them, although the period 1991-2001 has registered some increase in both absolute literacy and relative literacy rates, no state has yet attained full literacy and perfect equality.

It is also felt that gender equality may ensure gender empowerment. In order to achieve that it is essential that women are given equal opportunities in all economic pursuits including employment, ownership of firms and so on. **Kishor Goswami** attempts to address this vital issue in chapter 8 while analyzing the level of participation of women in decision-making taking a case of silk trade in Sualkuchi of Assam. According to the author, greater women's participation in decision-making *inter alia* may be considered as increased women's empowerment. His study finds that there is an increase in women's participation in decision-making process over the period of study. The increase pronounced in household related activities, financial matters, children's education, healthcare, purchase of assets, day to day activities, and weaving related activities. However, the rate of increase is relatively high only amongst the women involved in silk trade. The overall gender empowerment index is recorded to be 0.63. The author feels that if women are given better economic opportunities, greater empowerment can be guaranteed to them.

In India, besides education and employment, there are many other contentious issues where gender inequality continues to exist. It is viewed that women are underrepresented, suppressed and are denied their humanistic rights more particularly in the cultural context. Making a probe into persisting gender inequality in India, **Kumar Das and Banishree Das,** in chapter 9, assert that the current and past researchers blinded by populist sympathy for the poor often overlook the social and cultural dynamics which endorses the gender relations of inequality. According to them, economic prosperity does not necessarily imply a healthier unisex society. Higher education, reservations of seats and jobs for women do not necessarily ensure gender equality. Higher family cohesiveness or lesser degree of divorce does not imply gender fairness either. The authors argue that it is not possible or necessary to undergo gender vertigo to arrive at a transformation of the gender relations and it is also not necessary to imitate the western route either. What is most essential is to create an awareness building that would ensure women liberation by a slow and steady process of social transformation.

On similar footing, **Meera Panigrahi and Sudhakar Panda** in the next chapter (chapter 10) attempt to suggest that growth strategies, whether it is planned growth in a command economy backed by coercion, or profit-driven growth in a market economy, it should have multi-dimensional orientations inclusive of a socio-cultural perspective. Their paper examines the impact of the development strategies in centrally planned economies and free market economies on social well-being, human welfare and above all on humanistic culture. An attempt is made to suggest a path of development consistent with culture and humanism. They advocate for a human approach to development and a middle path to progress.

Chapter 11 authored by **Saundarjya Borbora and Arghya Mukherjee** aims to analyse the magnitude of child labour in India focusing on some important dimensions like rural-urban, gender differences and the regional variation across major Indian states. The paper makes an attempt to look at the determinants of child labour in the country on the basis of some quantitative variables, although some qualitative variables may have been equally important. The authors identify high school dropouts, low literacy rate, low SDP per capita and high poverty as the significant factors that promote child labour in India. The authors put forward the view that a multi pronged strategy is necessary for reduction of child labour and the members of the civil society have to play an active role in containing the growth of child labour.

Another important dimension of labor that has been a matter of concern is the exodus of people from rural to urban areas. In the next chapter (chapter 12), the author **Mihir Kumar Mahapatra** maintains that in the absence of adequate provision for development of human entity and opportunities to grow, migration of workers from a backward region to the developed one along with the emergence of 'jobless growth' has become an inevitable outcome. The author studies the situation of persistent regional disparity and emergence of 'jobless growth' in his attempt to analyze the pattern of migration in Karnataka. Among the economic factors considered to examine the rationale of migration to cities of Karnataka, 'employment' is assigned adequate importance. The pattern of migration between the regions provides interesting observations. The people are relatively more mobile in the developed southern region as compared to its underdeveloped northern region, though 'push factor' plays a role in the process of migration. In addition, inter-district migration is confined to the region itself and not from underdeveloped to developed ones or vice-versa. Besides, inter-censal inter-district net migration indicates that flow of migration is towards Bangalore and majorities of the out-migrants are from some of the districts of the southern region.

Part III - Management of Natural Resources and Environmental Protection: Development must ensure sustainable use of natural resources. Sustainability implies that while attempting to meet the needs of the present generation we must optimize the use and conservation of natural resources so that the future generations can avail of resources for maintaining their livelihood. Management of natural resources thus remains at the core. This section tries to deal with that from various perspectives.

Who should then manage natural resources? Over the last two decades, there has been apparent change in policy from the traditional state-managed top-down approach to the community level approach which is basically fueled by the recognition of the limits of government agencies in managing resources at the local level. International and national donor agencies are heavily involved in promoting these policy reforms believing that community management can ensure twin objectives: (i) improved livelihood; and (ii) better conservation of natural resources. Though related, the first reason predominates in development parlance and the second in conservationist stance. The power to local communities has been strengthened either through power-sharing arrangements with the state, more legal access to natural resources, or decentralization within government institutions that ensure more power to local communities.

In this context, **Damodar Suar, Himadri Sinha and Laxmi Bilash Hota** attempt to address how natural resources can be best managed and conserved. In chapter 13, they argue that improvement in eco-efficiency remains at the centre. Their study while discussing how natural resources can be used and conserved for sustainable development of the disadvantaged people e.g. poor, scheduled castes, scheduled tribes, and women, suggests that the improvement in eco-efficiency calls for mutually reinforcing cooperation and principles in society, institution, technology, and network. Society brings in 'sufficiency' while justifying nature, conditions and volume of social needs to be fulfilled. Institution refers to organizational arrangements in fulfilling the needs and thereby improving the 'effectiveness'. Technology ensures 'efficiency' while providing the means to fulfilling the needs. Finally, network acts as a 'catalyst' that indicates functional relationship with institutions which helps acquire knowledge and support. The authors point out that realization of these derived principles can further the conservation of land, water and forest resources and ensure the sustainable development of the disadvantaged.

Given the above backdrop, in chapter 14, **Bhagirath Behera** attempts to analyze and examine the use of JFM forests by the participant households for collection of firewood and livestock grazing, and identifies the determinants of distribution of benefits among different sections. The study is based on data collected from sample households within JFM communities of Andhra Pradesh.

The solid waste management truly becomes an issue of immediate concern particularly in the economies which are getting increasingly urbanized. India is no exception to it, where urbanization is taking place with leaps and bounds and consequently, unmanaged urban solid waste continues to pose a serious threat to public health and the quality of life for urban people, especially for socially and economically weaker sections of the society. In this backdrop, **C. S. Shylajan and Souvik Bhattacharjya** discuss the problem of solid waste and environmental policies related to waste management in India and major environmental policy instruments which have been in practice internationally for solid waste management (chapter 15). This paper alludes to various instances of successful use of economic instruments and incentives for effective solid waste management.

On the basis of the EKC hypothesis, **Trupti Mishra and Bani Chatterjee** in the last chapter (Chapter 16) attempt to examine the relationship between economic development and environmental degradation in Indian economy. The study estimates fixed and random effects of the panel data of 20 major Indian states for the period 1995-2005. The study uses per capita SDP as the representative variable for economic development. Three major water pollutants namely, BOD, COD and TSS for both industrial and residential locations are considered as the representatives of environmental degradation. The authors find that economic growth generates environmental pressure and there exists an inverted U-shape relationship between environmental pressure measured in terms of COD and TSS for industrial locations only. However, the other measure of environmental degradation shows a weak inverted N-shape relationship with economic growth.

In all, the book is an attempt to bring various facets of development to a unified whole. This enables us to judge the development from all perspectives differently yet in unison.

The book is an attempt to address some of these pertinent

issues in a wholesome way. The editors of the book are convinced that in order to address the various development perspectives, it is imperative to integrate them with adequate vigour. The editors owe a lot to the contributors to this volume for their academic rigour and commitment to this vital issue.

The book sees the light of the day for the support, inspiration and academic inputs that the editors have received from a host of persons from its inception till date. To name a few, our special thanks goes to Professor Sudhakar Panda, visiting professor, Department of Humanities and Social Sciences, IIT, Kharagpur for reviewing some of the papers and providing invaluable suggestions from time to time.

Mr. Falguni Pattanaik, research Scholar in the Department, has helped immensely in course of our editing. He deserves a special applause. Editors are also grateful to Dr. Bhagirath Behera, Assistant Professor, Department of Humanities and Social Sciences, IIT, Kharagpur, for his editorial guidance and valuable suggestions.

The editors keep on record the constant support and guidance that they have received from their colleagues, staff and students from within and outside the Department.

Indian Institute of Technology,
Kharagpur

Narayan C Nayak
Kishor Goswami
Bani Chatterjee

June 12, 2007

LIST OF CONTRIBUTORS

Arabinda Mishra	Associate Professor Department of Natural Resources, TERI School of Advanced Studies, New Delhi.
Arghya Mukherjee	Research Scholar, Department of Humanities and Social Sciences, Indian Institute of Technology, Guwahati.
Bani Chatterjee	Dean (Continuing Education) and Professor and Head, Department of Humanities and Social Sciences, Indian Institute of Technology, Kharagpur.
Banishree Das	Research Scholar, Asian Institute of Technology Bangkok.
Bhagabata Patro	Reader in Economics, P.G. Department of Economics, Berhampur University, Ganjam, Orissa.
Bhagirath Behera	Assistant Professor, Department of Humanities and Social Sciences, Indian Institute of Technology, Kharagpur
Bimal K. Mohanty	Reader in Economics, Ravenshaw College, Cuttack.
C. S. Shylajan	Centre for Development and Environment Policy, Indian Institute of Management, Calcutta.
Damodar Suar	Professor, Department of Humanities and Social Sciences, Indian Institute of Technology, Kharagpur.

Debabrata Samanta	Research Scholar, Department of Humanities and Social Sciences, Indian Institute of Technology, Kharagpur.
Gopal Krishna Sarangi	Research Scholar, Centre for Multi-Disciplinary Development Research, Dharwad.
Himadri Sinha	Professor, Department of Research, Xavier Institute of Social Service, Ranchi.
Himanshu Sekhar Rout	Lecturer in Economics, Dr. SRK Government Arts College, Yanam, Pudducherry.
Jagannath Lenka	Reader in Economics, North Orissa University, Baripada.
Kishor Goswami	Assistant Professor, Department of Humanities and Social Sciences, Indian Institute of Technology, Kharagpur.
Kumar Das	Professor, Department of Analytical and Applied Economics, Utkal University, Bhubaneswar.
Laxmi Bilash Hota	Research Scholar, Department of Humanities and Social Sciences, Indian Institute of Technology, Kharagpur.
Meera Panigrahi	Reader in English, Rama Devi Women's College, Bhubaneswar.
Mihir Kumar Mahapatra	Assistant Professor in Economics, Goa Institute of Management, Ribandar, Goa.

Minati Mallick	Lecturer in Economics, North Orissa University, Baripada.
Narayan C Nayak	Associate Professor, Department of Humanities and Social Sciences, Indian Institute of Technology, Kharagpur.
Nilachala Acharya	Research Scholar, P.G. Department of Economics, Berhampur University, Ganjam, Orissa.
Sarit Kumar Rout	Fellow, Health and Population Innovation, Population Council, New Delhi.
Saundarjya Borbora	Associate Professor, Department of Humanities and Social Sciences, Indian Institute of Technology, Guwahati.
Sharmita Dhar	Research Scholar, Department of Humanities and Social Sciences, Indian Institute of Technology, Kharagpur.
Souvik Bhattacharjya	Centre for Development and Environment Policy, Indian Institute of Management, Calcutta.
Sudhakar Panda	Visiting Faculty, Department of Humanities and Social Sciences, Indian Institute of Technology, Kharagpur.
Trupti Mishra	Assistant Professor, Department of Humanities and Social Sciences, Indian Institute of Technology, Kharagpur.

CONTENTS

Part I: Economic Reforms and Social Sectors

1

Development Index of Non-special Category States of India

Bhagabata Patro, Sarit Kumar Rout and Nilachala Acharya

Introduction

Rising inequality in the process of development has been a major challenge to the development economists since long. This phenomenon has both national and international dimensions. Conventionally, inequality is measured with the help of income criterion, i.e. specifying a minimum level of income below which a person is designated as `Below Poverty Line'. As the value of money keeps on declining over the years, this minimum income required for a pre-determined level of living is revised at regular intervals. Poverty measurement with the help of per capita income has many limitations. Particularly, money income may not reveal the true picture for international comparisons. Some oil-rich countries have high per capita income, yet they are not regarded as developed if we apply some objective criteria of development.

Alternative criteria of understanding inequality do not have, however, unique acceptability. Level of industrialization (Thirlwall, 2003) and imbalance between factors of production and factor under-utilization (Furtado, 1964) are two other measures to compare unequal development between regions.

Human Development Index (HDI), a concept of recent origin, has been widely used to measure the index of development and infer on the nature of inequality. The United Nations Development Programme defines human development as a 'process of enlarging people's choices' (UNDP, 2001). In addition to per capita income, HDI includes other social indicators like life expectancy at birth and educational attainment. An attempt has also been made to measure Human Poverty Index (HPI) to understand the state of deprivation in an economy. The HPI is calculated by taking into account the percentage of population not expected to survive up to the age of 40 years (P_1), the adult literacy rate (P_2) and a deprivation index (P_3). Formula for HPI is equal to $[1/3\ (p_1^3+p_2^3+p_3^3)]^{1/3}$. As per Human Development Report, 2004, India ranks 127th in the HDI and 48th in the HPI (UNDP, 2004).

More recently, an alternative measure of welfare was developed which is known as 'Basic Welfare Index (BWI). This index has three components i.e. education, health and nutrition. The index is constructed by using nine indicators selected from all these three components (Dholakia and Dholakia, 2004).

Scope and Methodology

Keeping in view the importance of HDI as mentioned in the preceding section, this paper makes an attempt to analyse the role of development spending in influencing human development index of the non-special category states of India. In India, government allocates huge amount of resources for the welfare of masses through budget allocation. The outcome of public spending in improving the human welfare depends upon a number of variables like functioning of different institutions, the participation of community in development programmes, the mechanism of transparency and accountability practiced by public institutions and the role of civil society organizations. It is always a gigantic task to define and examine the role of these sets of variables.

The study is confined to measure the inequality of development among the states (non-special category) in India. There is wide difference in the achievements of various human development indicators among various states of the country. States like Kerala, Gujarat, Maharashtra, Punjab and Haryana have progressed much faster than Orissa, Bihar, Madhya Pradesh,

Rajasthan and Uttar Pradesh (excluding Orissa the other states are popularly known as BIMARU states). Particularly, states like Orissa and Bihar lag far behind others in many of these indicators in spite of decades of planning and flow of large amount of resources (Economic Survey, GOI, 2004-05).

By using elementary statistical tools, this paper attempts to connect the development spending of the states with their HDI figures. For analytical purposes, the states are categorized into three groups: (a) Maharashtra, Punjab, Gujarat and Haryana as high-income states; (b) Kerala, Tamil Nadu, Karnataka, Andhra Pradesh and West Bengal as middle-income states; and (c) Orissa, Bihar, Madhya Pradesh, Rajasthan and Uttar Pradesh as low-income states. The development of these three categories of states is analyzed and compared over a period of 11 years i.e. from 1991-92 to 2001-02.

Pattern of Development Spending

The public expenditure of a state is made on the items of (i) general services, (ii) social services, and (iii) economic services. The general services include general administration, police, home, interest payments and meeting the pension liabilities of the government. The social services include education, sports, art and culture, health, water supply and sanitation, welfare of scheduled castes and scheduled tribes, etc. The economic services cover agriculture and allied activities, irrigation and power, rural development etc. The expenditure on social services and economic services constitute developmental spending, and that on general services constitute non-developmental spending. The spending on social and economic services is considered to be developmental because the social services enhance the capability of human beings to lead healthy and decent lives. Moreover, the investment on primary education and health directly benefits the poor. Similarly, the expenditure on economic services increases the productive capacity of an economy by providing people with livelihood opportunities and in turn helping to raise their incomes as well as the income of the state.

As it is evident from Table 1.1, in India, the development spending has increased significantly in many States. In absolute terms, development spending has gone up by more than two times for the states like Gujarat, Haryana, West Bengal, Karnataka, Andhra Pradesh, Bihar and Madhya Pradesh. It is between one and two times for Maharashtra, Kerala, Orissa, Uttar Pradesh and Rajasthan. The rise is less than 100 per cent for Punjab and Tamil Nadu. The average rise of development spending per annum is the highest for West Bengal followed by Andhra Pradesh, whereas it is the lowest in Punjab. Orissa is in the middle with average growth of around 13 per cent. The average share of development spending in the pre- and post-reforms period has been presented in Table 1.2.

High Income States

It is interesting to observe that the share of development spending has started declining in case of most of the states during the later part of nineties. Among the advanced states, there exist wide fluctuations in the share of allocation towards development purposes. In 1991-92, the share of development spending of Punjab was 77 per cent of its total spending, which came down to 44 per cent in 2001-02. During the initial five years of reforms i.e. from 1991-92 to 1995-96, the average share of development spending of Punjab was 57 per cent and it has declined to 48 per cent in the next phase of reforms i.e. from 1996-97 to 2001-02 (Table 1.2). In case of Maharashtra, the decline started after 1996-97. In the initial years of reforms, the average share of development spending was 71 per cent, which fell down to 63 per cent during the period 1996-97 to 2001-02 (Table 1.2).

The pattern of development spending is consistent in case of Gujarat, which, on an average, is 71 per cent of total spending. Among fourteen states, Gujarat allocates the highest percentage of total resources for development purposes. It is also evident that in Punjab, there is wider fluctuation in the share of development spending. Haryana allocates 60 per cent of its total spending for development purposes with no variation in the average figures for the two phases.

Table 1.1: Development Spending of Non-Special Category States of India (Rs. crore)

Sl. No	State	1991-92	2001-02	Increment Col.4 – Col.3	% rise (Col.5/Col.3)100	Average growth Col.6/11
1	2	3	4	5	6	7
1.	Punjab	3,879	6,981	3,102	80	7.3
2.	Gujarat	5,139	17,355	12,217	237	21.5
3.	Maharashtra	8,408	24,561	16,153	192	17.5
4.	Haryana	1,852	6,814	4,962	268	24.4
5.	W.B.	3,939	14,953	11,014	280	25.5
6.	Tamil Nadu	7,422	14,082	6,660	90	8.2
7.	Karnataka	4,505	14,352	9,847	218	19.8
8.	A.P.	5,409	20,280	14,871	275	25.0
9.	Kerala	2,422	6,673	4,251	176	16.0
10.	Orissa	2,473	5,958	3,485	141	12.8
11.	Bihar	4,391	13,747	9,356	213	19.4
12.	M.P.	4,723	14,555	9,832	208	18.9
13.	U.P.	8,388	21,020	12,632	151	13.7
14.	Rajasthan	4,141	10,919	6,778	164	14.9

Source: Compiled from Handbook of Statistics on State Government Finances, RBI, Mumbai, 2004

Table 1.2: Average Share of Development Spending to Total Spending for Non-special Category States of India

	Average 1991-92 to 1995-96	Average 1996-97 to 2001-02
High Income		
Maharashtra	70.86	63.11
Punjab	57.31	48.24
Gujarat	72.27	70.40
Haryana	59.67	59.20
Middle Income		
Andhra Pradesh	71.38	66.76
Karnataka	71.01	66.59
Kerala	61.71	58.64
Tamil Nadu	71.34	61.35
West Bengal	63.31	59.51
Low Income		
Bihar *	61.61	58.50
Madhya Pradesh *	69.82	65.70
Orissa	66.72	59.14
Rajasthan	68.24	61.28
Uttar Pradesh *	59.05	54.02

* Refers to the undivided Bihar, Madhya Pradesh and Uttar Pradesh
Source: Compiled from Handbook of Statistics on State Government Finances, RBI, 2004,

Middle Income States

The middle-income states like Andhra Pradesh, Karnataka, and Tamil Nadu spend around 71 per cent of total resources on development head. Table 1.2 reflects clearly that there is a decline in the allocation towards development head for all the middle-income states in the second half of reforms.

In the case of Andhra Pradesh, the allocation for development head remained more or less stable up to 1997-98 after which it started declining. Similarly, in case of Kerala, there was consistency up to 1998-99 and after which it started declining. In

West Bengal, there was consistency in the allocation of resources up to 1996-97 and after which the deceleration started. A higher fluctuation was noticed in case of Tamil Nadu with average development spending reduced to 61 per cent in the second phase from a high of 71 per cent in the first phase.

Low Income States

Among the low-income states, Madhya Pradesh allocates a higher proportion of total resources for development purposes followed by Rajasthan, Orissa, Bihar and Uttar Pradesh. A declining trend is observed in the share of development spending of each state. In case of Orissa, the share of development spending declined substantially from 68 per cent of total expenditure in 1991-92 to 49 per cent in 2001-02. In the first five years of reforms, the average share of development spending was 67 per cent of total spending, which declined to 59 per cent in the next six years (Table 1.2).

Among BIMARU states, Madhya Pradesh and Rajasthan paid more attention for improving the human development. Madhya Pradesh allocated, on an average, 70 per cent of total resources for economic and social services in the first five years of reform and there was consistency in allocation of resources during 1991-92 to 1995-96. For the next six years, the average share of development spending reached 66 per cent of total state spending. Rajasthan allocated around 68 per cent of total resources for developmental heads in the first phase and it decreased to 61 per cent in the second phase. Uttar Pradesh spent the least among the low-income states and its average share was 56 per cent only. Bihar allocated a little higher share for developmental heads in comparison to Uttar Pradesh and it was around 60 per cent during the period under study.

The low-income states should have spent a larger share of budgetary resources for human development i.e. on social and economic services. However, it is found that in these states, around 40 per cent of total budgetary allocation is spent on general services, which include administration, interest payment, and pension liability. The middle-income states comparatively spend less on general services and their average spending is 34 per cent during 1991-92 to 2001-02. Similarly, the high-income states together allocate 35 per cent of total expenditure for general services. In case of low income states, the administrative expenditure, pension and interest liability is mounting over the years.

The analysis of share of development spending for different categories of states indicates that low- and middle-income states in general have better and consistent allocation towards developmental spending. For all the states, the average share for the second phase (1996-97 to 2001-02) shows a declining trend. This implies that in the post-reform period, development spending is reduced which is contrary to the objective of economic reforms in the country. Among high-income states, the average share for Haryana is low due to substantial flow of resources towards payment of state lotteries in 1994-95. In case of Punjab, the reduced share is due to heavy repayment burden of the central loans.

Real Per Capita Development Spending

Analysis of real per capita development spending takes care of rise in population of the states. Among fourteen major states, the average real per capita development spending of Gujarat is the highest and it is the lowest for Bihar. While Gujarat spends, on an average, Rs. 1,710 per capita during the eleven years of our analysis, Bihar spends a mere Rs. 561 during the same period, which is less than one third of the former. Among the middle-income states, the average per capita development spending of Tamil Nadu is the highest (Rs. 1,367) and it ranks fifth in India (Table 1.3).

Rajasthan, a low-income category state, spends more in per capita terms than West Bengal, which is a middle-income category state. The rank of West Bengal is 12th whereas it is 9th for Rajasthan. There are four states viz. Uttar Pradesh, West Bengal, Bihar and Madhya Pradesh whose real per capita development spending is less than Orissa. All the middle-income states except West Bengal spend well in real per capita terms over the years.

Table 1.3: Annual Average Growth Rate of Real Per Capita Development Spending of Selected States

State	Average real per capita DP (Rs.)	Rank	Annual Average growth rate	Rank
Andhra Pradesh	1255.49	7	5.09	4
Bihar*	560.93	14	2.13	10
Gujarat	1710.49	1	5.81	2
Haryana	1528.16	3	5.35	3
Karnataka	1335.13	6	3.64	6
Kerala	1267.52	8	4.71	5
Maharashtra	1478.22	4	2.59	7
Madhya Pradesh*	912.98	11	2.31	8
Orissa	962.06	10	2.27	9
Punjab	1577.50	2	0.69	12
Rajasthan	1126.22	9	1.24	11
Tamil Nadu	1367.56	5	0.64	13
Uttar Pradesh*	694.58	13	0.51	14
West Bengal	881.87	12	7.04	1

DP = Development Spending.

* Relates to undivided Bihar, Madhya Pradesh and Uttar Pradesh.

Source: Compiled from Handbook of Statistics on State Government Finances, RBI, 2004.

The annual growth rate of real per capita development spending of various states reveals many interesting features (Table 1.3). For West Bengal, it is 7.04 per cent, which is the highest among all the states even though in absolute figures it is well below among other middle income states. Contrarily, the growth rate for Uttar Pradesh is 0.51 per cent, which is the lowest among all the states of the country. There are only four states viz. West Bengal, Gujarat, Andhra Pradesh and Haryana, whose annual growth rate of real per capita development spending is more than 5 per cent. For rest of the states, it varies between 2 to3 per cent except Kerala where it is 4.71 per cent and its position is 5th among all the states. Among the middle-income states, Andhra Pradesh, with a growth rate of 5.09 per cent, ranks 4th at the all India level. There are three states viz. Tamil Nadu, Punjab and Uttar Pradesh whose per capita growth rate is less than one per cent. For Punjab, the growth rate of per capita development spending is only 0.69 per cent per annum, whereas with regard to average real per capita development spending it occupies 2nd place among all states. Orissa with an average spending of Rs. 962 ranks 10th among the States and its growth rate is 2.27 per cent which ranks 9th rank among all the states.

Human Development Index and Developmental Spending

The HDI of the states are available for the years of 1992 and 2002. For other years the calculation is done by applying an extrapolation method. The assumption that development spending influences the HDI of a state is then subjected to a regression analysis. For each state the regression line is fitted and the regression coefficient is estimated. The fourteen states under study have spent different amounts and achieved differently in HDI over the 11-year period.

Table 1.4 gives the HDI for 1992 and 2002 for 14 major states. Among all the states, Kerala ranks top and Bihar lies at the bottom in the HDI ranking both in 1992 and 2002. There is no change in the positions of these two states. The variation in HDI is, however, different for different states over the period.

Conclusion

Public spending has important implication for human development of the states. The regression results suggest that the role of development spending is different for different categories of states. Development spending largely influences HDI in middle-income states like Kerala, Tamil Nadu and Karnataka. Among the low-income states, the performance of Bihar, Madhya Pradesh and Uttar Pradesh is commendable and the regression result shows that the development spending has a positive role in influencing the human development indicators. However, in case of high-income states like Punjab, Haryana, Gujarat and Maharashtra, the role of development spending is not encouraging. Interestingly, in case of Punjab and Haryana, the role of development spending is too weak to bring changes in HDI. The influence of development spending on HDI is not satisfactory for Orissa and Rajasthan.

Table 1.4: Variation in HDI of Non-special Category States of India

Sl. No	States	1992	2002	Increment Col.4 – Col.3	Percent rise (Col.5/Col.3)100
1	2	3	4	5	6
1.	Punjab	0.481	0.543	0.062	13
2.	Gujarat	0.436	0.484	0.048	11
3.	Maharashtra	0.459	0.530	0.071	15
4.	Haryana	0.450	0.515	0.065	14
5.	W.B.	0.411	0.479	0.068	17
6.	Tamil Nadu	0.473	0.537	0.064	14
7.	Karnataka	0.419	0.485	0.066	16
8.	A.P.	0.381	0.420	0.039	10
9.	Kerala	0.596	0.643	0.047	8
10.	Orissa	0.357	0.416	0.059	17
11.	Bihar	0.314	0.373	0.059	19
12.	M.P.	0.334	0.401	0.067	20
13.	U.P.	0.321	0.395	0.074	23
14.	Rajasthan	0.355	0.432	0.077	22

Source: Compiled from National Human Development Report, 2002.

Thus, the analysis brings valid inputs for public policy decisions. Allocation of resources will not automatically lead to the improvement of development indicators unless there is a change in governance mechanism and delivery of public services. There is also an increasing realisation of the fact that the per capita income alone is not a sufficient condition to raise HDI. The inadequacy of per capita income as a measure of enhancing welfare is proved with the fact that HDI in states like Punjab, Haryana and Andhra Pradesh has not changed significantly though there has been a rise in the per capita income of these states. Andhra Pradesh is adjudged as the state that has achieved rapid income growth in the last two decades but its human development growth is not satisfactory.

References

Dholakia, A. R. and Dholakia, H. R. (2004), 'Expenditure Allocation and Welfare Returns to Government A Suggested Model', *Economic and Political Weekly,* Vol. XXXIX, No 23.

Furtado, C. (1964), *Development and Underdevelopment*, University of California Press, Berkeley.

Gupta, S., Bendict Clements and Erwin Tiongson (1998), '*Finance & Development'*, Volume 35, Number-3, A Quarterly Magazine of IMF.

Government of India (2005), 'Economic Survey (2004-05)', Ministry of Finance, New Delhi.

Government of Orissa (2003-04), *Budget at a Glance.*

Government of Orissa (various years), '*Finance Accounts', Various Issues during 1990-91 to 2001-02.*

Government of India (2002), '*National Human Development Report - *2001', Planning Commission, Oxford University Press, New Delhi.

Premchand, A. (2004), 'Ethical Dimensions of Public Expenditure Management', *Economic and Political Weekly,* Vol. XXXIX, No. 8.

Reserve Bank of India (2004), *Handbook of Statistics on State Government Finances.*

Thirlwall, A. P. (2003), '*Growth and Development (Seventh Edition)'*, Palgrave McMillan, New York.

UNDP (2001), '*Human Development Report 2001*', Oxford University Press, New Delhi.

UNDP (2004), '*Human Development Report 2004*', Oxford University Press, New Delhi.

2

Economic Reforms and Public Expenditure on Social Services

Arabinda Mishra and Gopal Krishna Sarangi

Introduction

Since the beginning of the 1980s, many developing countries faced with mounting debt burdens, high rates of inflation and severe balance of payments problems, have been trying to achieve that elusive goal of sustainable fiscal balance through reformist structural adjustment programmes. By their very nature, such economic reform measures involve a paradigm shift in the role of the state vis-à-vis the economy. The two fundamental dictums underlying this shift are that of 'fiscal efficiency' and 'fiscal prudence'. While the dictum of efficiency prompts the government to reorient its resource allocation, that of prudence makes it obligatory on the part of governments to remain committed to an expenditure constraint. The repercussions of such fundamental changes in economic policy are wide-ranging and unlikely to remain limited to the conventional spheres of economic activity.

Of particular concern is the 'spillover' of the impact of reform measures to human welfare and development. The likely conduit of such a spillover is public spending on social services. For poor states, in particular, reduction in public spending on social services and the consequent deterioration in the quality of life is likely to have long-run adverse consequences on labour productivity and economic growth. In their pioneering study on the social impact of economic reforms in sub-Saharan Africa, Cornia *et al* (1987) highlight the adverse repercussions of structural adjustment policies on the condition of children and propose a 'human face' to the conventional World Bank policies of structural adjustment in developing countries. Empirical studies on the impact of economic reforms on public social sector spending present evidence that points to significantly different experiences across countries. Generally, countries in Latin America and sub-Saharan Africa have turned out to be poor performers compared to South-East Asian countries in ensuring a 'human face' to their structural adjustment programmes (Stewart, 1992; Jayarajah *et al*, 1996).

The most common justification for government intervention in provisioning of social services is with reference to the presence of significant externalities in such provisions. Even when privatization options are politically feasible and economically efficient, there would still be a strong need for government intervention in the social sector on grounds of equity. Reforms-related stress on state finances and the consequent squeeze on social sector expenditures run contrary to the above requirement. Ravallion and Rao (1992) point out that the impact of economic reforms on social sector spending may take place through three processes: (i) a proportionate reduction in allocations to all sectors including the social sector; (ii) a reduction in proportionate spending on other-than-social sectors, keeping allocations for social sectors intact; and (iii) a more than proportionate reduction in social sector allocation, keeping spending on other sectors intact. For poor regions, scenarios (i) and (iii) are likely to be disastrous as far as human development is concerned. Even maintaining the existing level of public expenditure on social services (scenario ii) may not be enough to counter the retarding influences on human development, since gains from research and superior technology cannot be realized without improved allocations. In a country like India, with a large population below poverty line and vital human development indicators still reflecting low levels of performance in many states, the impact of curtailed public spending on vital inputs to quality of life would be most adverse on human development.

In the case of India, any analysis of the fiscal impact of macro-economic reforms has to take into account the federal structure of the country's fiscal system. Among the Indian states, there is great disparity in terms of fiscal strength and stability. This is in large measure a reflection of inter-state differences in economic performance and fiscal governance. Intuitively it seems reasonable to suppose that the swiftness of change in the fiscal structure of a state, or the 'fiscal responsiveness', is directly related to the level of economic development of the state as well as the strength and stability of its finances. Poorer states with unstable fiscal systems and thin resource bases are especially vulnerable to reforms-induced perturbations in the resource generation and transfer systems in a federal setup. Thus, for instance, Ahluwalia (2003) argues that with liberalization of investment control and much stronger pressure of competition especially from imports, investment flows to states in India in the post-reform period have begun to be influenced to a much greater extent by economic considerations.

The resulting reallocation of investment could lead to a substantial increase in investment in the better performing states and a consequent increase in their growth rates with a corresponding reduction in investment in less well endowed or less well governed states and a deceleration in their growth. On a similar vein, Reddy (2002) puts up a case for discriminating resource transfers from the Centre to the States in India since, in the reform period, states that already have a reasonably well developed institutional support base and strong fiscal position can garner resources from the market and consequently reduce their dependence on central transfers. This issue becomes all the more important when one considers declining central transfers to the states in the reform period.

In addition to the possible reforms-induced changes in fiscal systems, it may also help to underscore some common inherent features of government finances in India that have become evident during the past two decades. Since the mid-1980s, fiscal profligacy has been the underlying theme of fiscal (mis)management in India. Despite frequent policy pronouncements to the contrary and the adoption of a comprehensive macro level structural adjustment programme in 1991, there is very little to show in terms of containment, if not reduction, in unproductive public expenditure. Reforms in the tax domain have failed to boost public revenues, mainly due to deficiencies left un-addressed in the administration system. Worsening fiscal health of the governments, especially at the state levels, is likely to build pressure on the public authorities to adopt hard options involving fiscal retrenchment and adjustment. The content of such a fiscal containment programme will be having significant implications for macro- and micro-economic performances in the social sectors of the economy.

In the above context, the present study aims at adding to our understanding of the impact of economic reforms on public social sector spending by addressing the following questions: What have been the reform period trends in public social sector spending at the state level in India? More importantly, from the analytical point of view, is there a pattern to such trends for states belonging to different developmental categories? Further, to what extent one may link up the possible reform-induced changes in the fiscal structure of different state categories with the respective trends in public social sector spending?

In the following sections, the answers to the above questions are sought from an analysis of the finances of 14 major Indian States that are categorized as high income group (HIG), middle income group (MIG) and low income group (LIG). The categorization of States follows the classification adopted by the Eleventh Finance Commission: HIG States are Punjab, Haryana, Maharashtra and Gujarat; MIG States are Andhra Pradesh, Karnataka, Kerala, Tamil Nadu and West Bengal; and LIG States are Bihar, Orissa, Madhya Pradesh, Rajasthan and Uttar Pradesh. The various issues of Reserve Bank of India Bulletin on "Finances of State Governments" from 1980-81 to 2003-04 form the main data source for the study. The period of analysis is divided into a 'pre-reform period' from 1980-81 to 1990-91 and a 'reform period' from 1991-92 to 2003-04 (however, in deriving reform period average estimates, 2003-04 is excluded since the relevant fiscal data for the year are available only in terms of budget estimates and not actuals).

A caveat is necessary at this point of the discussion. It must be recognized that fiscal reforms are only one component of the structural adjustment process in India and there are other dimensions that have also influenced the magnitude as well as the content of resource flow from the governments to the social sector. Thus, for instance, in the case of the health sector in India, Baru (2003) argues that the reform induced growth of multinational corporations has influenced the government's developmental funding to the sector. Rather than focusing on public health and preventive programmes, they have encouraged greater funding to curative and drug based programmes. Moreover the trends of the real per capita public spending on health in major states and their distribution among primary, secondary and tertiary health care shows that between the period 1985-86 and 1998-99 per capita public spending increased at the primary and the secondary levels by about 50 per cent while spending levels increased by more than 100 per cent on the tertiary sector (Misra et al 2003). Similarly, considerable dilution of the scope of the drug price controls and the introduction of product patents is likely to have contributed to increased drug prices for a large number of drugs during the nineties (Kumar and Pradhan, 2003). All this is likely to have caused significant adverse effects on the health care access by the poorer population groups in the country during the reform period.

Public Spending and Social Sector Achievements in India

In India we find both the public and private sectors involved in providing social services to the people. What are these social services? The budgetary classification of receipts and expenditures under different heads such as 'Economic Services', 'Social Services', 'Fiscal Services', etc is a convenient starting point and, accordingly, the present paper has accepted the following services as constituting the 'social sector' in India.

1. Education, Sports, Art and Culture.
2. Medical and Public Health.
3. Family Welfare.
4. Water Supply and Sanitation.
5. Housing.
6. Urban Development.
7. Welfare of Scheduled Castes, Scheduled Tribes and Other Backward Classes.
8. Labour and Labour Welfare.
9. Social Security and Welfare.
10. Nutrition.
11. Relief on account of Natural Calamities.
12. Others (includes information and publicity, secretariat-social services, other social services, etc).

It is generally accepted that there has occurred significant progress in the country with respect to many of the core social sector services that contribute to human development. In Table 2.1, we present the progress in India's social sector performance over time and at the level of the states in terms of two indicators – the infant mortality rate and the female literacy rate – that lie in the very heart of the Millennium Development Goals. The 14 major states for which the data is presented differ significantly in terms of economic status and if we follow the common perception that there is always an economic basis to social sector achievements, it is to be expected that there will be a pattern to the spread of the indicators establishing that richer States are better achievers of human development. On the contrary, as the data shows, low income group States like Orissa, Rajasthan and Madhya Pradesh have performed well above the average to bring down IMR and increase FLR in the 20 year period since 1981. Similarly, the below par performance of high income and middle income category States like Gujarat and Andhra Pradesh, respectively, in bringing down infant mortality rate or that of Gujarat and Kerala in increasing female literacy rate is a pointer to the fact that there are factors other than economic growth

Table 2.1: Social Sector Performance Indicators for 14 Major States of India in 1981, 1991 and 1998.

State	Infant Mortality Rate (IMR)				Female Literacy Rate (FLR)			
	1981	1991	1998-99	Changes in 1998-99 over 1981	1981	1991	2001	Changes in 2001 over 1981
Maharashtra	119	74	44	-75	41	52	68	27
Gujarat	115	78	63	-52	38	49	59	20
Punjab	127	74	57	-70	40	50	64	24
Haryana	126	52	57	-69	27	40	56	29
Andhra Pradesh	91	74	66	-25	24	33	51	27
Karnataka	81	42	52	-30	33	44	57	24
Kerala	54	54	16	-38	76	86	88	12
Tamil Nadu	104	62	48	-56	40	51	65	24
West Bengal	95	75	49	-46	36	47	60	24
Bihar	94	133	73	-21	17	23	34	17

Contd...

Madhya Pradesh	150	125	86	-64	19	29	51	32
Orissa	163	87	81	-82	25	35	51	26
Rajasthan	141	99	80	-61	14	20	44	30
Uttar Pradesh	130	77	87	-43	17	25	43	26
ALL INDIA	115		68	-47	30	39	54	24

Note: IMR is defined as number of deaths by age 1 year per 1000 live births; Female literacy rate has been estimated for age 7 years and above population.

Source: IMR Figures for 1981 and 1991 are from Occasional Paper No 1 of 1997, Table-3, Page 112-113, Census of India; IMR Figures for 1998-99 are taken from the National Family Health Survey (NFHS) – 2, 1998-99; Female Literacy Rate Figures are from Census of India, relevant years.

influencing social sector performance of States.

In the above context, Prabhu's (1996) study points out that social sector expenditures by State governments are crucially dependent as much as on their success at additional resource mobilization as the political commitment towards goals of human development. Her analysis of the Social Allocation Ratio (defined as the per cent of public expenditure earmarked for social services) in 15 major states of the country and covering the first 4 years of structural adjustment reveals a declining trend in the ratio for the majority of the states. At the individual States' levels, Prabhu's (2001) study concentrates on two States, Maharashtra and Tamil Nadu, which are comparable in terms of social sector attainments but differ significantly in terms of their social policies and political orientations. For the reforms period, it was found that allocational priorities in the two States did not experience any substantial shifts. Within the social sector, the study failed to find any significant evidence of restructuring of allocational priorities towards basic facilities.

The experiences of countries in sub-Saharan Africa, Latin America and South East Asia relating to the incorporation of a 'human' dimension to reform measures have been found to be influenced by 3 factors: (i) initial macro–economic conditions; (ii) growth performances of the countries during reforms; and (iii) the level of political commitment to social sectors (Prabhu, 2001). It is argued that, while the first two factors are important, it is again the degree of political commitment to social sectors that ultimately determines the extent to which public sector allocations to these sectors are protected during a period of stringent fiscal conditions. Studies by Stewart (1992) and Jayarajah *et al* (1996) on the contrasting experiences of south-east Asian countries and countries in Latin America and sub-Saharan Africa also underscore the importance of the political factor.

In contrast to Prabhu's conclusion about unchanging allocational priorities in the major Indian States during the reform period, Mishra's (2003) analysis of a set of expenditure indicators does reveal a significant and secular shift in the resource allocation priorities during the reforms period for the three categories of HIG, MIG and LIG States. The general pattern emerging from Mishra's study is that, while the HIG and LIG States may have reoriented their allocational priorities in a way that have adversely affected their relative social sector expenditures, in the case of MIG States there may have been efforts to maintain the status quo or even to improve allocations to social services.

Even allowing for political commitment and other governance-related issues that may be having strong influences on the utilization of public resources allocated to social services, it remains to be established that the level of government spending on social services enjoys significant correlation with social sector indicators such as IMR and FLR. In an economy in which public and private providers of social services function side by side, it is not easy to isolate the relative contribution of the public sector to human development. Indicators such as the infant mortality rate, maternal mortality rate, couple protection rate, birth rate and disease specific survival rates are more likely to be directly and immediately affected by changes in government policy, than other indicators like Body Mass Index, height for weight across different age groups, etc (Panchamukhi, 2001). Thus, even if we get significant correlation between government spending on social services and some selected indicators linked to social sector performance, it is not enough to establish that the relation is symptomatic of a more general linkage between public spending and social sector performance. Added to this, of course, are issues linked to the efficient and equitable utilization of government resources that are usually absent in any analysis (including the present one) of public spending on social services.

It is in the light of the above discussion that the correlation estimates presented in Table 2.2 need to be considered. Though the signs and values of the estimates suggest that public spending on social services is strongly correlated with social sector performance, it is quite possible that the observed relationship is peculiar to the indicators chosen. Even then, it is interesting to observe that over time, as the correlation between per capita public spending on social services and infant mortality rate has grown stronger, a reverse trend is found for the correlation between per capita public spending on social services and female literacy rate.

Table 2.2: Correlation between Social Sector Performance Indicators and Per Capita Public Expenditure on Social Services in 14 Major States of India

Year	Correlation between IMR and per capita public expenditure on social services in 14 major states of India	Correlation between female literacy rate and per capita public expenditure on social services in 14 major states of India
1981	-0.31	0.76
1991	-0.51	0.67
2001	-0.55	0.60

Note: For IMR, correlation estimate has been derived for 1998-99

In the Indian context, Sen's (1993) analysis of the data on public expenditures over a 15-year time period (1974-75 to 1989-90) is one of the first studies that seek to identify the extent of government involvement in human development in India. At the aggregated level, with public expenditure of the Centre and States combined together, the trend in public sector allocation to the social sector was found to be growing over time, though at a slow rate. In real per capita terms, nearly all the social service items were found to have grown at rates greater than 5 per cent per annum between 1974-75 and 1989-90, with education and public health putting up impressive performances at 5.84 per cent and 6.27 per cent respectively. Despite their rising trends, expenditures on human development sectors remained at low levels by international standards over the 15-year period analyzed, both in terms of their share in total expenditure and in real per capita terms. Further, the study's disaggregated analysis at the states' level exposes substantial inter-state variations in the trends in public expenditure on social services. Significantly, the study finds evidence of an inverse relationship between SDP and the ratio of SDP spent by governments on social services on the one hand, and a positive correlation between per capita SDP and per capita outlay on social services on the other.

Though the per capita public spending on social services for all the States under consideration appears to have increased continuously over the period 1981-82 to 2001-02, there is a decline in terms of the percentage increase in the per capita estimates for all States in 2001-02 over 1991-92 as compared to the corresponding percentage increase in 1991-92 over 1981-82. Further, there appears to be a pattern in this decline with the LIG States recording on an average the largest decline in the percentage increase in 2001-02 over 1991-92 as compared to the percentage increase in 1991-92 over 1981-82, followed in order by the MIG and HIG State categories.

Public Spending on Social Services at the State Level

In India economic policies began their orientation towards deregulation and liberalization from the mid-1970s. This move was particularly evident in exchange rate management. The IMF supported adjustment programme of 1981 marked the beginning of an "incremental approach to reforms" (Ahluwalia, 1994), involving relaxation of quotas and ceilings, industrial delicensing, broad banding of industrial investments and import liberalization. The policy changes of this period have been shown to increase industrial outputs and efficiencies and, thereby, stimulating industrial investment in the economy (Joshi and Little, 1994). This appears to have created a climate for further change. Consequently, the Rajiv Gandhi government (with an unprecedented electoral mandate for support) introduced the New Economic Policy (NEP) in 1985 with an explicit focus on economic efficiency and its components related to the dismantling of the control regime, liberalization of foreign trade and foreign investment and privatization of public sector enterprises. The

1985 Long Term Fiscal Policy (LTFP) aimed at a drastic restructuring of the fiscal system, particularly of the existing tax regime.

It is an irony that, throughout the 1980s, along with the efforts at restructuring of the country's economy, a severe macro-economic crisis was in the making that finally erupted in 1991. For the record, Indian economy's GDP growth rate of 5.5 per cent per annum during the 1980-1990 decade far bettered its 3.6 per cent per annum growth performance of the 1965-1980 period. However, much of this growth was powered by large deficits in the public expenditure of both central and state governments. The gross fiscal deficit of the central and state governments taken together averaged 9.5 per cent of GDP during 1985-90 and touched 10.1 per cent in 1990-91. What made this increase in fiscal deficit ominous was the trend in its revenue deficit component. As a ratio of the central governments' gross fiscal deficit, revenue deficit nearly doubled from an average of 17.0 per cent in 1980-85 to 31.5 per cent in 1985-90. Over the entire decadal period (1980-1990), revenue deficit as a ratio of the combined gross fiscal deficit of all state governments averaged at a high level of 15.02 per cent (moving from an average surplus position of -16.8 per cent in 1980-85 to an average deficit value of 8.1 per cent in 1985-90). A growing revenue deficit component of the fiscal deficit implies that the rise in fiscal deficit largely owes to increased non-capital expenditure, which is inherently inflationary when continued over a prolonged period. Thus, the fiscal basis of the 1991 macro-economic crisis was in the making throughout the 1980s.

The 1991 crisis compelled the government to introduce far-reaching structural adjustment programmes. However, as it happened in the later half of the 1980s, much of the post-1991 period has been witness to major slippages in fiscal containment, both at the central and state government levels. At the central government level, gross fiscal deficit as a ratio of GDP averaged 6.7 per cent during 1990-95 and 5.1 per cent in 1995-1998. The corresponding values of the gross fiscal deficit for all states taken together during the two periods are 2.9 per cent and 3.5 per cent respectively. In 1999-2000, the combined gross fiscal deficit of all states amounted to 4.9 per cent of GDP (revised estimate), and the total outstanding debt to GDP ratio was 21.5 per cent. As a ratio of the central government's gross fiscal deficit, revenue deficit increased from an average of 48.1 per cent in 1990-95 to 55.3 per cent in 1995-2000. Corresponding average values in case of all states put together are 24.7 per cent and 42.5 per cent respectively, for the periods 1990-95 and 1995-2000.

The above discussions about the reforms in India and its impact on government finances lead us to the conclusion that reforms in India have definitely exerted pressures on the revenue and expenditure sides of States' finances, but not in the directions that are usually expected, following the rationale behind economic reforms. The arguments rationalizing reforms invariably run in terms of revenue expansion and expenditure (of the non-investment type) contraction in the public sector domain. From available evidence, it can in no way be asserted that reforms in India have had their *desired* fiscal impact. Table 2.3 presents some such evidence at the aggregated level for the 3 different State categories – HIG, MIG and LIG States – that distinguishes between the relative fiscal performances of these groups of States in the pre-reform (1980-81 to 1990-91) and reform (1991-92 to 2002-03) periods. The three fiscal performance indicators chosen for the purpose are: (i) Gross Fiscal Deficit as per cent of Aggregate Gross Disbursements (total public spending termed as "aggregate gross disbursements", AGD, equals the sum of total revenue expenditure and total disbursements on the capital account); (ii) State's Own Resources as per cent of Aggregate Gross Disbursements; and (iii) the Net Devolution of Resources from the Centre as per cent of Aggregate Gross Disbursements.

The percentage changes in the mean values of the chosen fiscal indicators given in Table 2.3 for the reforms period over the corresponding values in the pre-reforms period point to a highly disappointing, if not perverse, picture of the fiscal impact of reforms in India at the level of States.

Table 2.3: Gross Fiscal Deficit (GFD), State's Own Resources (SOR) and Net Devolution of Resources from Centre (NET DEV) as Per Cent of Aggregate Gross Disbursements (AGD): Pre- and Post-reforms Averages for HIG, MIG and LIG States

State Category	Period	GFD as Per cent of AGD	SOR as Per cent of AGD	NET DEV as Per cent of AGD
HIG States	Pre-reform Period Average	20.1	57.2	23.3
	Reform Period Average	24.1	58.7	9.8
	% Change	4.0	1.5	-13.5
MIG States	Pre-reform Period Average	16.0	49.8	28.2
	Reform Period Average	23.9	47.7	21.4
	% Change	7.8	-2.1	-6.8
LIG States	Pre-reform Period Average	20.0	36.4	39.9
	Reform Period Average	24.7	34.4	33.2
	% Change	4.7	-2.1	-6.7

Pre-reform period is 1980-81 to 1990-91; Reform period is 1991-92 to 2002-03.

For all 3 State categories, the deficit indicator (GFD as per cent of AGD) shows substantial increases in the reform period. The resource position of both MIG and LIG States is found to have weakened during the reforms period in terms of revenue generated from own sources as well as transfers received from the centre. For the HIG States, though own resource generation is found to have marginally improved in the reform period over the pre-reform period position, there has been at the same time a huge decline in the net resource flow from the centre to these states. Thus, in general, all the 3 State groups appear to have suffered significant deterioration in their revenue positions in the reform period. The growing fiscal deficit at the same time suggests that, as it happened during the mid-eighties, States are following the deficit-financing route to fulfill their expenditure compulsions.

So what have been the implications for social sector spending by the State governments in the above background of falling resources and increased deficits? Usually, in the face of reforms-laid constraints (pegging the GFD to a particular per cent of the GDP/SDP is one example), one would expect governments with weak resource bases to take the 'soft options' like cutting-back on capital outlays and spending on social services.

Table 2.4 looks at the percentage changes in the mean values of indicators related to total expenditure on social services and its constituents in the reforms period for the 3 State categories. Interestingly, both the HIG and LIG States are found to have in fact marginally *increased* their relative spending on social services (relative to respective AGDs) in the reforms period. However, in the LIG States, the reform period increase in social sector spending occurs only in the revenue account and is accompanied by a decline in the capital outlay on social services in the same period. For the MIG States, the strategy appears to have been to cutback on total social sector spending while more or less maintaining the division between its revenue and capital account components.

It can be observed from Table 2.4 that the revenue account contains more than 90 per cent of the total social sector spending by the State governments. This prompts a question regarding the impact of reforms and the consequent structural shifts in the States' fiscal systems on resource allocation for social services *within* the revenue account. In the analysis to follow, the study looks at changes in State governments' social sector expenditures on the revenue account during the reforms period. Capital account expenditures are left out because it is difficult to identify any trend pattern from them.

Table 2.4: Public Expenditure on Social Services in HIG, MIG & LIG State Categories: Pre-reform and Reform Period Averages

State Category	Period	Total Revenue Expenditure on Social Services as % of TESS	Total Capital Outlay on Social Services as % of TESS	Total Loans and Advances for Social Services as % of TESS	TESS as % of Aggregate Gross Disbursements
HIG States	Pre-reform	92.2	3.8	4.1	29.6
	Reform	93.4	4.2	2.4	30.1
	Per cent Change	1.3	0.4	-1.7	0.5
MIG States	Pre-reform	93.7	2.8	3.6	36.0
	Reform	93.1	3.2	3.6	33.3
	Per cent Change	-0.5	0.4	0.1	-2.7
LIG States	Pre-reform	91.6	6.2	2.2	30.5
	Reform	93.3	5.0	1.7	31.4
	Per cent Change	1.7	-1.2	-0.5	0.9

TESS = Total Expenditure on Social Services.

Note: Pre-reform period is 1980-81 to 1990-91; Reform period is 1991-92 to 2002-03.

Further, between the two types of revenue expenditure – plan and non-plan – the present analysis limits itself to non-plan revenue expenditure. It is reasonably safe to assume that non-plan expenditure is more likely to be targeted by a fiscal containment programme than plan expenditure. More specifically, the study concentrates on the total non-plan revenue expenditure (NPE), the total non-plan developmental expenditure on the revenue account (NPDE) and the total non-plan expenditure on social services on the revenue account (NPESS). While total non-plan revenue expenditure (NPE) is normalized with respect to aggregate gross disbursements (AGD), the total non-plan developmental expenditure on the revenue account (NPDE) and the total non-plan revenue expenditure on social services (NPESS) are normalized, respectively, with respect to total non-plan revenue expenditure (NPE) total non-plan developmental expenditure on the revenue account (NPDE).

Thus, we have three fiscal indicators - NPEAGD: Non-plan Expenditure on all services taken together on Revenue Account (NPE) as a ratio of Aggregate Gross Disbursements (AGD); NPDENPE: Non-plan Developmental Expenditure on Revenue Account (NPDE) as per cent of Non-plan Expenditure on all services taken together on Revenue Account (NPE); and NPESSNPDE: Non-plan Expenditure on Social Services (NPESS) as per cent of Non-plan Developmental Expenditure on Revenue Account (NPDE) – that are expected to reveal the relative *containment effect* of reform measures on public spending on social services (NPEAGD) as well as the relative *allocative effect* of reforms on public spending on social services (NPDENPE and NPESSNPDE).

From Table 2.5 it is clear that the reform period has witnessed substantial decline in the non-plan developmental expenditure on the revenue account in case of all the 3 State categories. This is associated with increased non-plan revenue expenditure for HIG and LIG States, which would imply that for these States the increased non-plan spending during reform period has been on non-developmental heads and not on social and economic services

Table 2.5: Non-plan Expenditure, Non-plan Development Expenditure and Non-plan Expenditure on Social Services: Pre-reform and Reform Period Averages for HIG, MIG and LIG States

State Category	Period	Non-plan Expenditure as Per cent of Aggregate Gross Disbursements	Non-plan Development Expenditure as Per cent of Total Non-plan Expenditure	Non-plan Expenditure on Social Services as Per cent of Non-plan Development Expenditure
HIG States	Pre-reform	68.5	66.9	47.6
	Reform	74.2	55.1	56.6
	Per cent Change	5.7	-11.7	9.0
MIG States	Pre-reform	71.4	70.2	51.6
	Reform	69.5	55.5	61.9
	Per cent Change	-1.8	-14.7	10.3
LIG States	Pre-reform	62.5	65.0	52.4
	Reform	68.9	50.7	64.8
	Per cent Change	6.4	-14.3	12.4

Note: Pre-reform period is 1980-81 to 1990-91; Reform period is 1991-92 to 2002-03.

that taken together constitute developmental services in the conventional budgetary parlance. On the other hand, with the MIG States suffering from a decline in both total non-plan revenue expenditure and non-plan developmental expenditure on the revenue account, it appears that the reforms impact has been the most severe on this category as far as the containment of non-plan spending is concerned. However, and this holds true for all 3 categories of States, as far as the distribution of non-plan developmental revenue expenditure on social and economic services is concerned, there is no doubt that social services have been favoured during the reform period. In fact, judging by the per centage change in the NPESSNPDE indicator for the 3 State categories, it appears that the shift during reforms period in resource allocation towards social services within the non-plan developmental domain has been the most in case of LIG States, followed in order by the MIG and HIG States. This pattern is more clearly brought out in figure 1, which presents the year-wise percentage values of the NPDENPE and NPESSNPDE indicators for the 3 State categories.

Conclusions and Policy Implications

The analysis of the present study holds true at an aggregate level, where States with differing fiscal strengths have been grouped together solely on the basis of their economic performance. It is possible that within a particular State group, there are individual exceptions to the general pattern. However, from the policymaking point of view, it is the identification of trends and patterns at some aggregated level that is very often useful.

There are three major conclusions coming out from the present study. First, that in terms of the per capita spending on social services, public expenditure has grown by a lesser extent in the 1990s as compared to its increase in the earlier decade. The pattern that emerges on this aspect is that per capita public spending on social services has grown the least in LIG States, followed in order by the MIG and HIG States. The second major conclusion is that whatever growth in public spending on social services has taken place at the States' level in the reforms period has probably been deficit financed. Here also there are indications that the LIG States may have been compelled to cutback on capital outlays on social services in the reforms period. Thirdly, there is strong evidence of all States being impacted by the containment effect of economic reforms, as far as non-plan developmental expenditures are concerned. At the same time, there appears to have taken place significant shifts in resource allocation in favour of social services within the non-plan developmental expenditure domain during reforms, which may have acted in neutralizing or even overtaking the containment effect of reforms. Again, there is a pattern to such shifts, with the LIG States making the most effort to allocate more resources on social services within a shrinking non-plan developmental expenditure domain, followed in order by MIG and HIG States. However, judging by the trends in per capita public spending on social services for the LIG States, the shift in resource allocation in favour of social sector appears to have been inadequate.

What then are the policy implications of the above findings? The National Health Policy 2002 plans for increasing the share of Central grants to constitute at least 25 per cent of total health spending by the year 2010, up from the existing 15 per cent. Any policy prescription that calls for an increased quantum of budgetary support to social sector by the state governments need to take into account the ground realities relating to their capacity for: (i) additional resource mobilization; (ii) prudent fiscal management; and (iii) setting resource allocation priorities. State governments have limited capacity to raise extra resources. This constraint acts with varying degrees of severity on public investment programmes for different states. For the LIG states, especially, the need for Central support through additional resources is more pressing. While increasing its budgetary commitment to the social sector, the Central government should take into account inter-state disparities, both in terms of facilities and needs.

The state governments cannot sustain a higher level of public investment in the social sector unless they work towards restoring the fiscal balance in their budgets. The requirements of prudent fiscal management should be dovetailed into public social sector expenditure programmes. A basic pre-requisite to this is the proper identification of public expenditure items that can be contained/cut-back (as part of the reforms programme), without affecting adversely the level and quality of public provisioning of social services.

Resource allocations of the state governments to social sector reflect the priority given to social services by the political establishment. State governments generally tend to follow the easy option of cutting down on social sector spending, when forced to work with a deficit constraint. This puts down the status of social services as an 'afterthought' in the priority matrix of the policy makers. Reversing the tendency requires from the state governments clearly stated long-term budgetary commitments, after taking into account the gaps and imbalances in the social sector.

References

Ahluwalia, M. S. (1994), 'India's Economic Reforms', in *India, the Future of Economic Reforms,* (Eds. R. Cassen and V. Joshi), Oxford University Press, Oxford.

Ahluwalia, M. S. (2003), 'State Level Performance under Economic Reform in India', in *Economic Policy Reform and the Indian Economy,* (Ed. A. O. Kruger), Oxford University Press, Oxford.

Baru, R.V. (2003), *Privatization of Health Care in India: A Comparative Analysis of Orissa, Karnataka and Maharashtra States,* CMDR Monograph No. 43, CMDR, Dharwad, Karnataka.

Census of India (1997), 'Occasional Paper', No 1, pp. 112-113, Office of the Registrar General of India, New Delhi.

Census of India (1981, 1991 & 2001), 'Female Literacy Rate', Office of the Registrar General of India, New Delhi.

Cornia, G. A., R. Jolly and F. Stewart (1987), *Adjustment with a Human Face: Protecting the Vulnerable and Promoting Growth,* Vol. 1, Oxford University Press, Oxford.

Government of India (1999), 'National Family Health Survey-2, 1998-

99', Ministry of Health and Family Welfare, New Delhi.

Jayarajah, C., W. Branson and B. Sen (1996), *Social Dimensions of Adjustments: World Bank Experience, 1980-83,* A World Bank Operations Evaluations Study OED, Washington D. C.

Joshi, V. and I. M. D. Little (1994), *India: Macroeconomics and Political Economy, 1964 – 1991,* Oxford University Press, Oxford.

Kumar, N. and J. P. Pradhan (2003), *Economic Reforms, WTO and Indian Drugs and Pharmaceutical Industry: Implications of Emerging Trends*, CMDR Monograph No.42, CMDR, Dharwad, Karnataka.

Mishra, A. (2003), *Economic Reforms, Government Finances and Public Spending on Social Sector: An Analysis of the Health Sector in India*, CMDR Monograph No.37, CMDR, Dharwad, Karnataka.

Misra, R., R. Chatterjee and S. Rao (2003), *India Health Report*, Oxford University Press, New Delhi.

Panchamukhi, P. R. (2001), 'Economic Reforms and the Health Sector: Analysis of the Nexus in the Context of Karnataka', in *Refashioning the New Economic Order: Karnataka in Transition,* (Ed. A. P. Bali), Indian Council of Social Science Research, New Delhi.

Prabhu, S. K. (1996), 'The Impact of Structural Adjustment on Social Sector Expenditure: Evidence from Indian States', in *Economic Reforms and Poverty Alleviation in India*, (Eds. C.H. Hanumantha Rao and H. Linnemann), Indo-Dutch Studies on Development Alternatives – 17, Sage Publications, New Delhi.

Prabhu, S. K. (2001), *Economic Reform and Social Sector Development: A Study of Two Indian States,* Sage Publications, New Delhi.

Ravallion, M. and K. Subba Rao (1992), 'Adjustment and Human Development in India', *Journal of Indian School of Political Economy*, Vol. 4, No.1, pp. 55-79.

Reddy, Y. V. (2002), 'Fiscal Reforms at State Level: Review and Prospects', in *A Decade of Economic Reforms in India: The Past, The Present, The Future*, (Eds. R. Kapila and U. Kapila), Academic Foundation, New Delhi.

Reserve Bank of India (Various Issues from 1980-81 to 2000-2001), 'Finances of State Governments', in *Reserve Bank of India Bulletin,* Mumbai.

Reserve Bank of India (2004), *Handbook of Statistics on State Government Finances*, Mumbai.

Sen, T. K. (1993), 'Public Expenditure on Human Development in India: Trends and Issues', in *Human Development and Structural*

Adjustment, (Eds. K.S. Parikh and R. Sudarshan), Macmillan.

Stewart, F. (1992), 'The Many Faces of Adjustment', in *Development Finance and Policy Reform,* (Ed. P. Mosley), St. Martin's Press, New York.

3

Public Expenditure on Social Services: Evidence from Orissa

Bimal K. Mohanty

Introduction

The central theme of all programmes of development particularly in third world countries has been the promotion of human development. Since independence, India has been making all possible efforts to ensure a decent living to its citizens through the promotion of human development. Indian planning mechanism which works with a well-designed objective to achieve growth with social justice has the main focus on this aspect of development. In order to achieve this broad objective, both the national and sub-national governments in India have been implementing several programmes of action which include central plans, centrally sponsored plans and state plans in addition to several sub-plans with very specific description and fields of application. Promotion of social justice is directly linked with social sector development which ultimately culminates at human development. India and its constituent states are making all possible efforts to promote human development.

The Human Development Report 2002 (UNDP, 2002) has shown that India has shifted from Low Human Development to Medium Human Development status. Though some tangible achievements are seen to have been reaped by India in respect of the promotion of human development, Orissa still remains backward in this area. The Planning Commission of India in its National Human Development Report 2001 has computed Human Development Indexes (HDI) for fifteen major states[1] at three different points of time each at an interval of a ten-year period

(Table 3.1). A scrutiny of the ranks computed and assigned to the Indian states on the basis of their scores reveals that over a twenty-year period, Orissa has not shifted its position and is seen to have remained almost stagnated at being a Low Human Development state of India. Orissa's performance in the social sector development over years thus has remained far from being satisfactory.

Table 3.1: Planning Commission's Ranking of States on the Basis of HDI*

State	Ranking for 1981	Ranking for 1991	Ranking for 2001
Andhra Pradesh	9	9	10
Assam	10	10	14
Bihar	15	15	15
Gujarat	4	6	6
Haryana	5	5	5
Karnataka	6	7	7
Kerala	1	1	1
Madhya Pradesh	14	13	12
Maharashtra	3	4	4
Orissa	11	12	11
Punjab	2	2	2
Rajasthan	12	11	9
Tamil Nadu	7	3	3
Uttar Pradesh	13	14	13
West Bengal	8	8	8

* The method of inverse ranking has been followed.

Source: National Human Development Report, Planning Commission, New Delhi, 2002, Government of India

Any action programme intended to promote human development must assign priority to the development of social sector. Social sector development delivers social goods for common consumption. A country having provided for these goods in adequate quantity and in appropriate quality, other aspects of development being simultaneously realized, is believed to have achieved success in the provision of social services. This ensures a decent living to its residents. Since social goods are unlikely to be provided by the private initiatives and market failure is exhibited in respect of their distribution, the role of government becomes inevitable in the provision and distribution of these goods. Hence public action is one of the immediate solutions to the problem of underdevelopment particularly in countries with vast amount of disparities existing between masses and classes. How far the government is committed to the promotion of this sector is readily and immediately acknowledged from the actual (accounts) outlays provided for this sector out of the budget heads.

The development economists, more particularly those believing in balanced growth strategy, are of the opinion that there has been a strong and irrefutable inter-linkage between economic and social sector development. Indian planning also emphasizes on an integrated approach to development. The Seventh Five-Year Plan laid stress on a package approach to development whereby economic betterment of the nation could be continued with 'social support services'. The Tenth Five-Year Plan almost dittoed the same theme but in different language. In addition to the quantitative target of 8 per cent GDP growth rate during 2002-07, the Approach Paper of the Tenth Five-Year Plan states, "targets relating to poverty, employment, social and environmental indicators should also be considered as being central to the attainment of the objectives of the Plan". These are all human-development related targets of the Plan. Thus for an overall prosperity of the Indian economy, a synchronized development of both economic and social sectors should have to be organised and achieved. Orissa being one of the Low Human Development states of India has to adhere to the perspectives of the national planning by assigning priority to social sector development in order to shift its position at least to a Medium Human Development state within a reasonable length of time.

Theoretically, there exists a strong linkage between growth and development. This relationship is not one-way directed. Development cannot be anticipated without growth. Similarly, growth is not the only cause of development. Only when growth is translated into enhanced capabilities, development takes place. Now the question is whether increased economic standard automatically gets translated into increased capabilities in an expanding economy (measured in terms of increasing per capita income) or it requires the intermediation of an agent. The automatic percolation of the gains from increased income to human development is ruled out on the ground that market mechanism is extremely conservative in converting economic benefits into social benefits. Had it been the fact, countries with relatively larger per capita income would have been equally rich in terms of human development. Ironically, in these countries, the relationship between growth and social opportunities is extremely weak. There are countries which have grown very fast in terms of GDP production and therefore per capita income but are still worse in terms of social sector development. Most of the oil rich Middle East countries fall within this category.

It is now proved that economic growth does not automatically get translated into human development. The latter is primarily achieved through rapid economic growth of type that is favourable and conducive to human development as well as through direct and well-planned state interventions (Hirway, 2000). Unless government plays a decisive role, there is all likelihood that social sector development will remain at an all-time low level in spite of tremendous income gains. Economists like Pigou who were the ardent supporters of market mechanism, have upheld the role of government in the promotion of social welfare. Pigou is of the opinion that government policy ought to be devoted to securing a growth path which is Pareto optimum (Sen, 1970). Graff (1957) strongly opposed the policy of fiscal neutrality of a government. Its strict observance by any government particularly of LDCs would be a serious cause of imbalance between growth and social sector development (social justice) as market forces are weak enough to respond to social causes. In a recent article, Sachs (2004) reiterates the relevance of planning (state intervention) in LDCs for accelerating economic growth and making it socially responsive.

More than a decade ago, India introduced pro-market reform measures. The present study is motivated by a desire, among others, to examine the connection, if any, between economic growth and social sector development on the background of economic reforms and at the same time to focus on the trend of expenditure borne by the Government of Orissa on several divisions of social services. This objective emanates out of the controversy whether pro-market reform measures can coexist with state interventions in the promotion of social sector development and poverty alleviation. One school of thought (normally the believers in the affluence of market forces) holds that the process of economic reforms which assigns priority roles to market mechanism automatically withdraws the involvement of the state from some of the less important economic activities and thereby the surplus resources so generated can be more effectively put into those lines which are socially desirable and conducive to human development.

On the contrary, the adversaries of market mechanism cast their doubts in the efficacy of pro-market reform measures in less developed regions to promote the production and distribution of social services and to alleviate poverty as these measures are biased in favour of minimal involvement of the government. Befitting the objectives, post-reform data on Orissa finance has been used throughout the study. Orissa is chosen for the obvious reason that this state is one of the backward states of India and has scored a very low rank on the human development scale (Table 3.1) for which both growth and social sector development are of utmost necessity to fight economic as well as human poverty.

Methodology and Data Sources

The central idea behind this study is to present empirical evidence either in support of or in opposition to the hypothesized connection between growth and social sector development in Orissa in the post-reform period. While growth is to be measured by the movement in the production of gross state domestic product (GSDP), social sector development is to be proxied by the expenditure of the Government of Orissa on several heads of social services as furnished in the budget papers. The latter is based on the empty hypothesis that social sector development is a monotonically increasing function of the expenditure on social services and its proper management. The principal aim of the current exercise is to determine whether growth causes social sector development proxied by expenditure on social services or the latter causes the former. With a view to confirming the explanatory power of a time-series variable in a bivariate framework, regression, causality and cointegration approaches have been chosen. The reason for using multiple approaches lies in exploring the sensitivity of the results to the choice of econometric tools. Moreover, the three sets of conclusions having derived from the application of three different approaches may reveal the presence of a common element in them and on the basis of this regularity, the policy implications would be more convincing.

Regression technique is used in the study of bivariate data for drawing causal relationship between the two variables. It can do so only when one of the variables is pre-specified to be endogenous and the other as exogenous. There is complete absence of a built-in mechanism in regression approach to determine the endogeneity and exogeneity nature of the variables from and within the data set. Moreover, regression technique excludes the possibility of feedback between the variables. The existence of feedback results in bilateral causality between the variables. Regression technique entirely fails to account for the same. In the presence of feedback, the most popular test to ascertain endogeniety and exogeneity of the variables from and within the data set is the test of causality (Granger, 1969).

However, causality test by itself is not fool-proof. Its refined version is the unit root test for stationarity available under cointegration approach to the study of time-series. The test is used to examine whether a time-series is stationary or non-stationary. It is called stationary only when with shift in time, with or without error correction mechanism, the series converges into equilibrium (trend). In the study of time-series, if non-stationarity is not ruled out, it may result in spurious regression and thereby it disturbs the conclusion. The present study is essentially a study of time-series data. Optimum inference can thus be drawn if all these three approaches like regression, causality and cointegration are applied.

The study is based on secondary data. The major sources of data include Budget Papers of the Government of Orissa 1990-91 – 2004-05, Orissa Budget at a Glance 2000-01 – 2004-05, White Paper on Orissa State Finances 2001 and publications of the Reserve Bank of India on State Finances - A Study of Budgets.

Trends in Social Sector Expenditure in Orissa

While dealing with trends in social sector expenditure in Orissa, the time chosen is the post-reforms period, 1990-91 – 2002-03. This section is arranged under three sub-sections, each dealing with the trend analysis but from different view points.

Broad Item-wise Expenditure Trends: Disbursements out of revenue are made by the sub-national governments in India on major heads like general services, social services, economic services and grants-in-aid and contributions. Of all, the disbursements made to the general service sector comprise those ones which are ordinarily unavoidable like the expenses on organs of state, fiscal services mostly costs of collection of taxes, interest payment and servicing of debt, administrative services, and pensions and retirement benefits. The disbursements in the form of grants-in-aid and contributions include compensation and assignments to local bodies and Panchayati Raj institutions which are absolutely essential in order to strengthen democracy at the grass root level and to empower weaker sections of the society. Accordingly, any transference of disbursements if required can only be organised between social service sector and economic service sector.

The Government of Orissa's actual allocations to the last two services above out of its own revenue have increased by 1.04 per cent and 0.65 per cent per annum respectively. If capital expenditure outside the revenue account is considered, the corresponding annual average increase is seen to have been 0.97 per cent and 0.41 per cent respectively. While the disbursements out of revenue to social services as a percentage of GSDP of Orissa have increased marginally from 7.72 in 1990-91 to 7.74 in 2002-03, to economic services it has diminished from 5.94 in 1990-91 to 3.59 in 2002-03. The percentage share of social services in total disbursements out of revenue has diminished from 38.44 in 1990-91 to 34.55 in 2002-03, while that of economic services it is marked to have also reduced from 29.59 in 1990-91 to 16.00 in 2002-03. The additional burden caused to the state finance by the implementation of the recommendations of the Fifth Pay Commission and the unsustainable interest liability which arose from 364.67 crore (3.34 per cent of GSDP) in 1990-91 to 2885.58 crore (6.46 per cent of GSDP) in 2002-03 (little more than 691 per cent increase) has affected the disbursements out of its current revenue to both social and economic services but it has fallen stronger on the latter (GOO, Annual Financial Statements).

Social services have several components like (1) education, sports, art and culture, (2) health and family welfare, (3) water supply, sanitation, housing and urban development, (4) information and broad casting, (5) welfare of S.C., S.T. and O.B.C., (6) labour and labour welfare, (7) social welfare and nutrition and (8) others. Of these divisions, more important ones are those which have direct implications for human development. In this category, education; health and family welfare; water supply, sanitation and housing; and nutrition capture primary relevance. Table 3.2 presents the shares of each of these items during 1990-91 – 2002-03 in actual provisions for social services both in revenue account and capital account. More than 70 per cent of the total disbursements on revenue account and more than

Table 3.2: Shares in Total Disbursements (Both Revenue and Capital) to Social Services

Year	Education	Health and Family Welfare	Water Supply, Sanitation and Housing	Nutrition	Total	Others
1990-91	52.47(23.75)	16.03(12.97)	6.15(51.59)	1.51(0)	76.16(88.31)	23.84(11.69)
1991-92	51.44(8.29)	15.06(29.74)	7.17(47.59)	1.42(0)	75.09(85.62)	24.91(14.38)
1992-93	50.72(24.92)	14.35(8.71)	8.45(50.57)	1.61(0)	75.13(84.20)	24.87(15.8)
1993-94	50.93(12.99)	14.15(9.06)	6.34(66.27)	1.86(0)	73.28(88.32)	26.72(11.68)
1994-95	53.64(14.51)	14.48(31.49)	7.17(46.18)	1.52(0)	76.81(92.18)	23.19(7.82)
1995-96	50.49(6.09)	13.89(19.42)	7.06(63.57)	4.95(0)	76.39(89.08)	23.61(10.92)
1996-97	52.24(16.13)	13.58(12.81)	6.50(64.05)	4.67(0)	76.99(92.99)	23.01(7.01)
1997-98	53.91(3.58)	13.42(15.71)	7.58(73.76)	3.11(0)	78.02(93.05)	21.98(6.95)
1998-99	53.59(6.11)	14.74(9.22)	8.84(76.25)	2.77(0)	79.94(91.58)	20.06(8.42)
1999-00	47.63(18.30)	10.64(12.31)	6.16(61.83)	1.69(0)	66.12(92.44)	33.88(7.56)
2000-01	55.10(15.35)	13.90(20.98)	6.34(57.63)	1.70(0)	77.04(93.96)	22.96(6.04)
2001-02	52.56(15.15)	12.93(19.10)	6.86(61.49)	1.43(0)	73.78(95.74)	26.22(4.26)
2002-03	53.78(13.33)	14.58(23.94)	6.95(56.61)	1.86(0)	77.17(93.88)	22.83(6.12)

Note: Figures in the parentheses indicate percentage shares in capital expenditure for that year

Compiled from: Annual Financial Statements 1992-1993 – 2004-2005, Finance Department, Government of Orissa.

85 per cent of expenditure on capital account are seen to have been provided for these sectors. While education has the largest share in revenue expenditure on social services, water supply, sanitation and housing claim the highest share in total capital expenditure. During the period under study, the actual expenditure of the government on general education has increased on an average by 1.08 per cent per annum and that on technical education by 0.23 per cent per annum. There exists a wide gap between these two.

In Orissa, most of the institutions providing technical education are privately owned. Thus, they do not depend on the grants and subsidies from the government. On the contrary, schools and colleges which provide general education are either fully financed (government institutions) or fully or partly aided (non-government aided institutions) by the government. The financial liabilities for running these institutions are borne by the state. In the allocation to general education, primary education has the largest share followed by secondary and higher education. Table 3.3 shows the trends of such shares. In absolute terms, there have been increases in expenditure by the government in all three components of general education, but it has increased faster in higher education contrary to the requirements. There are strong arguments in favour of the financing of primary or elementary education up to seventh standard as it is a public good and is effective in promoting equity and social justice. Moreover, education bears strong positive externality. As per 2001 census, Orissa's literacy rate (63.6 per cent) is still below the national average of 65.4 per cent (GOI, 2001). The annual average growth rates in expenditure out of revenue on primary education, secondary education and higher education have increased by 1.10 per cent, 1.07 per cent and 1.21 per cent respectively against the state average for general education of 1.11 per cent per annum (Table 3.3). The spurts in expenditure for higher education have taken place from 2000-01 due basically to the implementation of the revised pay for college teachers and other staff working in these institutions.

Table 3.3: Disbursements to the Components of General Education out of Revenue

(Rs. crore)

Year	Primary Education	Secondary Education	Higher Education	Total General Education
1990-91	244.68 (57.89)	112.92 (26.72)	65.04 (15.39)	422.64 (100.00)
1991-92	313.07 (61.25)	116.68 (22.83)	81.41 (15.92)	511.16 (100.00)
1992-93	354.56 (61.02)	139.48 (24.00)	87.02 (14.98)	581.06 (100.00)
1993-94	391.21 (60.26)	166.52 (25.65)	91.47 (14.09)	649.20 (100.00)
1994-95	444.46 (58.02)	193.14 (25.21	128.49 (16.77)	766.09 (100.00)
1995-96	509.43 (57.24)	228.83 (25.71)	151.68 (17.04)	889.94 (100.00)
1996-97	581.52 (57.39)	270.44 (26.69)	161.28 (15.92)	1013.24 (100.00)
1997-98	683.05 (59.12)	297.10 (25.72)	175.20 (15.16)	1155.35 (100.00)
1998-99	804.38 (56.77)	416.69 (29.41)	195.81 (13.82)	1416.88 (100.00)
1999-00	1139.89 (67.03)	370.97 (21.82)	189.66 (11.15)	1700.52 (100.00)
2000-01	1033.43 (62.19)	365.98 (22.03)	262.23 (15.78)	1661.64 (100.00)
2001-02	996.14 (58.93)	372.43 (22.03)	321.82 (19.04)	1690.39 (100.00)
2002-03	1089.55 (57.33)	479.05 (25.20)	332.11 (17.47)	1900.71 (100.00)
Annual Average %age Growth Rates	1.10	1.07	1.21	1.11

Sources: (1) White Paper on Orissa State Finances, 2001, Finance Department, Government of Orissa (2) Orissa Budget (2004-2005) at a Glance, Finance Department, Government of Orissa.

Health and family welfare is another pertinent item in the list of social services. Most discouraging feature of the trend of expenditure on this head is that disbursement for this sector has diminished from 16.03 per cent of the total expenditure on social services in 1990-91 to 14.58 per cent in 2002-03 (Table 3.2). It clearly reveals that the health sector of Orissa has not received adequate attention. As per 2001 census, annual death rate in Orissa is the highest - 9.1 as against the national average of 8.1 out of 1000 population - and also infant mortality rate is the highest in Orissa - 87 against the national average of 64 out of 1000 live births (GOI, 2001).

The National Health Policy, 2002 envisages the provision of an acceptable standard of health for general population of the country. The Policy emphasizes on increasing the state expenditure on health to the extent of 2 per cent of GDP. However, the actual disbursements of the Government of Orissa out of revenue to health and family welfare have increased from 0.99 per cent of GSDP in 2001-02 to 1.03 per cent in 2002-03. If capital expenditure is included, these percentages will be 1.06 and 1.11 respectively (GOO, Annual Financial Statements).

Water supply, sanitation and housing are few other important dimensions of social sector. Since such items are the basic amenities of life, their adequate provision ensures a decent living. In Orissa, access to safe drinking water is highly limited (Table 3.4). The state has much to do in this vital respect.

While the percentage share of water supply, sanitation and housing in the total actual outlay met out of revenue for social service sector is relatively small, it is the highest on capital account. The former has increased from 6.15 per cent in 1990-91 to 6.95 per cent in 2002-03 but the latter from 51.59 per cent in 1990-91 to 56.61 per cent in 2002-03. The Government of Orissa assigns priority to water supply and sanitation in relation to housing which is confirmed by the fact that the share of the former in total allocation to both has increased from 61.59 per cent in 1990-91 to 70.30 per cent in 2002-03 with an annual average growth rate of 1.20 per cent. For housing, revenue expenditure has increased only at an annual average growth rate of 0.86 per cent (GOO, Annual Financial Statements). In spite of the government's commitment to provide safe drinking water, it has still remained much below the national standard.

Table 3.4: Percentage of Population Having Access to Safe Drinking Water

States	Year	Rural	Urban	Combined
Orissa	1981	9.47	51.31	14.58
	1991	35.32	62.83	39.07
Punjab	1981	81.80	91.13	84.36
	1991	92.09	94.24	92.74

Compiled from: (1) Kundu A., S. Bagchi and D. Kundu (1999): Regional Distribution of Infrastructure and Basic Amenities in Urban India: Issues Concerning Empowerment of Local Bodies, Economic and Political Weekly, Vol.34, No. 28. (2) Economic Survey 1990-91 – 1992-93, Government of Orissa

Nutrition now comprises one of the basic divisions of social welfare. The Ninth Five-Year Plan defines the concept of nutritional security as "people's access to basic nutritional requirements, both physically and economically". Since this problem is particularly acute with the poor and in the inaccessible regions, public action is inevitable. The tribes of Orissa living in deep forests are the permanent victims of nutritional deficiency who need to be brought under the protection and care of the state. The expenditure borne by the Government of Orissa in nutrition is very small which is met out of revenue account only. In the post-reform period, there has been an increase in such provision from 0.12 per cent of GSDP in 1990-91 to 0.17 per cent in 2002-03 with an average growth rate of 1.35 per cent per annum (GOO, Annual Financial Statements). The annual growth rate in expenditure on nutrition is not unsatisfactory as compared with other heads of allocations but as a percentage of GSDP it is deficient.

Trends of Plan and Non-Plan Expenditure on Social Services: India's shifting to a market dominated regime since mid-1991 may itself be a major cause of change in expenditure allocations by the states to different budget heads. This necessitates an examination of the pattern and trend of growth of expenditure of the Government of Orissa both in plan and non-plan heads on social services. While the aggregate expenditure on social services on plan head has increased by 0.88 per cent per annum during 1990-91 to 2002-03, on non-plan head, it has increased by 1.05 per cent against an overall increase of 1 per cent per annum (RBI, 2004). The rise in non-plan expenditure over the plan expenditure points to an increase in maintenance cost of government establishments and a diminution in the current provision for expansion and quality improvement in the services.

During the period 1990-91-2002-03, plan expenditure out of revenue as a percentage of GSDP of Orissa has not shifted its base. During this period, the compound growth rate of GSDP of Orissa has been 1.04 per cent per annum, while the average growth rate of disbursements out of revenue to social services on plan heads has been 0.88 per cent per annum. Such galloping difference in these two rates of growth has been due to unwarranted increase in allocations out of revenue to 'general services' in general and interest payment and servicing of debt in particular. While the former has increased by 1.47 per cent per annum, the latter has registered an increase by 1.58 per cent per annum (RBI, 2004).

In order to better understand the situation of the pattern of allocations, the present study makes an account of plan and non-plan heads to important items of social services by the Government of Orissa in the Ninth Five-Year Plan (1997-98 to 2001-02). Table 3.5 presents such allocations as a percêntage of GSDP to prime sub-sectors of social sector of the state.

It is revealed that in Orissa, plan expenditure on education, sports, art and culture has diminished from 1.40 in 1997-98 to 1.02 in 2001-02 having generated an inverted V pattern and assumed its peak in 1999-2000. However, non-plan expenditure

Table 3.5: Government of Orissa's Expenditure (Plan and Non-Plan) on Important Heads of Social Sector as a Percentage of GSDP During the Ninth Plan Period (1997-98 to 2001-02)

Items of Expenditure	Heads	1997-98	1998-98	1999-2000	2000-01	2001-02
Education, Sports, Art and Culture	Plan	1.40	1.49	1.77	1.37	1.02
	Non-Plan	2.57	2.86	3.57	3.17	3.12
Elementary Education	Plan	0.31	0.28	0.64	0.29	0.16
	Non-Plan	1.85	2.08	2.78	2.40	2.16
Medical and Public Health	Plan	0.18	0.23	0.22	0.27	0.27
	Non-Plan	0.60	0.72	0.76	0.72	0.64
Rural Primary Health and Prevention/Control of Diseases	Plan	0.12	0.14	0.11	0.14	0.14
	Non-Plan	0.25	0.28	0.29	0.27	0.23
Family Welfare	Plan	0.20	0.24	0.21	0.20	0.15
	Non-Plan	0.00	0.00	0.00	0.00	0.00
Water Supply and Sanitation	Plan	0.46	0.46	0.39	0.37	0.39
	Non-plan	0.13	0.29	0.28	0.20	0.20

Sources: (1) Orissa Budget (2003-2004) at a Glance, Finance Department, Government of Orissa. (2) Orissa Budget (2004-2005) at a Glance, Finance Department, Government of Orissa

has increased having assumed a sharp displacement upward in the year 1999-2000. Both plan and non-plan expenditures on elementary education of the state have also exhibited the same trend as the general head of education. Expenditure on medical and public health on both plan and non-plan heads has increased during the Ninth Plan period, but the latter has increased faster than the former.

Actual allocation to rural primary health and prevention/control of diseases on plan heads has increased slightly during the Ninth Plan period but non-plan expenditure has increased till 1999-2000 and thereafter has diminished. The share of expenditure on family welfare has diminished during that period. While proportion of expenditure on water supply and sanitation on plan head has diminished, on non-plan head, it has increased from 0.13 per cent to 0.20 per cent. All this shows that during Ninth Plan period, the government expenditure on plan head as a percentage of GSDP of Orissa on an average has diminished and non-plan expenditure has increased.

Evidence from Other States

The ranking, made by the Planning Commission, of the fifteen major states of India on the basis of their scores on the HDI scale assigns the first position to Kerala and the 15th position to undivided Bihar irrespective of the year of computation (Table 3.1). In 2001, Orissa's rank is 11th which is just one rank higher as compared to that in 1991. This section makes an effort to present a comparative picture of the trends in social sector expenditure borne by the Governments of Kerala, Bihar and Orissa during 1990-91–2001-02. The annual average growth rates of expenditure on social services both in revenue and capital accounts excluding ways and means advances on plan heads by the Governments of Orissa, Bihar and Kerala have been 1.02, 1.69 and 1.10 per cents respectively against 1.34, 1.54 and 0.97 per cents on non-plan heads. While the growth rate in expenditure allocation to social services, on both plan and non-plan heads, is the highest in Bihar, the same for Orissa is higher for allocation to non-plan heads than the plan heads. But for Kerala, the expenditure allocation to social services on plan heads rises faster than that on non-plan heads (RBI, 2004).

Kerala's success in social sector development lies *inter alia* in controlling its non-plan expenditure. In spite of tremendous spurts in allocations to social services by Bihar, it has never been displaced beyond the 15th position among the 15 major states in terms of HDI during the last two decades (Table 3.1). This testifies that higher allocations at present may not necessarily bring about higher social sector development if there were no or negligible efforts in the past. Kerala's experience testifies the proposition. Since Kerala in previous decades provided minimum level of education to all, it is now reaping its benefit both in economic and human development fronts (Kannan and Mohan, 2004). The international labour migration from Kerala to Gulf countries, possibly as an outcome of universal education, not only brought huge quantities of remittances but also aroused consciousness among the residents about the development of human resources. Thus such a development is basically the outcome of the build up capacity of a state in the provision of social services carried forward over time.

Orissa spends at a much faster rate on non-plan heads than on plan heads. This is in no way an indication of progress in social sector development. In each case, a polynomial trend has been fitted to the data for its known advantage over linear trend. While the former indicates both the nature of curvature and tilt of the trend, the latter presents only a simple tilt of the data which does not help draw more rigorous inferences. The trend path of the expenditure allocations to social services on plan heads for Orissa is concave but mildly increasing, while it is convex and also mildly increasing for non-plan allocations over the years. For Bihar, both paths are sharply increasing and convex. For Kerala, while the trend path for plan expenditure is mildly increasing and concave, the trend path for non-plan expenditure is almost a mildly rising one approximating a straight line. This explains the success story of Kerala's achievements in the provision of social services. The growth of both plan and non-plan expenditure on social sector development of Orissa presented by the polynomial trends approximately resembles with that of Kerala excepting that the latter has almost stabilized the non-plan expenditure at the same rate throughout on these items while for the former such expenditure exhibits a continuously rising trend.

The decadal changes in per capita expenditure on social services by these three states have been presented in Table 3.6. Per capita plan expenditure on social services for Bihar irrespective of the year of enquiry is less than the corresponding figures for Orissa and Kerala taken separately. But per capita non-plan expenditure on social services for Bihar irrespective of the year is always above that for Orissa but below that for Kerala.

Table 3.6: Trend of Per Capita Expenditure on Social Services

States	Year	Plan Expenditure (in Rs.)	Non-Plan Expenditure (in Rs.)	Total (in Rs.)
Orissa	1991	114.97	169.15	284.11
	2001	320.65(17.89)	664.16(29.26)	984.81(24.66)
Bihar	1991	42.62	194.45	237.07
	2001	219.76(41.56)	855.61(34.00)	1075.37(35.36)
Kerala	1991	73.35	389.80	463.15
	2001	235.09(22.05)	1083.94(17.81)	1319.03(18.48)
All-India	1991	92.60	287.20	379.80
	2001	356.17(28.46)	946.50(22.96)	1302.67(24.30)

Note: Figures in the parentheses indicate the annual (simple) average percentage changes during the decade 1991-2001.

Compiled from: Handbook of Statistics on State Government Finances 2004, Reserve Bank of India

The annual average percentage increase in Orissa's per capita plan expenditure (17.89) during 1990-2001 is less than the corresponding figure for Kerala (22.05) but such increase in non-plan expenditure (29.26) for Orissa is above that for Kerala

(17.81). But an extreme peculiarity is found in respect of Bihar's distribution of per capita expenditure on social services. In both plan or non-plan heads, annual average percentage increase in per capita expenditure for Bihar is always above the corresponding figures for Kerala. It, thus, confirms the hypothesis that a mere increase in per capita expenditure on social services does not necessarily ensure improvement in human development. It is in fact the time bound commitment with adequate provision for social services, which has happened for Kerala, is the key to the success story of improving human development index.

Conclusion

Orissa is one of the Low Human Development states of India. In order to improve its position, it is urgently needed to speed up social sector development. The government's commitment to the development of social sector is reflected through its expenditure provisions for the purpose. The trend of such provisions is likely to be affected by any major shift in policy measures. More-than-a-decade ago, pro-market reform measures were introduced. It is expected that such a major structural change might have affected the trend of expenditure on social services in Orissa. The disbursements out of revenue to social services as a percentage of GSDP of Orissa have increased marginally from 7.72 in 1990-91 to 7.74 in 2002-03.

More than 70 per cent of the total disbursements out of revenue and more than 85 per cent of capital account disbursements for social services are seen to have been provided for the sectors, like education, health, family welfare, water supply, sanitation, housing and nutrition which have direct impact on the development of human capital. While education has the largest share in total expenditure out of revenue borne on social services by the Government of Orissa, water supply, sanitation and housing claim the highest share in total capital expenditure on social services. The actual disbursements of the Government of Orissa out of revenue to health and family welfare have increased from 0.99 per cent of GSDP in 2001-02 to 1.03 per cent in 2002-

03. If expenditure borne out of capital account is included, these percentages become 1.06 and 1.11 respectively.

Hence Orissa's actual provisions to health and family welfare are much below the one prescribed by the National Health Policy, 2002 (2 per cent of GSDP). Punjab is seen to have provided safe drinking water facility to largest number of households both rural and urban among the fifteen major states of India. In comparison to Punjab, Orissa's achievements in this regard are highly inadequate. In 1991, Punjab could provide the facility of safe drinking water to 92.74 per cent of its population while Orissa could do it only for 39.07 per cent of its population. All this shows that the expenditure on social services as a percentage of GSDP of Orissa has not been encouraging during the post-reform period. Another feature of the expenditure of the Government of Orissa on social services is that on an average, plan expenditure as a percentage of GSDP has not increased during 1990-91 – 2002-03 but the non-plan expenditure has shown an upward shift. Unless non-plan expenditure as a percentage of GSDP is stabilized, it will be too hard to realize expenditure effectiveness in social services. Kerala's experience stands as evidence.

The empirical analysis of the behaviour of social sector expenditure in Orissa in the post-reform period has presented no encouraging trend. But at least in two situations, some hopes are cherished. The actual allocations to social services out of budget heads are seen to be elastic with respect to GSDP. The other one consists of the stationarity of the time-series in social sector expenditure in Orissa. Feedbacks are proved to be present between GSDP and social sector expenditure of which GSDP causes social sector expenditure stronger than how it is caused by the latter. Since the expenditure in social services over the thirteen year period (1990-91 – 2002-03) is stationary, any departure from the trend under the pressure of stochastic forces will be transient and will vanish soon to force back the series to equilibrium. For a poor state like Orissa, it is no less an achievement which stands as an evidence of government's commitment to promote social sector development.

References

Dev, M. S. and J. Mooij (2002), 'Social Sector Expenditures in the 1990s: Analysis of Central and State Budgets,' *Economic and Political Weekly*, Vol. 37, No. 9, pp. 853-866.

Dickey, D. A. and W. A. Fuller (1979), 'Distribution of the Estimators for Autoregressive Time Series with a Unit Root', *Journal of the American Statistical Association,* Vol. 74, pp. 427-431.

Government of India (2001), *'Census of India'*, Office of the Registrar General of India, New Delhi.

Government of India (2002), *'National Human Development Report'*, Planning Commission, New Delhi.

Government of Orissa (2001), *White Papers on Orissa State Finances,* Finance Department, Bhubaneswar.

Government of Orissa (2003), *Annual Financial Statements (2002-03),* Finance Department, Bhubaneswar.

Government of Orissa (2004), *Orissa Budget (2003-2004) at a Glance*, Finance Department, Bhubaneswar.

Government of Orissa (2005), *Orissa Budget (2004-2005) at a Glance*, Finance Department, Bhubaneswar.

Government of Orissa (various years), Directorate of Economics and Statistics, Bhubaneswar.

Government of Orissa, *Economic Survey (1990-91 – 1992-93),* Bhubaneswar.

Graff, J. de V. (1957), *Theoretical Welfare Economics*, Cambridge University Press.

Granger, C. W. J. (1969), 'Investigating Causal Relations by Econometric Models and Cross-Spectral Methods', *Econometrica,* July, pp. 424-438.

Hirway, I. (2000), 'Dynamics Development in Gujarat', *Economic and Political Weekly*, Vol. 35, Nos. 35 & 36, pp. 3106-3120.

Kannan, K. P. and R. Mohan (2004), 'Twelfth Finance Commission: View from Kerala', *Economic and Political Weekly*, Vol. 39, No. 23, pp. 2361-2375.

Kundu, A., S. Bagchi and D. Kundu (1999), 'Regional Distribution of Infrastructure and Basic Amenities in Urban India: Issues Concerning Empowerment of Local Bodies', *Economic and Political Weekly*, Vol. 34, and No. 28.

Mohanty, B. K. (2004), 'Econometrics of Money Output and Price Behaviour in India', Unpublished Major Research Project in Economics, University Grants Commission, New Delhi.

Mohanty, B. K. (2004), 'Fiscal Situation in Orissa: A Review', R. K. Panda (ed) '*Reviving Orissa Economy: Opportunities and Areas of Action*', pp. 117-150, A. P. H. Publishing Corporation, New Delhi.

Reserve Bank of India (2004), Handbook of Statistics on State Government Finances.

Sachs, I. (2004), 'From Poverty Trap to Inclusive Development in LDCs', *Economic and Political Weekly*, Vol. 39, No. 18, pp. 1802-1811.

Sarma, A. (2000), 'Gujarat Finances: Reform of Budgetary Management', *Economic and Political Weekly*, Vol. 35, Nos. 35&36, pp. 3125-3136.

Sen, A. K. (1970), *Growth Economics*, Penguin Books.

UNDP (2002), *Human Development Report*, Oxford University Press, New York.

4

Human Development in Rural Orissa

Minati Mallick and Jagannath Lenka

Introduction

Human Development (HD) in fact is at the heart of today's policy agenda of governments the world over. It is vindicated by the fact that in addition to several regional reports, more than 360 national and sub-national Human Development Reports have been prepared by 120 countries. These reports have injected the human development concept into national policy dialogues not only through human development indicators and policy recommendations but also through the country specific process of consultation, data collection and report preparation. Furthermore, there are more than one Human Development Index (HDI) such as Income inequality adjusted Human Development Index (IHDI), Gender related Development Index (GDI), Gender Empowerment Measure (GEM), Capability Poverty Measure (CPM) and Human Poverty Index (HPI) constructed for different purposes. Indeed the Human Development Reports (HDRs) have helped to put forward forcefully the message that economic development has no meaning unless it expands human choices.

Fundamental to enlarging these choices is building human capabilities – the range of things that people can do or be in life. The most basic capabilities for human development are to lead a long and healthy life, to be knowledgeable, to have access to the resources needed for a decent standard of living and to be able to participate in the life of the community. However, the practical usefulness and relevance of HDI may be seriously restricted if it is not used to facilitate disaggregated analysis and policy actions.

The overall index of a country/state conceals the fact that

different regions within the country/state have very different levels of human development whereas disaggregated HDIs reveal a more detailed profile of human development. One important aspect of disaggregated analysis is that it becomes clear precisely what the deficiencies in human capabilities in different regions and what specific aspect of human development should concern policy-makers in future regional plans. It is realized that in every component of HDI (whether income, education and health) there are glaring interstate and intrastate disparities in India. When coupled with rural dimensions this disparity seems to be more intensified. The affluence in the urban centres has no assurance of development in the peripheries.

The aim of this paper is to reflect the underlying features of human development in rural Orissa. The paper is structured as follows. Materials and methods of the analysis is followed by salient features of human development across the districts of rural Orissa and finally the findings and suggestions are presented in the end.

Materials and Methods

The present study makes use of secondary data collected from different publications of the Government of Orissa, Directorate of Economics and Statistics, and Planning Commission, Government of India. Since rural data relating to education, health and income are not available for the districts of Orissa, proxy variables have been used for analyzing the results. Per capita food grain production with one-third and the inverse of agricultural labourer as a percentage of total rural main workers with two-thirds weightage, rural literacy as well as rural female literacy with equal weight and inverse of infant mortality rate and number of rural medical institutions with equal weights have been used to construct the rural income index, education index and health index respectively for the districts of Orissa. Finally these three indices are used to construct a composite index called rural Human Development Index across the districts of Orissa. This is the Simple Arithmetic Mean of the income index, education index and health index.

The formula used for calculating the indices is as per the UNDP norms, i.e.

$$Z_i = \frac{\text{Actual } X_i \text{ value} - \text{Minimum } X_i \text{ value}}{\text{Maximum } X_i \text{ value} - \text{Minimum } X_i \text{ value}}$$

Where X_i refers to the value of the variable of ith district and Z_i is the corresponding index of the ith district. It may be noted here that the value of the indices lies in between '0' and '1' for which the value of HDI also lies in the same range for individual district. HDI does not measure the absolute level of human development rather assess the relative position of the districts and ranks them in relation to each other. This helps to know how far the districts have come from the lowest levels and how far they will have to travel towards present highest level of development on each of the three indicators.

Results and Discussions

The HDI value for each district indicates how far that district has to go to attain certain goals of human development or the present level of highest human development .The most desirable value of HDI is given as unity. The closer this value of a district is to one, the smaller the distance to be traveled by that district. UNDP has categorized human development into high HDI as above 0.8, medium as between 0.5 to 0.8, low as between 0.4 and 0.5, lowest as below 0.4. None of the districts in Orissa fall under the category of high HDI category of UNDP i.e. above 0.8. The present study has categorized human development into high HDI as above 0.6, medium as between 0.4 and 0.6 and low as below 0.4.

The income index, education index, health index and Human Development Index reflecting the rural characteristics of the districts of Orissa are shown in Table 4.1. In addition to these indices the rank of the districts based on the rural HDI and Rank of the districts as per District Domestic Product (DDP) are also shown in the table for a comparative analysis.

Table 4.1: Human Development Index for Rural Orissa

Sl. No.	Districts	Income Index	Education Index	Health Index	Rural HDI	Rank	Rank as per DDP
1	Angul	0.39	0.73	0.26	0.460	16.5	2
2	Bolangir	0.32	0.44	0.37	0.377	22	19
3	Balasore	0.33	0.81	0.61	0.583	9	28
4	Baragarh	0.58	0.66	0.41	0.550	11.5	17
5	Bhadrak	0.51	0.91	0.54	0.653	4	29
6	Boudh	0.38	0.49	0.35	0.407	20	21.5
7	Cuttack	0.52	0.90	0.36	0.593	6	7
8	Deogarh	0.35	0.61	0.80	0.587	7.5	14
9	Dhenkanal	0.43	0.80	0.15	0.460	16.5	13
10	Gajapati	0.36	0.19	0.20	0.250	26	8
11	Ganjam	0.39	0.53	0.25	0.390	21	15
12	Jagatsingpur	0.52	1.00	0.57	0.697	2	9
13	Jajpur	0.42	0.85	0.24	0.503	14	20
14	Jharsuguda	0.48	0.74	0.54	0.587	7.5	1
15	Kalahandi	0.28	0.26	0.51	0.350	23	26
16	Kandhamal	0.35	0.38	0.23	0.320	25	18
17	Kendrapara	0.52	0.96	0.59	0.690	3	3.5

Contd...

18	Keonjhar	0.34	0.56	0.44	0.447	18	11
19	Khurda	0.71	0.91	0.71	0.777	1	3.5
20	Koraput	0.39	0.00	0.30	0.230	28	13
21	Malkangiri	0.43	0.03	0.15	0.203	30	21.5
22	Mayurbhanj	0.33	0.40	0.97	0.567	10	24
23	Nawarangpur	0.40	0.06	0.26	0.240	27	30
24	Nayagarh	0.51	0.82	0.32	0.550	11.5	25
25	Nuapada	0.38	0.20	0.39	0.323	24	27
26	Puri	0.47	0.87	0.51	0.617	5	16
27	Rayagada	0.35	0.05	0.23	0.210	29	10
28	Sambalpur	0.50	0.67	0.28	0.483	15	6
29	Sonepur	0.47	0.61	0.22	0.433	19	23
30	Sundergarh	0.40	0.53	0.66	0.530	13	5
Average		0.43	0.57	0.41	0.469		
C.V		20 per cent	53 per cent	49 per cent	33 per cent		

It is observed that Khurda (0.71) tops the list followed by Baragarh (0.58) so far as income index is concerned. On the contrary Kalahandi is found to have lowest income index (0.28). Bhadrak, Cuttack, Dhenkanal, Jajpur, Jharsuguda Jagatsinghpur, Kendrapara, Nayagarh, Sambalpur, Sonepur and Sundergarh districts have this index between 0.4 and 0.6, while the rest of the districts have it below 0.4 indicating poor performance of the state in general and the districts in western Orissa in particular.

A cursory glance at education index reveals that rural literacy is highest in Jagatsinghpur followed by Kendrapara and Khurda and lowest in Koraput preceded by Rayagada and Nawarangpur. The mission of Total literacy is found to have made no headway in the districts of Bolangir, Boudh, Gajpati, Kalahandi, Kandhamal, Koraput, Malkangiri, Mayurbhanj, Nawarangpur, Nuapada and Rayagada. It may be pointed out that these districts are home to a large percentage of disadvantaged people, mostly scheduled tribes. Though the other districts have fared well but still they have to go miles compared to the national average.

So far as health index is concerned it is observed that Mayurbhanj district is at the top followed by Deogarh. Contrary to expectations these two districts have low infant mortality rate either due to the fact that a large number of Christian missionaries are working and providing health services in these districts or the mortality cases go unreported as these districts are dominated by Scheduled Tribes and Scheduled Castes. Health care and health provision facilities are found to be better in the districts of Balasore, Bhadrak, Jagatsinghpur, Jharsuguda, Kalahandi, Kendrapara, Khurda, Puri and Sundergarh for which the health index seems to be almost satisfactory in those districts. Rest of the districts fare badly and require immediate attention.

Looking to the Rural HD (Table 4.2) it is seen that among top five districts in terms of high rural HDI value are Khurda, Jagatsinghpur, Kendrapara, Bhadrak and Puri. These are all coastal districts with satisfactory values of income, education and health indices. The lowest positions are occupied by districts such as Malkangir, Rayagada, Koraput, Nawarangpur, Gajapati,

Kandhamal, Nuapada, Kalahandi, Bolangir and Ganjam with low rural HDI values less than 0.4.These districts are the backward and some of them are with Naxalite problems. The rest of the districts like Angul, Balasore, Baragarh, Boudh, Cuttack, Deogharh, Dhenkanal, Jajpur, Jharsuguda, Keonjhar, Mayurbhanj, Nayagarh, Sambalpur, Sonepur and Sundergarh have medium HDI values.

Table 4.2: Levels of Human Development

Districts	Levels of HD
Bhadrak, Jagatsinghpur, Kendrapara, Khurda, Puri	High
Angul, Balasore, Baragarh, Boudh, Cuttack, Deogarh, Dhenkanal, Jajpur, Jharsuguda, Keonjhar, Mayurbhanj, Nayagarh, Sambalpur, Sonepur, Sundergarh	Medium
Bolangir, Gajapati, Ganjam, Kalahandi, Kandhamal, Koraput, Malkangiri, Nawarangpur, Nuapada, Rayagada	Low

To note that the HDI values and rank of the districts as worked out and published in Human Development Report 2004, Government of Orissa is different from the corresponding figure of the present study. Since 85 per cent people live in rural Orissa, the present exercise gives better results compared to that given in HDR, 2004.

It is evident from Table 4.1 that the average HDI of the districts stands at 0.469, which reflects the poor human development of the state. This low average HDI is due to low average income and health indices. Though the average education index value is 0.57 which pushes up the average HDI, it is seen that the co-efficient of variation is maximum (53 per cent) for this index. The co-efficient of variation for income and health indices stands in the order of 20 per cent and 49 per cent. It may be construed that poor performance in income generation is widespread in rural Orissa. Education though seems to give some comforts is concentrated in non-backward districts. Health consciousness and health services are found to be dismal throughout.

Finally it is worked out that the correlation co-efficient between the HDI for rural Orissa and the District Domestic product (DDP) is very poor and stands at 0.28. This conveys the idea that economic growth is inadequate for human development.

Conclusion

The main findings that emerged from the present study are as follows.

- The value of HDI for rural Orissa as a whole turns out to be 0.469.This may be regarded as low by UNDP standard but as per our classification there is medium level of human development in rural Orissa. Of the three components of HDI, the education index has the highest weight (0.57) whereas the health index has lowest weight (0.41) and the income index (0.43) lies in between close to health index.
- Though the education index seems to be better, it has the highest variation of 53 per cent compared to 20 per cent and 49 per cent variation in income and health indices respectively.
- The District Domestic Product has a very poor rank correlation co-efficient with the HDI of rural Orissa indicating the fact that economic growth can hardly expand human choices if the income distribution is skewed.
- Districts such as like Bhadrak, Jagatsinghpur, Kendrapara, Puri and Khurda (the capital district of the state) have high HD values, while the industrially prosperous districts like Cuttack Sundergarh, Angul and, Jharsuguda fall in the medium category.
- As expected the KBK districts have the low levels of human development. It is disheartening to note that the measures taken by the central and state governments have not helped much even after more than one and half decades of economic

reforms.

This necessitates rethinking and reformulation of our policy approaches so as to break the vicious cycle of underdevelopment that is widespread in rural Orissa. Development of physical and social infrastructure is equally important. The sector that needs immediate attention is health sector. In addition to the existing literacy programmes, more health programmes are at the moment highly essential for human development in rural Orissa. This may be possible by organizing more health awareness camps in villages so as to help rural people give up superstitious beliefs and accept health related schemes launched by government from time to time. To accelerate income on a sustainable basis, the employment programmes are to be designed in such a way that physical infrastructure is created particularly for agricultural development that holds the key to rural development. These responsibilities are to be assigned to the panchayats where decisions of the local people matter to solve the local problems.

References

Gita Rani, P. (1999), 'Human Development Index in India: A District Profile', *Artha Vijnana* Vol. XLI.

Government of Orissa (2004), Human Development Report, 2004, Bhubaneswar.

Government of Orissa (2005), Economic Survey (2004-05), Bhubaneswar.

Human Development Report (2001), Oxford University Press, New York.

Kamdar, S. and Basak, A. (2005), 'Beyond the Human Development Index, Preliminary notes on Deprivation and inequality', *Economic and Political Weekly*, Vol. XL No. 34.

Meyer, P. (2001), 'Human Development and civic Community in India, making Democracy Perform', *Economic and Political weekly*, Vol. XXXVI No. 8, pp. 624-692.

Orissa Development Report (2002), Planning commission, Govt. of India, New Delhi.

Statistical Abstract of Orissa (2005), Directorate of Economics and Statistics, Orissa.

5

Impact of Income and Education on Health

Himanshu Sekhar Rout

Introduction

Macroeconomic Evidence: Since the publication of Adam Smith's *The Wealth of Nations*, economists have sought answers to a unique question as to why some countries are wealthy and others are poor. Why economic growth rates differ? The main empirical tool used to study economic growth is cross-country analysis of the relationship between economic growth and a range of variables that are believed to account for the latter (Sachs and Werner, 1997). The factors may include: level and pattern of educational attainment (schooling); population growth; density and age structure; natural resource base; personal and government saving (investment rate); physical capital stock; economic policy; quality of public institutions; the geography (location and climate of a country), etc.

Recent research has added several specific 'health indicators' to these factors, and looked at the links between them and economic growth. There are direct and positive links between economic performance and health indicators. Investing on health is a tool of macroeconomic policy as it enhances economic growth. Interestingly, economic historians have concluded that perhaps thirty per cent of the estimated per capita growth rate in Britain between 1780 and 1979 was a result of improvement in health and nutritional status (Fogel, 1997). A strong partial correlation exists between health (as proxied by life expectancy) and output per worker (and hence growth) (Knowles and Owen, 1997).

Microeconomic Analysis: Unlike macroeconomic studies

that compare the performance of countries over time, microeconomic analysis tests the link between health and the income of households and individuals. However, thus far, little attention has been given to the micro aspects of health economics by the researchers, government and policy makers. Little research has been done to examine the extent to which the money that poor families spend on health care affects their nutritional status and thereby the health and survival, particularly of women and children (Werner, 1995). Major theoretical contributions to health economics were made in the sixties and seventies (Padhi and Mishra, 2000). Recent individual and household level studies have, however, paid renewed attention to health and are reaching increasingly consistent findings (Strauss and Thomas, 1998). The present study is an attempt to add value to this micro level study. It examines the effects of income and education of households on their health care expenditures in Orissa, one of the poorest states in the eastern part of India.

Health and its Linkages: A Review

Health is a state of complete physical, mental and social well being and not merely the absence of disease or infirmity. While physical health implies complete absence of disease or infirmity, mental health refers to the complete freedom from tensions. On the other hand, social health is a broader concept which includes social cooperation, social values, and social relations (WHO, 1992).

Health is not an end in itself, but one of the essential means of achieving economic and social aims. It is one of the criteria for assessing the quality of development in a society. The growth of national income should be accompanied by a considerable decrease in the number of premature deaths that occur among the poor and by the eradication of malnutrition and a host of other problems that have their roots in a hostile physical environment, illiteracy as well as poverty (Senghor, 1987).

There are, however, skepticisms about the outcome. While it is hard to believe that economic growth would ensure higher public expenditure on health and other social services, it is also opined that economic growth and increased public expenditures can't, by themselves, ensure favourable socio-economic outcomes (Devarajan and Reinikka, 2002). Filmer et al (2000) look at the "weak links" between government spending and improved outcomes. There are also skepticisms that the present rate of growth may fail to achieve the desired outcome with regard to health, education, poverty, gender equality, etc within the stipulated time as envisaged in millennium declarations (Devarajan *et. al.*, 2002).

Indicators of Health

Health status cannot be directly measured, as it is a complex and multi-dimensional concept. Similar difficulty arises with respect to the determinants of health as it is not easy to quantify nutritional, behavioural and environmental factors. Information on conditions of health and their determinants can at best be characterized by indicator variables rather than the classical measurements of physical and biological sciences. The more that is learnt about determinants, it becomes clearer that health problem and social ills stem from common causes (Maranda and Clermont, 1998).

The earlier studies find that health is determined by a host of interrelated factors. It is influenced by income of the household, education, food, housing, basic sanitation, social practices, measures to control environmental hazards and communicable diseases. The human development outcomes like health and education depend on household characteristics, such as whether the mother is educated, or the family can afford to send the children to school (Devarajan, Miler and Swanson, 2002). Gupta and Dasgupta (2002) find that income and price are strongly correlated with one's choice of health care provider. Education is found to be an important determinant of provider's choice.

Of all the determinants of health, poverty is viewed as a major determinant of health. Poverty has profound effect on well-being. The concept of poverty is often mixed up with other terms such as deprivation, inequality, disadvantage, alienation and marginalization (Calman, 1997). Poverty invites malnourishment. Malnutrition has been identified as the "biggest single contributor to child mortality in developing countries" (FAO, 1970). The malnourished mother gives birth to a low weight baby. Malnourishment after birth lowers the child's resistance to disease. A malnourished child may suffer mental impairment and thus benefit less from any education that is provided. Malnutrition affects human growth and development by adversely affecting the normal shape and size of the body, and in early childhood it can result in serious retardation in mental development. In India, where children are expected to help in agriculture (as most of the people depend on it), the rates of school attendance is low, and poor health lowers it further. The child who is hungry while at school may gain little from education. Poverty and ill health waste educational resources. While it may be said that ill health is the cause of poverty, poverty is also viewed as a cause of ill health.

Earlier analysis of the British experience in the nineteenth century (McKeown, Brown and Record, 1972) and the Latin American experience prior to the 1930s (Arriaga and Davis, 1969) revealed that decline in mortality rate was closely related to improvement in living standards rather than medical breakthroughs. Since the 1930s to the 1960s, however, it was claimed that mortality reduction was independent of increase in living standards (Arriaga and Davis, 1969). In the latter studies, it is again suggested that per capita income is the widely discussed socioeconomic determinant of mortality, primarily because it is considered a summary of the ability of an economy to meet the needs of its citizens (Cochrane, 1980).

Poverty is a major cause of low health standard (Abel-Smith and Leiserson, 1978). Health expenditure of the household members of rural India is sensitive to changes in household income levels and the elasticity of health expenditure with respect to income is largest for high-income groups (Mathiyazhagan, 2003). Poverty, squatter and disease go together. Health status is a matter of economic power. More the capacity of persons to purchase the health and medical care services, the more is the likelihood of better health status to emerge. The poorer section of the population suffers badly in the maintenance of health because of poor financial status (Sharma, 2000). A wide gap between the rich and the poor amounts to higher mortality via the breakdown of social cohesion (Kawachi and Kennedy, 1997).

Ill health can also be an important cause of poverty because it can lead to loss of income, catastrophic health expenses, and orphanhood. Thus improvement of health can make a substantial contribution towards fulfillment of the millennium development goals, which aims to halve between 1990 and 2015 the proportion of people whose income is less than US$ 1 a day (Haines and Cassels, 2004). Overall economic growth - particularly poverty-reducing growth - and education are central to good health (World Bank, 1993).

Besides poverty, another key factor that affects health is education. The positive association between education and health is well established. Well-educated people experience better health (Ross and Wu, 1995). In contrast, low educational attainment is associated with high rates of infectious disease, chronic noninfectious disease, self-reported poor health, shorter survival rate while sick, and shorter life expectancy (Feldman et al, 1989; Guralnik et al, 1993; Morris, 1990).

Why is education associated with good health? The theoretical explanations fall into three categories: (1) work and economic conditions, (2) socio-psychological resources, and (3) healthy life style. According to the first, well educated people are less likely to be unemployed and more likely to have full time jobs, fulfilling work, high incomes, and low economic hardships. According to the second, the well educated have social and psychological resources, including a high sense of personal control and social support in addition to economic resources. As per the third, the well educated have healthier life styles. The well educated are more likely to exercise, to drink moderately, to receive preventive medical care, and less likely to smoke (Ross and Wu, 1995).

Mother's year of education is often positively associated with improved child health and nutritional status (Behrman, 1990). There are varieties of mechanisms through which mother's education could raise child health. First, direct acquisition of basic health knowledge in school may provide future mothers with information useful for diagnosing and treating child health problems. Second, literacy and numeric skills learnt in school may enhance mother's abilities to treat child illness conditional on health knowledge and also should help mothers increase their stock of health knowledge after leaving school. Third, exposure to modern society in general via schooling may change women's attitudes towards traditional methods of raising children and treating their health problems (Glewwe, 1998).

Schultz (1984) argues that mother's education can influence child health in five ways: (1) education may lead to a more efficient mix of health goods used to produce child health; (2) better educated mother may be more effective at producing child health for a given amount and mix of health goods; (3) schooling can affect parents' preferences in systematic ways – for example, educated mother tends to opt for fewer but healthier children; (4) more schooling should increase family income, either through higher wages or increased productivity in self employment, which should improve child health status; and (5) education raises the opportunity costs of time, which tends to increase the time mothers spent working outside the home and thus reduce both maternal time for child care and duration of breastfeeding.

Barrera (1990) found that better educated mothers tended to wean their children sooner, but they compensated for this shortened breastfeeding time with better care. Overall, their children were healthier as measured by higher height-for-age z-scores. Cochrane, et al (1980) envisages that maternal education is closely related to child health whether measured by nutritional status or infant and child mortality. The evidence on the significance of the relationship is unequivocal. The magnitude is more difficult to determine. Bivariate analysis of infant and child mortality indicates that on an average, an additional year of schooling for a mother results in a reduction of nine per thousand in mortality of her offspring.

Cochrane (1980) also suggests that although per capita income is highly correlated with life expectancy in all periods examined, the elasticity of life expectancy with respect to income levels has declined since the 1930s and 1940s. It is not completely clear whether income inequality in itself is important or the factors associated with more equal distribution of income, such as literacy or access to health services are important. In simple correlation analysis, literacy seems to be the most important variable explaining life expectancy. In all cases, literacy has a higher level of significance than the presence of doctors per capita. Gupta and Dasgupta (2002) find that while income and price are strongly correlated with one's choice of health care provider, education is found to be an important determinant of provider's choice.

It is evident from the health research literature that the impact of either income or education on health care expenditure is studied separately. The present study is an attempt to find out the impact of both income and education on health care expenditure simultaneously. Secondly, it is also found that large proportions of health research have concentrated on a few key states of India – Kerala, Madhya Pradesh, West Bengal and Uttar Pradesh – while paying less attention to others. The present study has conducted the study in Orissa, where the prevalence of poverty, illiteracy, high infant mortality rate, malnutrition, low life expectancy and many other related problems needs special attention.

Database and Methodology

The study is based on primary data collected from four districts of Orissa, namely Khurda and Cuttack (for urban areas), Jajpur (for rural areas) and Nawarangpur (for tribal areas). The households are used as the units of sampling. The total sample size consists of 375 households, with 125 households from each area as mentioned above. Under urban areas, Bhubaneswar and Cuttack are chosen on the basis of judgment sampling method as both the cities appropriately represent urban Orissa. Multi-stage sampling method is adopted to select households from each city. In the first stage, units are taken as the wards, and in the second stage, units are taken as the households. Ward No. 20 and 7 are selected from Bhubaneswar and Cuttack respectively on the basis of random sampling method. Sixty-five and sixty households are selected at random from the selected wards of Bhubaneswar and Cuttack respectively. Data of four households are deleted at the end because of lack of information and inconsistency in the responses.

To select a rural and a tribal district, out of thirty districts of Orissa, two categories of districts are made. Category I includes the top ten districts in terms of rural population as per 1991 census. Similarly, Category II includes the top ten districts in terms of tribal population as per the above census (Table 5.1). Jajpur from category I and Nawarangpur from category II are selected on the basis of random sampling method for rural and tribal representations respectively.

Table 5.1: Top Ten Rural and Tribal Populous Districts of Orissa According to Census 1991

Top Ten Rural Districts (Category I)		Top Ten Tribal Districts (Category II)	
No.	Districts	No.	Districts
01	Ganjam	01	Mayurbhanj
02	Mayurbhanj	02	Sundergarh
03	Balasore	03	Keonjhar
04	Cuttack	04	Koraput
05	Jajpur	05	Nawarangpur
06	Keonjhar	06	Rayagada
07	Puri	07	Kalahandi
08	Baragarh	08	Sambalpur
09	Bolangir	09	Kandhamal
10	Kendrapara	10	Bolangir

Source: Data compiled from District Statistical Handbook 1997 Jajpur.

After the selection of rural and tribal districts, multi-stage random sampling method is adopted to select households. In stage I, Rasulpur Block is selected at random out of ten blocks of Jajpur district. In stage II, Jabara and Singapur Gram Panchayats (GPs) are selected at random out of twenty six GPs of Rasulpur Block. In stage III, Jabara village, out of five villages of Jabara GP and Singapur village out of seven villages of Singapur GP are selected randomly. In stage IV, sixty seven households, out of four hundred twenty two households of Jabara village and fifty eight households, out of three hundred sixty six households of Singapur village are selected at random with proportional allocation. The sample size for rural Orissa is one hundred twenty five.

For tribal areas, in stage I, Kosagumuda Block is selected at random out of ten blocks of Nawarangpur district. In stage II, Rajore GP and Pand-Gura GP are selected at random out of twenty two GPs of Kosagumuda Block. In stage III, Rajore village, out of ten villages of Rajore GP and Kandapuri village out of twelve villages of Pand-Gura GP are selected randomly. In stage IV, eighty seven households out of four hundred twelve households of Rajore village and thirty eight households out of one hundred eight two households of Kandapuri village are selected at random with proportional allocation. The sample size for tribal Orissa is one hundred twenty five.

With a view to find out the effects of income and education on health expenditure, multiple regression analysis is used. Three variables used for the study are represented as household health expenditure, income of the household and education of the head of the household. Household health expenditure is measured by per head health expenditure (PHE) which is estimated by dividing total annual health expenditure of the household by the household size. Similarly, for the income of a household, per head income of the household (PHI) is estimated by dividing total annual household income by size of the household. Education is taken as a dichotomous Dummy by assigning value one for the head of the family who is educated and zero for the illiterate.

Results and Discussion

It is evident from the descriptive statistics that an average household in the study area spends 7.42 percent of the income on out-of-pocket health expenditure. In the studies of Sundar (1995) and George (1997), it was recorded as 5 per cent and 9.78 per cent respectively. The government spending on the health sector works out to be less than two per cent of the country's Gross Domestic Product (GDP) (Tulasidhar, 1992). The World Health Organization (WHO) has recommended that governments must spend at least 5 per cent of their GDP on health care. India is lagging far behind.

It is revealed from Table 5.2 that the per capita income in the study area is Rs.14,034.66 per annum with standard deviation of 16684.7095 where as the per head household health care expenditure (PHE) is Rs. 1,026.79 per annum with standard deviation of 1678.0469. The mean of education is 0.7062 with standard deviation of 0.4561.

Table 5.2: Descriptive Statistics

Variables / Descriptive Statistics	Per Head Income	Per Head Health Expenditure	Education
Mean	12647.47	938.98	0.7062
Standard Deviation	16684.71	1678.54	0.4561
Coefficient of Variation	01.32	01.79	0.65
Highest Value	140000.00	13100.00	1.00
Lowest Value	1428.57	21.43	0.00
Range	138571.43	13078.57	1.00

Source: Compiled From Primary Data.

To find out the impact of household income (PHI) and education of the head of the household (EDN) on the pattern of health care expenditure (PHE) a linear regression model was fitted as PHE = -323.2 + 0.82PHI + 0.07EDN with R^2 value 0.712, which states that, ceteris paribus, a rupee increase in household income brings eighty two paise increase in household health care expenditure and if an extra household's head is educated, it influences the household health care expenditure by seven per cent. This implies that income is more responsible than education for better health. Thus, the family having more income meets with better health conditions.

From the study it is found that as disposable income (Y_d) of the household increases, individual takes more care of his life, hence health care expenditure (H) increases but at a particular level of income, due to high life risk, health expenditure becomes independent of income and perfectly elastic, which is termed as "High Life Risk Path (HLRP)".

The health expenditure during HLRP depends on households' past savings (S) and loanable capacity (L).

To improve the health status of the people, extreme poverty and hunger should be eradicated which is the first goal of the Millennium Development Goals (MDGs). The health planners and administrators should be involved in the planning process of the government to reduce poverty and adopt policies for more equitable distribution of income. They can also recommend for a specific health tax (an earmarked or so-called hypothecated tax) devoted to health care. Again spending more on health services does not necessarily buy better health. It needs an efficient management and use of resources. The principle of equality for opportunity for access to services on the basis of need and equal risk, irrespective of ability to pay should be followed.

If efficiency and also economy in administrative costs are to be achieved, global financing of providers according to appropriate workload ought to be another guiding principle. This will share with equitable public health services more generally, to ensure that - within available resources - the money follows the patient. Hospital and other providers are funded according to workload but this should not be carried out on the basis of a market mechanism. Such a mechanism can undermine the cooperative ethic in very practical ways. This is not just a general altruistic objection but also an empirical statement based on the deleterious consequences of even public sector markets (for example, in diminishing cooperation between hospitals, between hospital and community services, and between purchasers and providers) (Paton, 1995).

Health is a function not only of medical care but also of the overall integrated development of socio-cultural, economic, educational and political factors. Therefore, in order to raise the health status and quality of life, a focused approach integrating the development of social, cultural, economical and educational needs to emerge to bring about the overall transformation of a society.

To tackle poverty and hence health, it is necessary to consider individual and community. Community development projects that involve people in improving the local environment can provide a useful vehicle within which a wide variety of approaches can be used. The approaches are (i) putting the subject of poverty on the agenda of groups and organizations, (ii) targeting resources and expertise appropriately, (iii) developing educational opportunities, (iv) introducing appropriate tax and benefit measures, (v) ensuring employment opportunities, (vi) changing the environment, and (vii) providing adequate housing. These measures are essential in providing both a better environment and opportunities for all. They all attempt to improve quality of life and self esteem (Calman, 1997).

Conclusion

Health is a complex and multidimensional concept. It is a function not only of medical care but also of the overall integrated development of socio-cultural, economic, educational, political and technological factors. Health is influenced by income of the households, educational level of the family members, food, housing, basic sanitation, social practices, measures to control environmental hazards and communicable disease, and government spending in clinical and public health. In this context, the present study reveals that income level of the households and educational level of the family members have strong positive correlation with household health expenditure. An average household spends 7.42 per cent of the income on out-of-pocket health expenditure in Orissa. The regression analysis finds that a rupee increase in household income brings 82 paise increase in household health care expenditure. Further, it reveals that if an extra household head is educated, it influences the household health care expenditure by 7 per cent. This proves that income is more responsible than education for better health. A family having more income can maintain better health condition.

Thus, health planners and administrators should be involved in the planning process of the government to reduce poverty and adopt policies for more equitable distribution of income. They can also recommend for a specific health tax (an earmarked or so-called hypothecated tax) devoted to health care. Again spending more on health services does not necessarily buy better health. It needs an efficient management and use of resources. The principle of equality for opportunity for access to services on the basis of need and equal risk, irrespective of ability to pay need to be followed.

References

Abel-Smith, B. and A. Leiserson (1978), 'Poverty, Development and Health Policy', *Public Health Papers 69*, World Health Organization, Geneva.

Arriaga, E. E. and K. Davis (1969), 'The Pattern of Mortality Change in Latin America', *Demography*, Vol. 6, No. 3, pp. 223-42.

Barrera, A. (1990), 'The Interactive Effects of Mother's Schooling and Unsupplemented Breastfeeding on Child Health', *Journal of Development Economics*, Vol. 34, No. 1, pp. 81-98.

Behrman, J. (1990), 'The Action of Human Resources and Poverty on one Another: What we have yet to Learn, Living Standards Measurement Study', Working Paper No. 74, The World Bank, Washington D.C.

Calman, K. C. (1997), 'Equity, Poverty and Health for All', *British Medical Journal*, Vol. 314, p. 1189.

Cochrane, S. H. (1980), 'The Socioeconomic Determinants of Mortality: The Cross National Evidence', Staff Working Paper No. 405, The

World Bank, 1818 H Street, Washington, D.C.

Cochrane, S. H., J. Leslie and D. J. O'Hara (1980), 'Parental Education and Child Health: Intra-country Evidence', Staff Working Paper No. 405, pp. 56-95, The World Bank, 1818 H Street, Washington, D.C.

Devarajan, S. and R. Reinikka (2002), '*Making Services work for Poor people*', Mimeo: The World Bank Group.

Devarajan, S., M. J. Miller and E. V. Swanson (2002), 'Goals for Development: History, Prospects and Costs', World Bank Poverty research Working Paper 2819.

Doornbos, G. and D. Kromhout (1990), 'Educational Level and Mortality in the 32 years follow up study of 18-year-old men in the Netherlands', *International Journal of Epidemiology*, No. 19, pp. 374-79.

Feldman, J. J., D. M. Makuc., J. C. Kleinman and J. Cornoni-Huntley (1989), 'National Trends in Educational Differentials in Mortality', *American Journal of Epidemiology*, No. 129, pp. 919-33.

Filmer, Deon, Jeffery S. Hammer and Lant H. Pritchett (2000), 'Weak Links in the Chain: a Diagnosis of Health Policy in Poor countries', *World Bank Research Observer*, Vol. 15, No. 2, pp. 199-224

Fogel, R. W. (1997), 'New findings on secular trends in nutrition and mortality: some implications for population theory', in M.R. Rosenzweig and O. Stark (eds.), *Handbook of population and family economics*, Vol. 1A, pp. 433-481, Elsevier Science, Amsterdam.

Food and Agriculture Organization (1970), *Lives in Peril*, p. 25, Rome.

George, Alex (1997), 'Household Health Expenditure in Two States', pp. 79, The Foundation for Research in Community Health, Mumbai/ Pune.

Gibson, R. (1990), *Principles of Nutritional Assessment*, Oxford University Press.

Glewwe, P. (1998), 'Why does Mother's Schooling Raise Child Health in Developing Countries? Evidence from Morocco', *The Journal Human Resources*, Vol. 34, No. 1, p. 125.

Gupta, I. and P. Dasgupta (2002), 'Demand for Curative Health Care in Rural India: Choosing between Private, Public and No Care', Working Paper No. 82, NCAER, New Delhi.

Guralnik, J. M., K. C. Land, G. G. Fillenbaum and L. G. Branch (1993), 'Educational Status and Active Life Expectancy among Older Blacks and Whites', *New England Journal of Medicine*, No. 329, pp. 110-116.

Haines, A. and A. Cassels (2004), 'Can the millennium development goals be attained?', *British Medical Journal*, Vol. 329, pp. 394 - 397.

Kawachi, I. and B. Kennedy (1997), 'Health and Social Cohesion: Why care about income inequality?', *British Medical Journal*, Vol. 314, p. 1037.

Knowles, S. and P. D. Owen (1997), 'Education and Health in an Effective-Labour Empirical Growth Model', *The Economic Record*, Vol. 73, No. 223, p. 326.

Lipworth, L., T. Abelin and R. R. Connelly (1970), 'Socioeconomic factors in the Prognosis of Cancer Patients', *Journal of Chronic Disease*, Vol. 23, pp. 105-116.

Maranda, M. A. and M. Clermont (1998), 'Health and well being under one umbrella,' *World Health Forum*, Vol. 19, p. 241.

Mathiyazhagan, M. K. (2003), 'Rural Household Characteristics and Health Expenditure in India; An Analysis', *Journal of Social and Economic Development*, Vol. V, No. 1, p. 86.

McKeown, T., R. G. Brown and R. G. Record (1972), 'An Interpretation of the Modern Rise in Population in Europe', *Population Studies*, Vol. 26, No. 3, pp. 345-82.

Morris, J. N. (1990), 'Inequalities in Health; Ten Years and Little Further on', *The Lancet*, No. 36, pp. 491-493.

Murthy, N., I. Hirway, P. Panchmukhi., and J. Satia (1990), 'How well do India's Social Service Programs serve the Poor?', World Bank Policy Research Working Paper WPS491, The World Bank.

Padhi, S. and S. Mishra (2000), 'Premature Mortality, Health Status and Public Health Care Facilities in Orissa: a Study in Accessibility and Utilization', Nabakrishna Choudhury Centre for Development Studies, Bhubaneswar.

Panerai, R. B. (1998), 'Validation of indicators for health policy research', *World Health Forum*, Vol. 19, p. 6.

Paton, C. (1995), 'Present dangers and future threats', *British Medical Journal*, Vol. 310, No. 13, May.

Qadeer, I. (1995), 'Primary Health Care – A Paradise Lost', *IASSI Quarterly*, Vol. 14, Nos.1 and 2, p. 2.

Ross Catherine E. and Chia-Ling Wu (1995), 'The Links between Education and Health', *American Sociological Review*, Vol. 60, pp. 719-745.

Rout, H. S. (1998), 'India's Health Sector: Present and Past', *Vision*, Vol. XVIII, No.1-2.

Sachs, J. D. and A. M. Werner (1997), 'Fundamental sources of long term growth', *American Economic Review*, Vol. 87, pp. 184-188.

Saigal, S. (2002), '*Literature Review on Service Delivery in India*', A Background Reference for The World Development Report 2004: 'Making Services Work for Poor People', Draft 2, The World Bank.

Schultz, T. P. (1984), 'Studying the Impact of Household Economic and Community Variables on Child Mortality', *Population and development Review*, Vol. 10, pp. 215-35, Supplement.

Senghor, L. S. (1987), 'Health for development', *World Health Forum*, Vol. 8, p. 3.

Shariff, A., P. Ghosh and S. K. Mondal (2002), 'State Adjusted Public Expenditure on Social Sector and Poverty Alleviation Programmes', *Economic and Political Weekly*, Vol. 37, No. 8, p. 767.

Sharma, O. P. (2000), '*Rural Health and Medical Care in India*', Manak Publication Private Limited, New Delhi.

Strauss, J. and D. Thomas (1998), 'Health, Nutrition and Economic Development', *Journal of Economic Literature*, Vol. 36, pp. 766-817.

Sundar, R. (1995), 'Household survey of Health Care Utilization and Expenditure', Working Paper No 53, p.37, NCAER, New Delhi.

Tulasidhar, V. B. (1992), '*State's Financing of Health Care in India, Some Recent Trends*', Notional Institute of Public Finance and Policy, New Delhi.

Werner, D. (1995), 'Turning Health into an Investment: Assaults on Third World Health Care', *Economic and Political Weekly*, Vol. 30, No. 3, pp. 147-151.

World Bank (1993), '*World Development Report 1993: Investing on Health*', The World Bank and Oxford University Press, New York.

World Health Organization (1992), *Basic Document*, 39th Edition, Geneva.

6

Universal Primary Education in India: Issues and Challenges

Narayan C Nayak and Debabrata Samanta

Introduction

Development must be all pervasive that encompasses not only upward changes in macro economic indicators like GDP growth rate, foreign currency reserves, FDI flows, etc, but also noteworthy achievements in social sector. This approach gains currency as about 1.2 billion people of the world live on less than $1 a day, more than 113 million primary school age children do not go to school, more of them being girls than boys, and more than 5 lakh women die every year during pregnancy and child birth, to mention a few (WDR, 2001). Mere upward movement of a few growth indicators may not be enough to reflect the real picture of an economy. The development process must be seen in an integrated way that embodies the overall health of the economy. Especially, the developing countries like India, while valuing the growth impetus, must ensure the basic amenities to the people. It must create an environment in which the people can develop their full potential and lead their productive and creative lives according to their needs and interests (UNDP, 2003). As Dreze and Sen opine, "basic education, good health and other human attainments are not only directly valuable as constituent elements of our basic capabilities, these capabilities can also help in generating economic success of a more standard kind, which in turn can contribute to enhance the quality of human life even more" (Dreze and Sen, 1999, p 6).

Among all the dimensions of social sector, education is a key element that needs special attention. In a globalised era, when markets of the international economies are getting integrated, if a large part of the population can not read or write or cannot access other communication services, the integration may fail inevitably. Lack of education would continue to remain as a potential threat to prosperity everywhere. In the 'growth-mediated' social progress, public education may prove to be both favorable to economic growth (through the expansion of the opportunity of economic expansion) and favoured by economic growth (through the generation of more resources for such support) (Dreze and Sen, 1999). Although some studies emphasize on the productive contribution of learning by doing or functional literacy and on the job training, the ability to receive these trainings largely depends on the formal basic education imparted at the schools at an early stage (World Bank, 1993). Education also makes people socially concerned about their rights and duties, and makes the social system more participatory so that the benefit of growth is distributed.

The achievement of Universal Primary Education has been included in the 'Millennium Development Goal' to ensure that boys and girls alike must complete primary schooling (UN, 2000). Basic health and education are considered the 'fundamental rights'. The Universal Declaration of human rights asserts an individual's right to a standard of living adequate for health and wellbeing of himself and of his family, including medical care and a right to education that is free at least at elementary stages (WDR, 2004).

However, in India, all is not well with education. India, a country poised for rapid industrial growth and aspiring to become a developed nation by the year 2020, is faced with serious challenges in this front. While it is interesting to note that at the macro economic front, some noteworthy changes have been brought about particularly in the post-reforms periods, these changes have left the social sector almost untouched or at best given scant attention. As a result, still a large size of the population of the country continues to remain illiterate, underfed, and malnourished. The issues are diverse and addressing them may require a multi-pronged approach.

This paper thus attempts to make an overview of the state of education in India and makes a critical insight to the associated problems. Accordingly, the paper is divided into following themes: one, addresses the problems related to education in India, second, analyses the dimensions of the causes of such problems in education and the third, concludes with necessary observations.

Education in India: Progress Thus Far

Article 45 of the Indian Constitution states, "The state shall endeavor to provide within a period of ten years from the commencement of this constitution for free and compulsory education for all children until they complete the age of 14 years". Ironically, that constitutional obligation was deferred-first to 1970, and then to 1980, 1990 and 2000 and also beyond (www.indiatogether.org). The 93rd amendment of the Constitution has made free and compulsory education a 'fundamental right' for all children in the age group of 6-14 years. In order to fulfill this constitutional obligation, Sarva Shiksha Abhiyan has been launched by the Ministry of Human Resource Development, Govt. of India in partnership with the states in a mission mode. This programme is an effort towards recognition of the need for improving the performance of the school system through a community-owned approach and ensuring quality elementary education to all children in the age group of 6-14 years by the year 2010. Besides, India has also been a signatory to the 'Millennium Development Goal', which has pledged to achieve *inter alia* universal elementary education by the year 2015 (UN, 2000).

Needless to say, India is far behind the goal post despite all the efforts made so far. Though in the post-reforms period, India has moved from 'Hindu Rate of Growth' to nearly 8 per cent rate of growth of real GDP during 2005-06 (CSO, 2006), the impact of such growth particularly on elementary education appears to be limited. Higher income growth is not yet translated into greater educational attainment. It is more so with the attainment of elementary education.

If we compare India with some other developing countries including those from Asia, we visualize a very interesting picture. India is lagging far behind many other developing countries in this regard (Table 6.1). While the countries like South Korea, Maldives and Vietnam have attained levels of literacy as high as 97.8 per cent, 96.3 per cent and 93.3 per cent respectively, India's literacy rate as per 2001 census has reached a mere 65.3 per cent, which is little higher than that of Nigeria (64.1 per cent). The other very disturbing aspect is that the gender disparity is more buoyant in India. India records one of the highest female-male literacy gaps in the world. Only 5 countries have higher gaps than India (Bhutan, Syria, Togo, Malawi, and Mozambique). The state of Rajasthan alone has a population as large as that of all the five countries combined and no country in the world has a higher female-male literacy gap than Rajasthan, where the literacy rate for women is a mere 5 per cent.

Table 6.1: Literacy Rates in Selected Countries of the World

	Literacy rate 15+ (per cent) (2000)		
Country	Total	Male	Female
South Korea	97.8	99.2	96.4
Maldives	96.3	96.3	96.4
Vietnam	93.3	95.7	91.0
Mexico	91.0	93.1	89.1
Malaysia	87.5	91.5	83.6
Indonesia	87.0	91.9	82.1
Brazil	85.3	85.1	85.4
China	85.0	92.3	77.4
Nigeria	64.1	72.3	56.2
India (2001 census)	65.3	75.8	54.1

Source: UNESCO 1999 Statistical Year Book (Estimates literacy Rates for the year 2000) courtesy: www.nlm.nic.in/lsi.htm.

It is interesting to note that in 1951, the gender disparity was very much in prevalence with a female-male literacy gap of 18.30. Over the decades, however, the disparity has widened which has reached 21.70 in 2001 with still increasing gaps in the preceding decades. Though in the period 1991-2001, the increase in the female literacy rate (14.87 per cent) was more as compared to that in the male literacy rate (11.72 per cent), this was not enough to bridge the gap (Table 6.2).

Table 6.2: Level of Literacy in India during 1951-2001

Year	Person	Male	Female	Male-Female gap in literacy rate
1951	18.33	27.16	8.86	18.30
1961	28.30	40.40	15.35	25.05
1971	34.45	45.96	21.97	23.98
1981	43.57	56.38	29.76	26.62
1991	52.21	64.13	39.29	24.84
2001	65.38	75.85	54.16	21.70

Source: Census of India (www.indiabudget.nic.in)

Added to this, at the elementary level of education, the enrolment rate is very low for girls (Table 6.3). Out of the estimated population of 205 million in the age group of 6-14 years in March 1, 2002, nearly 82.5 per cent got enrolled in schools as compared to 82.4 per cent in 2001-02. In the year 1999-2000, nearly 79 per cent attended schools in this age group. During 1991-96, the student retention rate at the primary school stage was about 58 per cent only. At the primary level, the drop-out rate decreased from 39 per cent in 2001-02 to 34.9 per cent in 2002-03, while at the upper primary level, the drop-out rate decreased from 54.6 per cent to 52.8 per cent over the same period. Despite the decline over the years, the drop-out rate still remains very high, especially with girls, for whom the rates in 2002-03 were 33.7 per cent and 53.5 per cent at the primary and the upper primary levels respectively (Economic Survey, 2004-05).

Table 6.3: Trends in Gross Enrollment Ratio in Primary (I-IV) Level (in per cent)

Year	Boys	Girls	Total
1970-71	95.5	60.5	78.6
1980-81	95.8	64.1	80.5
1990-91	114.0	85.5	100.1
1991-92	112.8	86.9	100.2
1992-93	95.0	73.5	84.6
1993-94	90.0	73.1	81.9
1994-95	96.6	78.2	87.7
1995-96	97.1	79.4	88.6
1996-97*	98.7	81.9	90.6
1997-98*	97.7	81.2	89.7
1998-99*	100.9	82.9	92.1
1999-00*	104.1	85.2	94.9
2000-01*	104.9	85.9	95.7
2001-02	105.3	86.9	96.3
2002-03	97.5	93.1	95.4

*Provisional

Source: Selected Education Statistics, 2000-01, MHRD; Economic Survey 2004-05.

There also remains disparity in the attainment of literacy across states. While in some states and union territories like Kerala (90.9 per cent), Mizoram (88.8 per cent), Lakshadweep (86.7 per cent), Goa (82 per cent) and Chandigarh (81.9 per cent), the level of literacy as attained is comparable to the best in the world, the states like Bihar (47 per cent), Jharkhand (53.6 per cent), Arunachal Pradesh (54.3 per cent), Jammu and Kashmir (55.5 per cent), Uttar Pradesh (56.3 per cent), and Dadra and Nagar Haveli (57.6 per cent) are lagging far behind. Added to this, in the latter states, the gender disparity is very acute. In Bihar, about 66.9 per cent females are illiterate followed by 59.8

per cent females in Dadra and Nagar Haveli, 57.8 per cent in Uttar Pradesh, 57 per cent in Jammu and Kashmir, 56.5 per cent in Arunachal Pradesh and 56.1 per cent in Rajasthan.

Identifying Issues

Given the plight of the situation with respect to education that we visualize in India, it may be worthwhile to address the issue in its totality. In our attempt to finding the crux of the problems, in addition to the supporting data, recourse to the earlier studies has been made throughout this section to substantiate the argument. Both the above drive home the fact that there exist two conflicting but interlinked dimensions with respect to education - demand side and supply side – that act as deterrent to the achievement of the target. While the former is believed to be driven by forces like income level, parental education, low opportunity cost, migration, etc, the latter may be represented through policy initiatives and their promptness, size and accountability and the like. Given the nature of problems that India is faced with, an analysis of these dimensions may give some direction to judging the state of Indian economy, polity and society.

Demand Side

Notwithstanding the fact that education is.imperative and one of the most valuable possessions, households often sacrifice education primarily due to low income and other associated problems. In addition, some parents value education less important due to their illiteracy, frequent migration and so on. An analysis of these dimensions particularly in the context of India would be in vogue.

Poverty: There is evidence to suggest that poverty leads to illiteracy. Grootaert and Patrinos (1999) in their cross country study argue that economic wellbeing of the households as measured by income and wealth indicators affects the likelihood of the children attending schools. They further argue that poorer households are prone to income shocks and they fail to insure themselves against that. In the process, children's labour becomes an important source of cushion for these families, which is supplied at the cost of schooling. In Indian context, analyzing NCAER data, Duraisamy (2002) finds that family income along with parental education and availability of middle schools in villages has a significant positive effect on child's school enrolment decisions. Dreze and Kingdon (2001) also find similar type of outcome for northern states of India.

In addition to low income, persistent inequality in the distribution of income also acts as a deterrent. It may be noted here that due to structural constraints, inequality in the distribution of income has become the rule in India. There thus remain two types of households: the rich and the poor. Both incur expenditure on education and other social sector services. However, the poor are expected to depend more on the public provision, while the rich are in a position to utilize the private services. The impact of such public services on social attainments depends on the extent to which such services are utilized, which in turn depends on the efficacy of the functioning of the delivery systems (Seeta Prabhu, 2001).

It is further evident that schooling outcomes are positively associated with per capita household expenditures. Mukhopadhyay and Chandrasekhar (2004) have found that the probability of a child from a household in the top non food expenditure quartile going to school is higher by over 11 per cent as compared to a child from the bottom wealth quartile. A study by NCERT finds that better economic condition of the household and parental ability to bear extra tuition costs, books, stationeries, and clothes contribute to continuation of schooling by girls. An overview of the levels of literacy in Indian states given their levels of per capita income clearly indicates that the states with higher per capita income have achieved higher levels of literacy. The Pearson correlation as estimated between per capita income and literacy rates of 20 major states and union territories confirm the same with a value 0.661 which is significant at 0.01 level (Table 6.4).

Table 6.4: Level of Literacy and Per Capita Income of the Selected Indian States & Union Territories

State/UT	Literacy Rate (2001)	Per capita Income (2001-02)
Kerala	90.92	11046
Chandigarh	81.76	28271
Pondicherry	81.49	18820
Maharashtra	77.27	15070
Himachal Pradesh	77.13	11936
Tamil Nadu	73.47	13108
Gujarat	69.97	14102
Punjab	69.95	15255
West Bengal	69.22	10376
Manipur	68.87	7976
Haryana	68.59	14075
Chhattisgarh	65.18	7647
Assam	64.28	5989
Madhya Pradesh	64.11	7635
Orissa	63.61	6105
Meghalaya	63.31	8827
Andhra Pradesh	61.11	10313
Rajasthan	61.03	8536
Arunachal Pradesh	54.74	9413
Bihar	47.53	3399

High Cost of Education: The costs associated with education create discrimination against the poor as they eat up a larger share of the household budget. The latter discourages or denies poor people to send their children to schools. In 1995-96, the expenditure per student receiving primary education in a government school of rural India was Rs. 219, while for students going to local body schools, private aided schools and private unaided schools it was Rs. 223, Rs. 622 and Rs. 911 respectively

(NSSO, 1998). As against the national average, there are wide variations across states and union territories in this respect with a high of Rs. 1,863 in Dadra and Nagar Haveli and a low of Rs. 132 in Karnataka. Among the states only, Nagaland (Rs.1,210) followed by Punjab (Rs. 890) and a few other north-eastern states spend more on primary education (Table 6.5).

Table 6.5: State and Union-Territory wise Average Expenditure of the Students Pursuing Primary Education in Rural India

State/Union Territories	Average Expenditure (Rs.)	State/Union Territories	Average Expenditure (Rs.)
Andaman & Nicobar	623	Lakshwadeep	228
Andhra Pradesh	234	Madhya Pradesh	193
Arunachal Pradesh	483	Maharashtra	266
Assam	199	Manipur	625
Bihar	230	Meghalaya	753
Chandigarh	635	Mizoram	639
Dadra & Nagar Haveli	1863	Nagaland	1210
Daman & Diu	1523	Orissa	199
Delhi	702	Pondicherry	529
Goa	550	Punjab	890
Gujarat	172	Rajasthan	316
Haryana	687	Sikkim	686
Himachal Pradesh	501	Tamil Nadu	267
Jammu & Kashmir	721	Tripura	456
Karnataka	132	Uttar Pradesh	320
Kerala	658	West Bengal	245

Source: NSSO, 1998.

Empirical study provides the evidence that higher schooling

expenses create hindrances for pursuing primary education. Tilak (1996) in his studies reported that contrary to the popular notion, the households in rural India spend a substantial amount of money on education of their children. Even the government primary schools do not provide complete free education. In another study, Tilak (2002) found that the households belonging to the lower strata of social and economic hierarchy having low income also spend significant amount especially on elementary education, which should have been otherwise made freely available. Interestingly, the Public Report on Basic Education in India (PROBE, 1999) in its study on northern India reported that respondents kept expensive schooling ahead of even child labour among the reasons cited for lack of education among the children. Using data from rural India on 46,430 children, it has been further found by Mukhopadhyay and Chandrasekhar (2004) that a unit increment in the logarithm of cost of primary schooling (Rs. 190) reduces the likelihood of going to school by 3 percentage points. This finding is robust across different measures of cost. Further, while cost is a significant deterrent for schooling for wealth groups, its effects are more on the lower wealth groups.

It is further emphasized that the family plays a crucial role in decisions about investment in education, particularly in developing countries. The reasons could be that education is expensive and there is limited scope for borrowing to invest in education. One can not borrow to invest in education because human capital provides very poor collateral and thus most of the financial investment in education has to be borne by the family (Banerjee, 2004).

Child Labour: Another important yet understated and unresolved dimension of low educational attainment in developing countries including India is the preponderance of child labour. The latter is promoted in the low income families as it contributes to their household earnings. Consequently, the opportunity cost of sending the children to school is assumed to be very high. It is found that the children are engaged in many household activities varying from attending younger siblings to going to field to assist their parents; and in this respect, generally the girl child suffers the most. India has one of the highest numbers of child labourers in the world, with estimates ranging between 14 and 100 million in various studies (http://www.hum-coolie.com/on-child-labour.htm). The official data reports that the magnitude of child labour has increased from 11.59 million in 1991 to 12.66 million in 2001 (Census, 2001). Although other unofficial reports present a much higher figure, the government's programmes – Sarva Shiksha Abhiyan, National Child Labour Project and Indus Project - do not even address effectively these 12.66 million child labour. According to the NCERT Sixth All India Educational Survey, a total of 111 million children of primary school age (6-14) were not attending school in 1993-94 (http://www.ncert.nic.in/sites/ educationalsurvey/saies.htm). Most of these children work in the unorganized domestic sector.

Alien Language of Instruction: The language as a barrier is often evident in the tribal areas of the country. The mainstream language at which the instruction is made is found to be alien to the children in the tribal areas. In a study undertaken in the state of Jharkhand, Rana and Das (2004) find that Hindi, the official language of Jharkhand, is as foreign to them as any other language. According to HDR (2003), teaching children in the appropriate language also improves educational outcomes, as high performing countries have already proved it. In those countries, the mother tongue is used for instructions at the primary level. Students learn to read more quickly when they are taught in the languages most familiar to them and can even learn a second language more quickly. In a vast country like India, which is endowed with so many languages and dialects, it has perhaps not been a realistic proposition to provide education in the local language of every child. That may have been one of the deterring factors towards attaining higher literacy in India.

Seasonal Migration of the Parents: In India, it is evident that due to lack of adequate rural non-farm employment opportunities, people migrate from the rural to urban areas in search of livelihood. In many circumstances, this becomes seasonal in nature. Consequently, the parents often take their children with themselves leading to discontinuation of their studies. Interestingly, the rural schools become reluctant to admit these children due to their long absence. Bhattacharyya (2005) reveals that the migratory families bring children with them to the work place. The older kids are put to work or made to look after the younger ones. The system of education in India leaves parents and kids helpless. From class IV onwards, village schools refuse to admit the children if they are absent for half of the year.

Characteristics of the Child: In India, the characteristic of child plays a crucial role in determining whether he or she should be provided education or not. As girls are given less weightage as compared to boys in the social hierarchy, naturally, parents often discriminate against the girls in almost all matters including education. The girls are pooled out of schools and asked to help in the domestic chores and look after their younger siblings. As mentioned earlier, in the wake of the increased schooling expenses, more girls are asked to sacrifice their studies as compared to the boys (Mukhopadhyay and Chandrasekhar, 2004). It is emphasized in the above-mentioned study that the more the number of children below the age of five in families, the greater the probabilities that the girls are denied schooling as the girls are required to take care of their younger siblings. In all social groups, the probability of a girl child going to school is lower by 16.4 per cent point. The gender bias is prominent primarily because of the perception that the return on the education on a male child is higher than that on a female child (Dreze and Sen, 1995).

The age of the child also plays a decisive role in enrolling him/her in the school. In their study, Mukhopadhyay and Chandrasekhar (2004) commented that the longer the delay in enrolling the child in school, the lower would be the likelihood of attendance. Grooteart and Patrinos (1999) argued that the older the child, the more likely that he or she would work for wages or within the household.

Lack of Education with the Parents: Education level of the parents is another pertinent aspect that needs serious attention.

The illiterate parents often fail to realize the importance of education of their children. Educated parents or household heads are more likely to send their children to school. There is evidence to suggest that mother's education improves girl child's schooling outcomes (Mukhopadhyay and Chandrasekhar, 2004). In their study, Grootaert and Patrinos (1999) found that parental education has a strong positive influence on schooling outcomes and in particular for the girl child. The impact of mother's education is more pronounced for the girl child than for boys. They concluded that the key factors affecting child labor are household size and composition, education and employment status of the parents.

Supply Side

Besides the demand driven problems, there are quite a few pertinent supply side dimensions that may require equal attention. The Supply side problems are linked to the roles of the government and other service providers. According to the HDR 2003, the developing countries face three main challenges in expanding primary education; viz. limited resources, poor implementation and poor infrastructure. India is no exception to that. An account of the nature and magnitude of problems related to these three aspects in the context of India may prove to be significant in addressing the issue in right direction.

Limited Resources: It is interesting to note that in India, while private expenditure on schooling is on the rise, which is beyond the reach of the poor households, the public expenditure is much below the desired level. The public expenditure on education as a percentage of GDP has reached 4 per cent in the year 2001-02. This attainment is much below the target of 6 per cent of GDP as set down first by National Policy on Education in the year 1968 and reiterated at the international level. This proportion is found to be less than that in many developing countries including the countries of Africa as well (Tilak, 2004). Over the successive five year plans, although there has been continuous increase in public expenditure allocation, it has never been sufficient to reach the target (Table 6.6). If we compare

India's spending on education with that in the other countries, according to the HDR, 2006, India ranks 103 with respect to share of the public expenditure on education as a percentage of its GDP (UNDP, 2006).

Table 6.6: Expenditure on Education in Five Year Plans

Five Year Plans	Elementary (Per cent)	Secondary (Per cent)	Higher (Per cent)
I	85(56)	20(13)	14(9)
II	95(35)	51(19)	48(18)
III	201(34)	103(18)	87(15)
IV	239(30)	140(18)	195(25)
V	317(35)	156(17)	205(22)
VI	803(30)	736(25)	530(18)
VI	2,849(34)	1,829(22)	1,201(14)
VIII	4,006.6(47)	1,538(18)	1,055.8(12.4)
IX	16,364.88(65.7)	2,603.5(10.5)	2500.0(10.0)

Note: The figures in parenthesis indicate per cent to total allocation.
Source: Five-Year Plans, Annual Plans and MHRD Reports.

While the total public expenditure is low, ironically, the states spend more on social sector than the centre, which leads to differential treatments according to the resource base of the states. It is evident that the per capital social sector expenditure is higher with richer states as compared to that with poorer ones (Table 6.7).

Interestingly, the education schemes which are in force to act as facilitators for higher enrolment in the schools are losing their vigour with the passage of time. As Tilak (2004) argues, in recent years, the fund allocations to the midday meal scheme are not in consonance with the increasing enrolment. The number of children covered by the scheme increased from approximately 3 crore in 1995-96 to about 10 crore 2002-03. Contrary to this, the allocation of funds has come down from Rs. 1,600 crore in 1998-

99 to less than Rs. 10 crore in 2002-03. This clearly indicates the non-committal approach of the government.

Table 6.7: Per Capita Expenditure on Total Social Services in 1998-99 (Current Prices)

States	Per Capita Expenditure (Rs)
Andhra Pradesh	973
Bihar	476
Goa	3069
Gujarat	1211
Haryana	1111
Karnataka	1001
Kerala	1096
Madhya Pradesh	942
Maharashtra	1045
Orissa	782
Punjab	1157
Rajasthan	1037
Tamil Nadu	1205
Uttar Pradesh	571
West Bengal	740
Weighted Average of 15 States	879

Source: RBI Bulletins; as cited in Dev and Mooij, 2002.

It is interesting to note that over the past few years there has been significant increase in the external aid towards promotion elementary education in India. It was Rs. 37 crore in 1993-94 which increased to Rs. 1,210 in 2001-02 (budget estimate as cited in Tilak, 2004). As a proportion of the central government's plan expenditure on elementary education, it has increased from 10 per cent to above 30 per cent during this period. While the figure indicates a significant attainment in this front for India, as Tilak (2004) asserts it leads one to doubt whether external aid does add to the spending on education or it acts as a substitute of the national spending, as no noticeable change in public spending on education is observed during this period.

Poor Implementation

In addition to inadequate allocation of funds, lack of proper implementation of the educational schemes has become another disturbing facet. In India, although a number of literacy programmes have been introduced from time to time, primarily the problems have cropped up at the stage of implementation. In a study conducted in West Bengal, Dutta (2004) identified challenges from four different fronts, apart from lack of coordination and formal linkages between programmes. In the first place, there is lack of effective participation of Panchayats and urban local bodies. Second, the political interest is not so focused on education as on the other activities. Third, the lack of political attention discourages bureaucracy to implement the programmes in adequate vigour. Fourth, there is lack of adequate community participation in the programme.

Another very pertinent dimension of education is the pattern of expenditure in education. In India, as mentioned in the previous section, government has been attempting from various sources to increase the funding for elementary education. Under the common minimum programme of the UPA led government, a 2 per cent education cess has also been imposed to raise revenue of about Rs. 5,000 crore to finance the basic education. Despite all the above attempts, the problem remains primarily due to the fact that 95 per cent of the allocated funds are used to pay salaries to the teachers only.

Poor Infrastructure

Availability of proper infrastructure has a positive effect on enrolment and attendance in the school (Foster and Rosenzweig, 2004). Contrarily, in India, a large number of schools are devoid of adequate infrastructure facilities. The PROBE survey (1999) found that 82 per cent of the schools needed repair. Two-thirds had roofs with leakages which was making it difficult to hold classes at the time of rains. In the government primary schools, it was found that nearly 11 per cent schools had no functioning toilets, 73 per cent did not have blackboards in every class, 58 per cent schools had no drinking water facilities and 52 per cent schools did not have playgrounds. The distance of the school has often influenced the parent's decision to send their children to school and in this respect; arguably, the girls are discriminated against the boys (Dreze and Sen, 1995). The closer the school, the higher are the chances that the children including the girls will go to schools (with the exception of girls belonging to scheduled tribe community) (Mukhopadhyay and Chandrasekhar, 2004).

Another alarming problem is the lack of teachers in schools. In India, with total number of 3.2 million teachers at elementary stage as in 2000-01, the teacher-pupil ratio was as high as 1:43 in 2001. About 75 per cent of the rural schools have one teacher for several classes. In Bihar, the teacher-pupil ratio is as high as 1:78.

The high teacher-pupil ratio results in lack of adequate personal attention to children at the early stages of their education and thus it may be acting as a de-motivating factor for the school going children. This problem gets further aggravated by the uneven distribution of teachers across schools. A large percentage of schools are reported to have got more than 1:50 teacher-pupil ratio. In some cases, it has even reached a staggering high of three digit figures.

Although it is claimed that the single teacher schools have been done away with since the introduction of the Operation Blackboard in 1986, the PROBE survey found in its sample that about 12 per cent of the schools were functioning with single teachers and another 21 per cent schools had single teachers present in the schools as other teachers were absent (PROBE, 1999). Thus, effectively nearly one-third of the schools were in the hands of single teachers.

Conclusion

To conclude, we may thus state that even after more than five decades of planned development, India's target of achieving universal primary education still remains a far cry. There remain problems both at the demand side and the supply side. Given the nature and complexity of the problems that surround this vital social sector, an integrated approach to the whole issue may bring about desired solutions.

References

Banerjee A. V. (2004), 'Educational Policy and Economics of the Family', Journal *of Development Economics*, June, Vol. 74, No. 1.

Bhattacharyya, M. (2005), 'Classroom Joys, caked in mud', The Telegraph, 10.05.2005.

Census of India (2001), *Primary Census Abstract*, Office of the Registrar General of India, New Delhi.

Central Statistical Organization (2006), National Accounts Statistics, Ministry Of Statistics and Programme Implementation, Government of India, New Delhi.

Dev, S. M. and J. Mooij (2002), 'Social Sector Expenditures in the 1990s: Analysis of Central and State Budgets', *Economic and Political Weekly*, Volume. 37, No. 9, pp. 853-866, March 2.

Dreze, J. and A. Sen (1995), *India: Economic Development and Social Opportunity*, Oxford University Press, Oxford.

Dreze, J. and A. Sen (1999), *Indian Development- Selected Regional Perspectives*, Oxford University Press, New Delhi.

Dreze, J. and G. Kingdon. (2001), 'School Participation in Rural India', *Review of Development Economics*, Vol. 5, No. 1, pp. 1-24.

Duraisamy, P. (2002), 'Changes in Returns to Education in India, 1983-1994: By Gender, Age-Cohort and Location', *Economics of Education Review*, Vol. 21, No. 6, pp. 609-622.

Dutta, P. (2004), 'Literacy, Development and Empowerment: the Experience of West Bengal' *Indian Social Science Review*, Vol. 6, No. 1, Jan-Jun 2004.

Foster, A. D. and Mark. R. Rosenzweig (2004), 'Technological Change Distribution of Schooling: evidence From Green Revolution in India', *Journal of Development Economics*, Vol. 74, No. 1, June 2004.

Government of India (Various Years), 'Analysis of Budget Expenditure on Education', MHRD, New Delhi.

——(1997-98), Selected Educational Statistics, MHRD, New Delhi.

——(2004-05), Economic Survey, 2004-05, Ministry of Finance, New Delhi.

——Department of Elementary Education and Literacy, MHRD, New Delhi, Courtesy:

——Five-Year Plans and Annual Plans, Planning Commission of India, New Delhi, Courtesy:

Grootaert, C. and H. Patrinos (eds) (1999), *The Policy Analysis of Child Labour: A Comparative Study*, New York: St Martin's Press.

Mukhopadhyay, A. and S. Chandrasekhar (2004), 'Does Cost of Primary Education matter? Evidence from Rural India', Working Paper Series, IGIDR and ISI, Delhi.

National Sample Survey Organization, (1998), 'Attending an Educational Institution in India: its level, Nature and Cost", *NSS 52nd Round Edition, July 1995-June 1996,* Report No 439, Department of Statistics, Government of India, New Delhi.

PROBE (1999), *Public Report on Basic Education in India*, Oxford University Press, New Delhi.

Rana, Kumar and Samantak Das, (2004), 'Primary Education in Jharkhand', *Economic and Political Weekly*, Vol. 39, No. 11, pp. 1171-78, March 13-19.

Seeta Prabhu, K. (2001), *Economic Reform and Social Sector Development: A Study of Two Indian States*, New Delhi: Sage Publications.

Tilak, J.B.G. (2002), 'Determinants of Household Expenditure on Education in Rural India: A Study based on the NCAER Survey on Human Development in India', NCAER Working Paper No 88, August.

——(2004), 'Education in the UPA Government Common Minimum Programme', *Economic ad Political Weekly*, October 23-29, Vol. XXXIX, NO 43.

——1996, 'How free is 'Free' Primary Education in India', *Economic and Political weekly*, Vol. 31, No. 5, pp. 275-282.

UNDP (2003), *Human Development Report*, 2003, Oxford University Press, New Delhi.

UNDP (2006), *Human Development Report, 2006*, Oxford University Press, New Delhi.

UNESCO (1999), *Statistical Year Book* (Estimates literacy Rates for the year 2000), Courtesy: www.nlm.nic.in/lsi.htm.

World Bank (1993), *The East Asian Miracle*, Oxford University Press, Oxford.

World Bank (2001), *World Development Report 2001*, Oxford University Press.

World Bank (2004), *World Development Report 2004*, Oxford University Press.

Part II: Women, Labour and Socio-Cultural Perspectives

7

Hierarchical Distribution of Female Education in India

Sharmita Dhar, Narayan C Nayak and
Bani Chatterjee

Introduction

Thus far, threshold education has been the priority in developing countries including India. The thrust on threshold point is the genesis of equity analysis of last quarter a century probably starting from Rawls' (1999) 'A Theory of Justice'. It is imperative to know what is below the minimum threshold point. In politics, it is mere voting right; in economic development, it is poverty line; and in education, it is literacy rate. Sen (1970) and Rawls (1999) are some of the proponents of this type of social welfare function. Rawls (1999) while suggesting a max-min policy argues that justice is guided by a policy of maximizing the minimum value, which becomes a social welfare index. This policy obviously leads to perfect equality of the relevant variable, be it justice, education, health or any other social indicator.

The approach as stated above is a social equity indicator. In education, the latter becomes meaningful provided equity beyond literacy in the hierarchical structure is maintained. It is in this context essential to analyse the distributional equity in the hierarchy of education particularly in India where attainment of mere literacy has failed to bear fruits. This paper attempts to address the same taking into account the level of education among women up to higher secondary level.

Database and Methodology

The study is based on secondary data. The major sources of

data include National Planning Commission of India (2001), Statistical Abstract (2002), Government of India, New Delhi, Annual Report (2004-2005), Department of School Education, Government of West Bengal, etc. The whole analysis is based on the concept of absolute as well as relative status of female population in India. To measure the relative status of females in comparison with males across different stages of education, number of girls' enrolment per 100 boys' enrolment at different stages has been estimated and also the ratio of girls' enrolment per 100 boys' enrolment between two successive stages has been computed. The latter ratio indicates the proportion of girls per 100 boys who are privileged or have chances of successive education from among the girls per 100 boys who have already attained previous level of education. If the ratio exceeds one it implies that the relative enrolment of girls improves as the level of education rises. If it is equal to one, the status of girl students remains unaltered over the stages and if it is less than one the situation becomes worse for the girls across successive stages of education. In the present study, an attempt is made to emphasize only on distributional equity i.e. the equity aspect of education in a multi-level hierarchical model of education.

To be precise, we may treat education as a commodity, which may be distributed among various age groups of women population. In the similar line, this distribution can be considered caste-wise, income-wise, etc. A general model of distribution of education across different age groups of population is given in Table 7.1. The study follows a tentative directional analysis, wherein a specific category i.e. gender is considered. To be more specific, the paper attempts to see the distributional equity in female education in India in the hierarchy of education.

Female Education in India: A Hierarchical Distribution

In order to understand the nature and extent of education that women have received in India, a multistage hierarchal model of education may be considered. The stages may include literacy, preliminary and primary education, secondary and intermediate education, and graduation in general as well as professional education. In the present study, an analysis from literacy level to secondary-higher secondary combined level has been made.

Table 7.1: Distribution of Education across Different Stages and Estimation of Privileged and Deprivation Ratio

Stages of Education	Primary (I – V)	Middle (VI – VIII)	Secondary and Higher Secondary combined (IX-XII)
Total No. of students	P_1	P_2	P_3
No. of girls' enrolment per 100 boys enrolment	F_1	F_2	F_3
Computed ratios	F_2 / F_1		F_3 / F_2

Literacy Level among Females: Attainment of literacy has always been a thrust area in our drive towards achieving development goals. Successive Human Development Reports have given emphasis to universal literacy along with gross enrollment ratio to measure education index as an important dimension of human development (UNDP, 2004). Millennium Development Goals (MDG) has also reiterated the importance of literacy while treating human development in its entirety (UN, 2000). In the process, goals towards achieving total literacy among women have gained momentum. India being a signatory of MDG has been attempting to eradicate illiteracy by all possible means by 2015. However, not much seems to have been achieved in this direction, particularly for women.

In the present context, two important dimensions of female literacy emerge viz. absolute rate and the relative rate that require our attention. While the former estimates the magnitude of literate population among women, the latter is a relative measure of comparison, which is defined as a ratio of female literacy to male literacy. If this ratio is unity, it becomes an ideal situation guaranteeing distributional equity across gender. If the ratio is greater than 1, female literacy outpaces male literacy, whereas if the ratio is less than 1, the vice-versa becomes true.

Table 7.2 presents a clear picture on absolute and relative female literacy rates in India. A comparison between 1991 and 2001 reveals that there has been some improvement in the level of literacy amongst females. For each state and union territory, the length of the bar representing literacy rate of 2001 is higher than that of 1991. However, none has yet achieved full literacy. In 2001, Kerala with 88 per cent female literacy topped the list of states followed by Mizoram with 86 per cent and Goa with 76 per cent. Against them, states like Bihar (34 per cent), Jharkhand (39 per cent), Uttar Pradesh (43 per cent) and Rajasthan (44 per cent) were lagging far behind in this respect.

Table 7.2: Literacy Rate in India in 1991 and 2001

Sl. No.	State/UT	Female Literacy Rate (per cent)		Female : Male Literacy Ratio	
		1991	2001	1991	2001
1.	Andhra	33	51	0.6	0.718
2.	Arunachal Pradesh	30	44	0.588	0.688
3.	Assam	43	56	0.694	0.778
4.	Bihar	23	34	0.442	0.567
5.	Chhatisgarh	-	52	-	0.667
6.	Goa	67	76	0.798	0.854
7.	Gujarat	49	59	0.671	0.728
8.	Haryana	40	56	0.58	0.709
9.	Hp	52	68	0.693	0.791
10.	J&K	-	42	-	0.636
11.	Jharkhand	-	39	-	0.574

Contd...

12.	Karnataka	44	57	0.657	0.75
13.	Kerala	86	88	0.915	0.936
14.	M.P	29	50	0.5	0.649
15.	Maharashtra	52	68	0.675	0.791
16.	Manipur	48	60	0.667	0.769
17.	Meghalay	45	60	0.849	0.909
18.	Mizoram	79	86	0.919	0.945
19.	Nagaland	55	62	0.809	0.861
20.	Orissa	35	51	0.556	0.671
21.	Punjab	50	64	0.758	0.842
22.	Rajasthan	20	44	0.364	0.579
23.	Sikkim	47	61	0.712	0.792
24.	Tamil Nadu	51	65	0.689	0.793
25.	Tripura	50	65	0.704	0.802
26.	Uttar Pradesh	25	43	0.446	0.614
27.	Uttaranchal	-	60	-	0.714
28.	West Bengal	47	60	0.691	0.769
29.	A&N Islands	65	75	0.8228	0.872
30.	Chandigarh	72	77	0.878	0.895
31.	D&N Haveli	27	43	0.5	0.589
32.	Daman& Diu	59	70	0.7108	0.796
33.	Delhi	67	75	0.8171	0.862
34.	Lakshadweep	73	82	0.8111	0.882
35.	Pondicherry	66	74	0.7857	0.831

Source: Statistical Abstract, Government of India, 2002

There have been marked improvements in the female-male literacy ratios between 1991 and 2001. However, none has yet attained perfect equality. While states like Mizoram (0.945), Kerala (0.9366) and Meghalaya (0.909) are heading towards perfect equality, Bihar (0.567), Jharkhand (0.574), Rajasthan (0.579), Uttar Pradesh (0.614), Jammu and Kashmir (0.636), Madhya Pradesh (0.649), Chhattisgarh (0.667) and Orissa (0.671) are lagging far behind the goalpost. The situation in the latter states thus demands immediate intervention. Contrary to the performance of states, all the union territories except Dadra and Nagar Haveli have performed consistently well during the period under study. There have been improvements in both absolute and relative literacy rates.

The situation becomes more worsening when we attempt to compare between rural and urban areas in the existing framework. Table 7.3 depicts the state-wise distribution of literacy rates across rural and urban areas for the year 1998. It is evident that attainment of literacy is highly skewed towards the urban areas both at aggregate and sub-aggregate levels. Given the fact that in absolute sense, literacy level among females is less as compared to their male counterparts in both rural and urban areas, the magnitude of biasness is more in rural areas, when judged from the angle of relative literacy. There exists more inequality in rural areas than in urban areas between males and females. Excluding Kerala, a few smaller states have performed well in this respect.

Table 7.3: Literacy Rates across Rural and Urban Areas in India in 1998

Sl. No.	State/UT	Female Literacy Rate (per cent)		Female : Male Literacy Ratio	
		Rural	Urban	Rural	Urban
1.	Andhra	37	68	0.6379	0.8095
2.	Arunachal Pradesh	47	71	0.7581	0.7717
3.	Assam	69	89	0.8118	0.9368
4.	Bihar	28	55	0.4912	0.6875
5.	Chhattishgarh	-	-	-	-
6.	Goa	78	93	0.8966	0.949
7.	Gujarat	50	75	0.641	0.8333
8.	Haryana	45	69	0.625	0.7753
9.	Hp	63	86	0.7778	0.8958
10.	J&K	42	54	0.6	0.6585

Contd...

11.	Jharkhand	-	-	-	-
12.	Karnataka	44	71	0.6567	0.8452
13.	Kerala	88	93	0.9362	0.9588
14.	M.P.	34	66	0.5484	0.7952
15.	Maharashtra	53	82	0.6883	0.8913
16.	Manipur	71	81	0.8256	0.9101
17.	Meghalay	81	94	0.9205	0.9792
18.	Mizoram	89	98	0.9674	0.9899
19.	Nagaland	79	78	0.8778	0.9176
20.	Orissa	41	74	0.6406	0.8315
21.	Punjab	57	77	0.8143	0.9277
22.	Rajasthan	24	66	0.3871	0.75
23.	Sikkim	64	84	0.7711	1.012
24.	Tamil Nadu	55	78	0.7237	0.8667
25.	Tripura	75	88	0.8523	0.9263
26.	Uttar Pradesh	35	58	0.5385	0.725
27.	Uttaranchal	-	-	-	-
28.	West Bengal	56	79	0.7273	0.8778
29.	A&N Islands	81	92	0.8901	0.92
30.	Chandigarh	63	83	0.7778	0.9765
31.	D & N Haveli	54	76	0.675	0.8539
32.	Daman & Diu	70	95	0.7527	1.1446
33.	Delhi	62	84	0.6263	0.9032
34.	Lakshadweep	78	82	0.8571	0.8367
35.	Pondicherry	88	81	0.967	0.8901

Source: Statistical Abstract, Government of India, 2002.

Surprisingly, the highest female literacy rate has been achieved in Mizoram (both rural and urban-89 per cent and 98 per cent respectively) and not Kerala (rural female literacy-88 per cent & urban female literacy rate-93 per cent) though Kerala is famous for having made the maximum progress in the field of education in the whole country. There are few other smaller states which have performed relatively well are Meghalay (rural-81 per cent and urban-94 per cent), Goa (rural-78 per cent and urban-93 per cent), Tripura (rural-75 per cent and urban-88 per cent), Manipur (rural-71 per cent and urban- 81 per cent). Although Sikkim, another smaller state in the north-east, has done relatively better in urban female literacy (84 per cent), its achievement in the rural front is not encouraging (64 per cent).

As compared to states, union territories have performed relatively well with exceptions of Delhi and Dadra and Nagar Haveli. To our surprise, rural female literacy in the union territory of Delhi (62 per cent) is one of the lowest and the female: male literacy ratio (0.63) is very low. Interestingly, in Delhi, while nearly 99 per cent of rural male population is found to be literate, only 62 per cent of rural females have been literate. Dadra and Nagar Haveli is another union territory, which has also been a poor performer at rural front (rural-54 per cent and urban-76 per cent). Among all the states and union territories, the rural women of Rajasthan have attained the lowest literacy rate in both absolute term (24 per cent) as well as in relative term (0.39) followed by Bihar (28 per cent, 0.49 respectively) and Uttar Pradesh (35 per cent, 0.54 respectively). It is interesting to note that in terms of rural female-male literacy ratio, none of the states or union territories has yet reached the stage of perfect equality. Only Mizoram, Kerala and Meghalaya are closer to the target. On the contrary, in the urban areas, interestingly, female literacy is greater than male literacy in Sikkim (1.012) and Daman and Diu (1.144).

Hierarchical Distribution of Education for Women from Primary to Higher Secondary Level

In India, a uniform structure of school education has been adopted by all the states and union territories. However, within the states and the union territories, there are variations regarding the age of admission to class one, number of years/classes at the primary, upper primary and secondary stages. The primary stage comprises of classes from I to V in 16 states and 4 union territories (viz. Andhra Pradesh, Arunachal Pradesh, Bihar, Haryana, Himachal Pradesh, Jammu & Kashmir, Manipur, Orissa,

Madhya Pradesh, Punjab, Rajasthan, Sikkim, Tamil Nadu, Tripura, Uttar Pradesh, and West Bengal among the states; and Andaman & Nicobar Islands, Chandigarh, Delhi, and Karikal & Yanam regions of Pondicherry among union territories), whereas in rest of the states and union territories including the Mahe region of Pondicherry, the primary stage comprises of classes from I to IV.

Similarly, the middle school stage of education comprises of classes from VI to VIII in some states, while in some others it is from classes V to VII, yet in others it is from classes VI to VII or from VI-VII. While most of the states and union territories treat classes IX-X as the secondary stage of schooling, few states and union territories including Andhra Pradesh, Assam, Goa, Gujarat, Karnataka, Kerala, Maharashtra, Orissa, Dadra and Nagar Haveli, Daman and Diu and Lakshadweep also treat classes VIII-X as the high school stage of education. There is, however, a uniform structure at higher secondary level across the country.

Making an account of the relative position of girls in comparison with boys in the hierarchy of education from class I to XII (Table 7.5), we observe that during the period 2002-04, the enrolment of girls per 100 boys is found to be extremely bad in Bihar (74, 54 and 41 at I-V, VI-VIII and IX-XI respectively) and Jharkhand (79, 67 and 56 at I-V, VI-VIII and IX-XI respectively) at all stages of education. Rajasthan is another state which has done relatively well at the primary stage in terms of enrolment of girls per 100 boys (82) has receded much below the desired level at the subsequent stages (53 and 42 at VI-VIII and IX-XI respectively). The States which have done extremely well are Sikkim (101, 106 and 97 at I-V, VI-VIII and IX-XI respectively) and Meghalaya (102, 109 and 100 at I-V, VI-VIII and IX-XI respectively) in north east which have even outperformed Kerala (96, 91 and 106 at I-V, VI-VIII and IX-XI respectively), the state which has recorded the highest literacy rate.

The above situation can be described more clearly with the help of the computed ratios (Table 7.5). The ratios in Table 7.5 have been computed on the basis of the data given in Table 7.4.

Table 7.4: State-wise Enrolment of Girls per 100 Boys during 2002-2004

Sl. No.	State/UT	No. of girls' enrolment per 100 boys' Enrolment in classes		
		I-V	VI - VIII	IX – XII
1.	Andhra	97	86	73
2.	Arunachal Pradesh	84	85	70
3.	Assam	93	92	85
4.	Bihar	74	54	41
5.	Chhattisgarh	93	76	59
6.	Goa	92	89	95
7.	Gujarat	85	73	69
8.	Haryana	84	80	69
9.	Hp	91	90	87
10.	J&K	83	76	71
11.	Jharkhand	79	67	56
12.	Karnataka	94	88	81
13.	Kerala	96	91	106
14.	M.P.	86	65	53
15.	Maharashtra	91	87	78
16.	Manipur	93	95	93
17.	Meghalay	102	109	100
18.	Mizoram	92	96	101
19.	Nagaland	91	93	90
20.	Orissa	90	81	75
21.	Punjab	89	90	90
22.	Rajasthan	82	53	42
23.	Sikkim	101	106	97
24.	Tamil Nadu	93	92	95
25.	Tripura	91	90	82
26.	Uttar Pradesh	86	70	57

Contd…

27.	Uttaranchal	94	87	75
28.	West Bengal	96	88	73
29.	A&N Islands	92	89	95
30.	Chandigarh	83	87	91
31.	D & N Haveli	84	61	69
32.	Daman & Diu	89	87	77
33.	Delhi	89	88	89
34.	Lakshadweep	82	79	92
35.	Pondicherry	94	92	99

Source: Annual Report 2004-2005, Department of School Education, Govt. of West Bengal

It is evident from the results that in the north-eastern states like Arunachal Pradesh (1.01), Manipur (1.02), Meghalaya (1.07), Nagaland (1.02), Mizoram (1.04) and Sikkim (1.05) where females play a dominant role in the society, the ratios of girls' enrolment per 100 boys between middle school and primary level exceed one, which implies that the relative position of girls has become better in the second stage of education as compared to the primary level. Among the larger states, Punjab (1.01) is the only state, which has shown similar type of situation. Among the union territories, Chandigarh (1.05) alone has performed well between the first two stages.

Table 7.5: Computed Ratios

Sl. No.	State/UT	F_2 / F_1	F_3 / F_2
1.	Andhra	0.89	0.85
2.	Arunachal Pradesh	1.01	0.82
3.	Assam	0.99	0.92
4.	Bihar	0.73	0.76
5.	Chhattisgarh	0.82	0.78
6.	Goa	0.97	1.07

Contd...

7.	Gujarat	0.86	0.95
8.	Haryana	0.95	0.86
9.	Hp	0.99	0.97
10.	J&K	0.92	0.93
11.	Jharkhand	0.85	0.84
12.	Karnataka	0.94	0.92
13.	Kerala	0.95	1.16
14.	M.P.	0.76	0.82
15.	Maharashtra	0.96	0.90
16.	Manipur	1.02	0.98
17.	Meghalay	1.07	0.92
18.	Mizoram	1.04	1.05
19.	Nagaland	1.02	0.97
20.	Orissa	0.90	0.93
21.	Punjab	1.01	1.00
22.	Rajasthan	0.65	0.79
23.	Sikkim	1.05	0.92
24.	Tamil Nadu	0.99	1.03
25.	Tripura	0.99	0.91
26.	Uttar Pradesh	0.81	0.81
27.	Uttaranchal	0.93	0.86
28.	West Bengal	0.92	0.83
29.	A&N Islands	0.97	1.07
30.	Chandigarh	1.05	1.05
31.	D & N Haveli	0.73	1.13
32.	Daman & Diu	0.98	0.89
33.	Delhi	0.99	1.01
34.	Lakshadweep	0.96	1.16
35.	Pondicherry	0.98	1.08

As compared to the above, the ratios of girls enrolled per 100 boys as estimated between secondary-higher secondary combined and middle school (Table 7.5) reveal that Kerala (1.16) and

Lakshadweep (1.16) outperform all the other states and union territories followed by Dadra and Nagar Haveli (1.13), Pondicherry (1.08), Goa (1.07), Andaman and Nicobar Islands (1.07), Mizoram (1.05), Chandigarh (1.05), Tamil Nadu (1.03) and Delhi (1.01). These are the only states and union territories, where the relative enrolment ratios of girls have improved at the secondary and higher secondary level combined against the middle school level. Punjab is the other state which has maintained statuesque. The rest of the states and union territories have shown ratios less than one.

However, the entire fact is not revealed from the above tables. They only represent the relative position of females to males across states and union territories. The dropout rates of different states rather show the absolute picture of girls' education in India (Table 7.6). It is interesting to note here that even though the relative position and literacy rates are impressive in north-eastern states, the dropout rates are very high in these states. Among the major states, West Bengal (88) records the highest dropout rate between I-X followed by Bihar (87), Rajasthan (83), Andhra Pradesh (79), Assam (75) and Madhya Pradesh (75). Kerala (19) records the lowest dropout rate between I-X. No other state is found to be close to Kerala's attainment in this regard. Besides Kerala, the performance is satisfactory for Goa, Pondicherry, and Chandigarh. The negative dropout rate with Delhi can be interpreted as the addition of students coming from the other parts of the country at higher classes of schooling.

Table 7.6: State-wise Dropout Rates in 1998-99

Sl. No.	State/UT	Girls Dropout Rates		
		I -V	I -VIII	I –X
1.	Andhra	47	74	79
2.	Arunachal Pradesh	45	66	79
3.	Assam	42	72	75
4.	Bihar	62	80	87

Contd...

5.	Goa	13	11	42
6.	Gujarat	34	65	75
7.	Haryana	16	29	56
8.	Hp	31	28	43
9.	J&K	34	44	70
10.	Karnataka	33	64	69
11.	Kerala	-7	-3	19
12.	M.P.	28	57	75
13.	Maharashtra	26	44	64
14.	Manipur	54	47	77
15.	Meghalay	64	78	64
16.	Mizoram	52	66	71
19.	Nagaland	35	39	61
20.	Orissa	48	72	62
21.	Punjab	22	29	44
22.	Rajasthan	58	68	83
23.	Sikkim	36	63	89
24.	Tamil Nadu	16	35	58
25.	Tripura	54	71	84
26.	Uttar Pradesh	56	58	73
27.	West Bengal	54	78	88
28.	A&N Islands	21	28	45
29.	Chandigarh	-4	-3	8
30.	D & N Haveli	44	63	79
31.	Daman & Diu	-0.32	7	46
32.	Delhi	28	9	-68
33.	Lakshadweep	7	25	55
34.	Pondicherry	-2	-2	36

Source: National Human Development Report, 2001.

Implications

As it is evident from the analysis, amongst the major states, excepting Kerala, no other states have done well in female literacy. Relatively smaller states like Mizoram, Sikkim and many union territories outperformed the rest in this respect. The level of achievement in states like Bihar, Uttar Pradesh, Jharkhand and Rajasthan is so low that it requires immediate intervention and may warrant special efforts. As far as relative disparity between females and males is concerned, there has been improvement in the status, which is quite significant in some states and union territories but very low in the other. In this respect, union territories have outpaced the states. The situation is no better in the hierarchical distribution until higher secondary level of education is reached. Excepting Kerala and Lakshadweep and Delhi, in all other states and union territories, the dropout rates among females are quite high at later stages of schooling. In all, poorer states record low women literacy, low female-male literacy ratios, low girls' enrolment ratios, low relative girls' enrolment ratios between successive stages of schooling and high dropouts.

Given the situations as cited above, we may attempt to draw some possible implications. They may provide some insight to the problems thereby helping us devise suitable strategies to address them.

It may be revealing to note that among the states, Kerala is the only bigger state that has been doing consistently well in the field of overall education including women's education. The success story of Kerala may be attributed to, as Sukumaran (2002) suggests, impressive educational structure, availability of schools in the immediate vicinity of the households (both rural and urban areas alike), widespread Christian missionaries, instruction in vernacular i.e. Malayalam, job opportunities and better socio-economic status. The other two most important factors may be the rise and spread of social reforms on the one hand and the ascent of left forces to power in as early as in 1957 on the other. According to Sukumaran (2002), in the early part of twentieth century, social reformers like Sri Narayan Guru, Sri Aiyyarkali etc, in their historic and revolutionary pursuit of uplifting the social backward sections in Kerala, had emphasized on the importance of acquiring formal education. Later, among upper castes, the need to educate women gained importance. In addition, with the advent of left forces to power in Kerala in 1957, there began serious intervention in the social transformation process with an ideological conviction leading to attainment of education at a faster rate.

Other than Kerala, a few north-eastern states and union territories record better performance in women's education. Explanation behind this phenomenon may lie in the fact that these states and union territories are smaller in size and very thinly populated. Consequently, the literacy programmes launched by the governments have been relatively more effective. Besides, like Kerala, in these state also, missionaries have played pivotal role in spreading education.

As compared to Kerala and some smaller states and union territories, the states like Bihar, Uttar Pradesh, Rajasthan and some other poorer states have been subjected to a number of socio-political and economic crises leading to poor performance in social sector front including women's education. To be precise, among the major states, BIMARU states are hard-hit. The low social sector development and particularly low level of education amongst females in these states can be attributed to their existing poor socio-political and economic character. There persists gender bias in our social hierarchy which deters women to attain the desired level of development. In this context, it may be worthwhile to compare the Gender Disparity Index (GDI) across states instead of their Human Development Indices (HDI). The GDI for states like Meghalaya (.807), Manipur (.815) having higher female literacy rate is much higher than that for states like Bihar (.469) and Uttar Pradesh (.52) having lower literacy rate (National Human Development Report, 2001).

The earlier studies prove that women are largely discriminated in our society at large and the discrimination is more pronounced in some states than the other. Velkoff (1998) finds that many parents view educating sons as an investment because the sons remain responsible for caring aging parents. On the other hand, parents may see the education of daughters as a waste of money because daughters eventually live with their husbands' families and the parents are not be benefited directly from their education. Also, in some states, it is apprehended that daughters with higher level of education are likely to have higher dowry expenses as they may want a comparably educated husband.

It has also been observed that in a patriarchal society of ours, women are subjected to seven different types of inequality, viz. mortality inequality, natality inequality, ownership inequality basic facilities inequality, special facilities inequality, professional inequality, and household inequality (Sen, 1990). Among all, the latter four inequalities may be posing as deterrents towards enabling females to achieve education on equal footing with their male counterparts.

Besides the above, there are some supply side hindrances that have restricted girls to become literate or receive formal schooling. According to Velkoff (1998) one of the barriers to education in India is the lack of adequate schools and class rooms. Many states simply do not have enough classrooms to accommodate all school-age children. Further, the classrooms that are available often lack basic utilities such as sanitary facilities and water. In Uttar Pradesh, a recent study found (World Bank, 1997) that 50 per cent of schools did not have water and 80 per cent did not have toilets. Lack of toilet facilities can be particularly detrimental to the attendance of girl students. In some states, the inadequacy of classrooms gets further compounded by the sheer number of students in the school-going age group due to high rate of population growth. In 1993, Uttar Pradesh needed to build 28400 additional classrooms to achieve total enrollment among the children between age group of 6-10 (World Bank, 1997).

Lack of female teachers is another potential barrier to female education. Girls are likely to attend schools and have higher academic achievements if they have female teachers. This is particularly true in highly gender-segregated societies such as India (Velkoff, 1998).

In addition to the factors as cited above which are specific to women's education alone, there exist a few very well pertinent economic factors that act as detriments to the social sector development which is inclusive of women's education. This may be analyzed across states and union territories to infer why some are doing well while the others are not. The economic factors may include Per Capita Net State Domestic Products, magnitude of public expenditure across states, etc.

Conclusion

We may thus conclude that level of achievement amongst women particularly in the field of education is not very encouraging. The level of women literacy is not only low at the country level but also the achievement in this respect is highly skewed towards the developed states or smaller states and union territories. Although there has been some improvements in female-male literacy ratio across states, high in some and low in the other, none of the states and union territories has yet achieved perfect equality. Rural women are found to be less educated as compared to their urban counterparts. There has been decline in girls' enrolment ratios per 100 boys in successive levels of schooling in large number of states and union territories. In a very few states, the relative enrolment ratios of girls have improved at the secondary and higher secondary levels combined against the middle school level and also between primary and middle schools levels. In regard to dropout rates, all the states excepting Kerala have shown bad performance.

Given the nature of the problems the country and its constituents are faced with, the issues to address are manifold and complex. What may be urgently required is to correct is the biasness in our approaches to deal with the problems. Besides, poorer states and union territories need special attention as they are facing multi-pronged challenges.

References

Census (2001), 'Evaluating the Trends: 2001', South Asian Voice, June.

Dev, S. M and J. Mooij (2002), 'Social Sector Expenditures in the 1990s: Analysis of Central and State Budgets', *Economic and*

Political Weekly, Vol. 37, No. 9, pp. 853-866, March 2.

EPW Research Foundation (2003), 'Finance of Government of India', *Economic and Political Weekly*, Vol. 38, No. 19, pp. 1887-1907, May 10.

Government of India (2001), 'Indian Public Finance Statistics', Ministry of Finance, New Delhi.

Government of India (2001), 'National Human Development Report', Planning Commission of India, New Delhi.

Government of India (2002), 'Statistical Abstract, 2002', Ministry of Statistics and Programme Implementation, New Delhi.

Government of West Bengal (2004-05), 'Annual Report, 2004-2005', Department of School Education, Kolkata.

Rajaraman, Indira (2001) 'Expenditure Reforms', *The Economic Times*, May 10.

Rawls, J. (1999), *A Theory of Justice*, Harvard University Press.

Sen, A. K. (1970), *Collective Choice and Social Welfare*, Holden-Day, San Francisco.

Sen, A. K. (1990), 'More Than 100 Million Women Are Missing', New York Review of Books, Vol. 37, No. 20, December 20.

Sukumaran, S. (2002), 'Education in Kerala: An Overview', The Education System, Vol. 9, January.

Swaroop, V., S. Jha and A. Rajkumar (2000), 'Fiscal Effects of Foreign Aid in a Federal System of Governance: The Case of India', *Journal of Public Economics*, No. 77, pp. 307-330.

UNDP (2004), Human Development Reports, Oxford University Press, Oxford.

United Nations (2000), Millennium Declaration, *United Nations*, New York.

Velkoff, V. A. (1998), 'Women's Education in India', US Department of Commerce, USA.

World Bank (1997), 'Development in Practice: Primary Education in India', Allied Publishing, New Delhi.

8

Silk Trade and Women in Decision Making

Kishor Goswami

Introduction

In many Asian countries, silk industry is one of the labour-intensive industries that possesses a greater degree of rural employment opportunities. The Agreement on Textile and Clothing (ATC) in 1994 has systematically eliminated textile and clothing quota restrictions from many developing countries by January 1, 2005. Countries with large economies, cheap labour, and technological prowess have turned the situation into their favour. However, more business with outdated technology has created more pressure on its workers to produce more in less time. Level of Technology in many Asian countries is outdated and is mostly hand spun or hand woven. Since most of the workers in the industry are women and work mostly as weavers, helpers, etc., with the expansion of the business, the pressure on women workers is bound to be more.

India continues to be the second largest producer of silk in the world. The total export earnings from silk items during April-February, 2005-06 have increased by 15 per cent to US$ 647.08 million from US$ 562.89 million in April-February, 2004-05 (Silk Export and Import Review, 2006). Among different silk exporting states in India, Assam plays an important role particularly in the export of *Pat* and *Muga* silks. Weaving is one of the largest and oldest industries in Assam. The state produces three unique varieties of silk viz., the Golden *Muga*, the White *Pat*, and the Warm *Eri*. The industry directly supported about 1.72 million weavers in 2003 (Pandey, 2003). The state exported silk products worth of Rs. 120 millions during 2005-06 through Assam Apex Weavers and Artisans Cooperative Federation Ltd (ARTFED).

Silk produce all over the state find their way to Sualkuchi, which is 32 kilometres away from Guwahati. It is the largest village in Asia and the largest silk producing village in the world (Kashyap, 2000). It produces over six million meters of muga and pat fabrics every year and exports them to various countries (Thakuria, 2004). With a population of about 50,000 the village has more than 13,752 weavers, 4,842 helpers, and 4,023 owners. More than 60 per cent of the workers in the industry are females. This explains the importance of weaving industry in the state and the role of women in the industry. The industry is known for generating women employment which is crucial for empowerment of women. But lives of the weavers are not easy in the world's largest weaving village. With expansion of trade, jobs are becoming contractual and exploitation of female labour is becoming common. Present study thus attempts to analyse the women empowerment and their decision-making in silk industry in Sualkuchi.

A Brief Review of Literature

Trade opens possibilities for new markets, goods and services, new factors of production and the benefits of increased efficiency due to competition (Durano, 1999). Although there are many proponents and opponents of globalisation of trade, there is hardly any doubt about the importance of free trade in modern world. The development of world trade has made the issues such as role of gender in trade, employment and wage policies, working conditions, etc., critical. Trade is generally believed to be gender-neutral. However, it is not the same in reality. Cagatay (2000) found that women and men are affected differently by trade policies and performances and gender inequalities impact differently on trade policy outcomes. Cagatay made a strong argument in favour of gender analysis in the formulation of trade policies to enhance gender equality and human development. Trade analysts often ignore that women and men do not have the same access to economic and social resources and therefore may be affected differently (Nageer *et al.*, 2003). This is more so because of asymmetric rights and responsibilities, reproduction and motherhood, gendered social norms, labour market segregation, consumption patterns, and time poverty (Gammage *et al.,* 2002).

The inequality of the position of women has largely benefited the market and the capitalist as women not only provide cheap labour, but also contribute to the survival of the economic systems through their unpaid labour (Kalima, 2002). Kurasini Declaration (24-28 June, 2002) on gender and trade also says that globalisation, trade liberalisation, and structural adjustment policies have been imposed on population at the expense of women's social and economic empowerment (Kurasini Declaration, 2002). They are denied the opportunity to learn skills, earn decent incomes and participate in civic and political life. Unemployment and poverty brake down the basic social structure and increased violence and exploitation of women. Studying on gender issues in international trade, Durano (1999) suggests for a more realistic view of the market to protect and empower the vulnerable group i.e., women.

The expansion of trade into different industries and regions makes the role of gender crucial in different trade related activities. When trade results in increased income and employment, this can reduce gender inequality (Williams, 2005). Williams (2001) predicts an increase in employment opportunity for women and expansion of business owned and operated by women at international level. This increases the income of women and ultimately their economic empowerment. In contrast, Cagatay (2000) argues that expansion of women's employment has not led to a closing of gender-based wage gaps and conditions of work have not improved. The author observes that women's jobs are still insecure and unstable as expansion has occurred in an era of loss of power by workers. In the same line, IFAD (2003) survey suggests an increase in women's access to and control over income through entrepreneurial skills, training, and access to land, credit, and improved market linkages.

Sources of Data and Methodologies

The brief literature review reveals that globalisation of trade creates beneficiaries as well as losers particularly among the women. The silk industry is no more different. There is thus a need to study how women are empowered in silk trade. Since men and women face the globalisation of trade in different ways, different mechanisms are needed to address their problems. The study is based on primary data collected from 200 respondents of Sualkuchi. The respondents include weavers, helpers and silk traders consisting both males and females. An interview schedule was prepared and purposive random sampling was used for collection of primary data. For this purpose, the area was divided into three strata viz. Pub (East) Sualkuchi, Madhya (Central) Sualkuchi, and (West) Paschim Sualkuchi. A total of 67 respondents were covered in Pub Sualkuchi, 33 in Madhya Sualkuchi and 100 in Paschim Sualkuchi.

Many weavers in the study area are migrated from nearby areas. Therefore, the study considers both migrant weavers and weavers from the same locality. Moreover, a few of them work in their own looms. Many owners even work as weavers and sell the products. They have complete control in marketing of their products. They have been considered as traders. Helpers in the industry are mostly unskilled workers. Most of them join the industry as helpers and learn the art of weaving. After two to three years, they become semi-skilled weavers. In addition to primary data, secondary data have been collected from different sources such as Directorate of Sericulture, Government of Assam (GOA), Central Silk Board, Government of India, ARTFED, etc. Opinion of the experts towards different aspects of the industry has been collected through Focus Group Discussions (FGD) and Participatory Rural Appraisal technique. The impact on women empowerment has been studied considering three different time periods i.e. Period I (before 2000), Period II (2000 to 2004), and Period III (2005 and after). Overall women empowerment in the industry has been measured using United Nations' Gender Empowerment Measure (GEM) (UNDP, 2006).

GEM = (EDEP for local government bodies' representation + EDEP for economic participation + EDEP for income) / 3

Where, EDEP = Equally Distributed Equivalent Percentage, and

EDEP = 1/ [{Female Population Share/ Female Index} + {Male Population Share/ Male Index}]

EDEP for local government bodies' representation measures the relative empowerment of women in terms of their political participation. Since the study is based on a small and remote place of India, instead of women's parliamentary representation, representation at the local bodies' i.e. *Panchayat* is considered for women's political participation. For political and economic participation and decision-making, the EDEP is indexed by dividing it by 50. In an ideal society, with equal empowerment between genders, the GEM variables would equal 50 per cent implying thereby that women's share would equal men's share for each variable (UNDP, 2006). EDEP for economic participation is calculated for women's and men's percentage share of positions as owners, managers in the industry, and another for women's and men's percentage share as weavers. The simple average of the two measures gives the EDEP for economic participation.

For measuring EDEP for income, annual earnings of the women and men in the industry are considered separately. The income measure indicates a person's capacity to earn income and capture women's economic independence. The earned income is measured for women and men separately and then indexed using the following formulae:

Income index = (earned income - minimum value) ÷ (maximum value – minimum value).

Impact of globalisation on Women's Empowerment (WE) has been studied using the following equation considering Women Empowerment in Period I, II and III as WE_1, WE_2 and WE_3 respectively.

$$WE_1 = \sum_{i=1}^{n} WR \text{ for all } j = 1 / \sum_{i=1}^{N} WR \text{ for all } j = 1 \text{-----} k$$

Where,

n = sample population responding question in positive,

N = sample population responding all the question,

WR= women respondent,

i = sample population, and

j = all the given options ranging from 1 to k (such as decision making for household activities, financial matter, children's education, healthcare, purchase of assets, day to day activities, weaving related activities, and marketing of silk).

The change in women empowerment is measured as

$\Delta WE = WE_2 - WE_1$ or $WE_3 - WE_2$ or $WE_3 - WE_1$

Results and Discussion

Study Area: Sualkuchi, the largest village in Asia and the largest silk producing village in the world, is located at $26^0\ 10^{/}\ 12^{//}$ north latitude of the equator and $91^0\ 34^{/}\ 11^{//}$ east longitude of the prime meridian. Sualkuchi plays a key role in the silk industry of Assam. The requirement of raw materials in the village is about 66 per cent of the total state consumption and in turn, the village contributes about 73.5 per cent of the total silk produce in the state (Table 8.1).

Table 8.1: Consumption of Yarn and Production of Silk in Sualkuchi in 2005-06

	Consumption in lakh kg			Total Production in lakh linear meter
	Mulberry	Muga	Total	
Sualkuchi	2.00	0.98	2.98	31.00
Assam	-	-	4.39*	42.19

* Also includes eri silk (Philosamis recini)

Source: ARTFED, 2006

In Sualkuchi village, ARTFED plays a major role for improving the market potential of different weaving products and increasing their share in global market. The organisation owns about 400 looms in Sualkuchi to produce *muga* and *pat* silks. In addition to their own production, ARTFED procures silk products from individual weavers, and self-help groups (SHGs). It has 59 showrooms/emporiums all over India that include cities like Kolkata, Kanpur, Jaipur, Indore, New Delhi and so on.

During 2005-06, ARTFED exported muga silk worth of Rs. 120 million from Sualkuchi to countries like USA, Japan, European countries, etc. In order to meet the domestic requirements, numerous handloom cooperatives, SHGs, NGOs and individual entrepreneurs are involved in production and marketing of different silk products. This helps mostly the traders to sale the products outside Assam as *silk from Sualkuchi*.

As per 2001 census, the village has 4,385 households. The total local population in the village is 22,147 excluding migrant weavers and other migrants. Of them, 49 per cent are males and 51 per cent are females (Population Census, 2001). With migrant weavers, the percentage of female in total population increases as most of the migrant weavers are females. Moreover, migrant weavers and other migrant labourers form a considerable portion of the total population in that village.

In Sualkuchi, there are 65 per cent male and 35 per cent female workers engaged in various occupations (Table 8.2). In case of main work, about 67 per cent are males, while the rest are females. In casual works, males (74 per cent) significantly outnumber females (26 per cent). Out of total main workers in the village, mere 1 per cent remains in agriculture, while a staggering 50.45 per cent remain in household works. Of the latter, about 58 per cent are males and 42 per cent are females. The household works basically include weaving activities in the informal sector. During 2002-03, about 17,000 workers were engaged in loom industry everyday of which about 15,000 were migrated workers (Pathak, 2003).

Gender, Marital Status, and Level of Literacy of the Respondents

In the study area, out of 200 respondents, 119 (59.5 per cent) were females and 81 (40.5 per cent) were males (Table 8.3). If we consider only weavers, the percentage of women weavers amongst the total weavers increases further as majority of the migrant weavers are females. As against this, males (including owner) are higher in number in silk trade.

Table 8.2: Distribution of Population According to Various Occupation Groups in Sualkuchi

Work Groups	Male	Female	Total
Total worker	5,691 (65.00)	3,040 (35.00)	8,731 (100.00)
Main worker	5,523 (67.00)	2,730 (33.00)	8,253 (100.00)
Casual worker	32 (74.00)	11 (26.00)	43 (100.00)
Main agricultural workers	65 (66.00)	34 (34.00)	99 (100.00)
Main household workers	2,428 (58.00)	1,738 (42.00)	4,164 (100.00)
Main other workers	2,998 (76.00)	949 (24.00)	3,947 (100.00)
Non workers	5,247 (39.00)	8,169 (61.00)	13,416 (100.00)

Note: Figures in parentheses represent percentages of the respective row totals.
Source: Compiled from Population Census 2001, Government of India.

Table 8.3: Distribution of Respondents According to Gender

Hamlet	Respondents		
	Female	Male	Total
Madhya	30 (90.91)	3 (9.09)	33
Paschim	49 (49.00)	51 (51.00)	100
Pub	40 (59.70)	27 (4C.30)	67
Grand Total	119 (59.50)	81 (40.50)	200

Note: Figures in parentheses indicate percentage of total

About 28.50 per cent of the respondents were married (Table 8.4). The percentage of unmarried respondents is more as many of the respondents are migrant weavers and incidence of late marriage and remaining single is relatively more among them. It was reported that many unmarried girls took the profession of weaving to make themselves economically independent.

Out of 119 female respondents, 20 (16.81 per cent) were illiterate, 21 (17.65 per cent) were having education up to primary level, 58 (48.74 per cent) up to middle school, 15 (12.61 per cent) up to high school and 5 (4.20 per cent) completed higher secondary level of education (Table 8.5). About 90 per cent of them were engaged as weavers, followed by 8.40 per cent as owners and silk traders, and mere1.68 per cent as helpers. Amongst female weavers, 17.76 per cent were illiterate, 15.89 per cent were having education up to primary level, 52.34 per cent had education up to middle school, 12.15 per cent were matriculate and mere 1.87 per cent had finished up to higher secondary level. No female weaver was having education beyond higher secondary level. The situation is not better with the female traders as well as helpers.

Women in Decision-Making

Role of Women in Decision-Making: Participation of women in the decision making process is an important indicator of women empowerment. However, analysing the role of female vis-à-vis male in the family decision making, it is found that out of 119 female respondents, 39 respondents have positive roles in period I (Table 8.6). This has increased to 68 (74.36 per cent) in period II and 85 (25.00 per cent) in period III. This indicates that females have a say in family decision-making and it has increased over the years signifying greater women empowerment in the industry.

There has been an increase in the participation of women in financial decision-making from 38 in Period I to 67 in period II and then to 70 in period III. Likewise, women's participation in children's education has also increased from 23 in period I to 42

Table 8.4: Distribution of Respondents According to Marital Status

Hamlet	Married		Total	Unmarried		Total
	Male	Female		Male	Female	
Madhya	2 (22.22)	7 (77.78)	9	2 (8.33)	22 (91.67)	24
Paschim	16 (55.17)	13 (44.83)	29	34 (47.89)	37 (52.11)	71
Pub	14 (73.68)	5 (26.32)	19	13 (27.08)	35 (72.92)	48
Grand Total	32 (56.14)	25 (43.86)	57	49 (34.27)	94 (65.73)	143

Note: Figures in parentheses indicate percentage of total.

Table 8.5: Distribution of Female Respondents According to the Level of Literacy

Hamlet	Illiterate			Primary			Middle Level school			Metric			Higher Secondary			Graduation			TOTAL
	W	ST	H	W	ST	H	W	ST	H	W	ST	H	W	ST	H	W	ST	H	
Madhya	8	0	0	3	0	0	14	0	0	4	0	0	1	0	0	0	0	0	30
Paschim	6	0	1	9	2	1	23	1	0	4	1	0	0	1	0	0	0	0	49
Pub	5	0	0	5	1	0	19	1	0	5	1	0	1	2	0	0	0	0	40
Grand Total	19	0	1	17	3	1	56	2	0	13	2	0	2	3	0	0	0	0	119

Note: W = Weaver; ST = Silk Trade (including owner); H = Helper.

in period II and 44 in period III. Similar trend prevails with respect to decision-making in healthcare. Here the increase is by 83.33 per cent between period I and period II, and by 4.55 per cent between period II and period III. In the decision to purchase assets, the number has increased from 27 in period I to 46 in period II. However, there has not been much change thereafter. This might be due to the small time lag between period II and period III.

Table 8.6: Distribution of Respondents in Decision Making Based on Positive Response

Category	Total Respondents	Period I	Period II	Period III
All Matters				
Female	119	39	68 (74.36)	85 (25.00)
Male	81	29	51 (75.86)	56 (9.80)
Total	200	68	119 (75.00)	141 (18.49)
Financial Matter				
Female	119	38	67 (76.32)	70 (4.48)
Male	81	28	49 (75.00)	51 (4.08)
Total	200	66	116 (75.76)	121 (4.31)
Children's Education				
Female	119	23	42 (82.61)	44 (4.76)
Male	81	27	46 (70.37)	47 (2.17)
Total	200	50	88 (76.00)	91 (3.41)
Healthcare Decision				
Female	119	24	44 (83.33)	46 (4.55)
Male	81	29	47 (62.07)	48 (2.13)
Total	200	53	91 (71.70)	94 (3.30)
Purchase of Assets				
Female	119	27	46 (70.37)	47 (2.17)
Male	81	29	48 (65.52)	49 (2.08)
Total	200	56	94 (67.86)	96 (2.13)
Day to Day Activities				
Female	119	23	41 (78.26)	44 (7.32)
Male	81	29	47 (62.07)	48 (2.13)
Total	200	52	88 (69.23)	92 (4.55)

Contd...

Weaving Related Activities				
Female	119	36	63 (75.00)	64 (1.59)
Male	81	33	53 (60.61)	54 (1.89)
Total	200	69	116 (68.12)	118 (1.72)
Marketing of Silk				
Female	10	2	5 (150.00)	7 (40.00)
Male	29	11	12 (9.09)	16 (33.33)
Total	39	13	17 (30.77)	23 (35.29)

Note: Figures in parentheses indicate percentage change over previous period.

In decisions related to day to day activities, the number of female respondents having a say has increased from 23 in period I to 41 in period II and thereafter to 44 in period III. It indicates that male respondents have a better position in these matters. In contrast, women have a better say in the decision-making process of weaving related activities. About 36 respondents have reported to have a say in period I which increased to 63 in period II and further to 64 in period III. The increasing participation of women in decision-making related to weaving may be largely attributed to the fact that most of the weavers in the industry are women.

The females' participation in decision-making in marketing of silk is studied for the respondents who are involved in silk trade including the owners. Out of 10 female respondents, only 2 female silk traders have reported to have some say in marketing of their products in period I. However, the number has increased to 5 in period II and to 7 in period III. This increase in participation reflects the possibility of creating more women entrepreneurs in future.

From the above findings, it may be inferred that there has been a positive change in matters related to the participation of women in decision-making leading to greater empowerment of women particularly in the silk industry. Although it is difficult to say that globalisation is the determining factor that influences positively in empowering women, it plays an important role particularly in the economic empowerment of women. Once females become economically stronger, they can accept greater responsibilities than males. These responsibilities may be with respect to financial matter, healthcare, children's education, day-to-day's activity, etc.

Measurement of Gender Empowerment

Gender Empowerment Measure (GEM) assesses three dimensions of gender empowerment such as political participation and decision-making power, economic participation and decision-making power, and command over economic resources. Analysing the GEM, it is found that the percentage share of women in local government bodies such as *panchayats* is 37 per cent. The indexed EDEP for representation at local government bodies is found to be 0.91 which indicates lower women representation in comparison to men. The EDEP for economic participation also exhibits similar trend. However, the EDEP for income indicates the existence of higher disparities in the earned income of women and men in the study area. The overall GEM in the industry is found to be 0.63.

The results indicate existence of inequality in gender empowerment. Since the analysis considers absolute average level of income between males and females, this may underestimate the value of GEM. Considering the relative income shares of males and females may improve the value for GEM. Moreover, the analysis did not consider care work where females play a major role. Studies of gender empowerment involving different time periods may provide useful information about gender empowerment in a particular area. Therefore, an attempt has been made to study the women empowerment in the industry involving three different time periods as mentioned earlier.

Summary and Conclusions

Major findings of the study can be summarised as follows:

Out of 200 respondents surveyed, 59.50 per cent are females and 40.50 per cent is males. About 71.5 per cent of the respondents are unmarried. About 79 per cent of the total respondents work as weavers followed by 19.5 per cent as owners cum silk traders and mere 1.5 per cent as helpers. The education of most of the workers is up to primary or middle school level only. A considerable proportion of them are illiterate.

There is an increase in women's participation in decision-making process over the period of study. The increase is more pronounced in household related activities, financial matters, children's education, healthcare, purchase of assets, day to day activities, and weaving related activities. The rate of increase is relatively high only amongst the women involved in silk trade. Higher women's participation in decision-making process may be considered as increased women's empowerment in the industry.

Measuring the gender empowerment, it is found that the overall GEM in the industry is 0.63. There has been about 77 per cent improvement in women's empowerment between period I and period II and about 92 per cent between period I and period III.

In silk trade, although women are becoming more and more empowered, the limited employment opportunities, poor level of education, etc., are the issues that demand immediate attention. Silk trade will be helpful when women involved in the industry become self-determined in their economic and social status, and they improve their basic standard of living.

References

ARTFED (2006), 'Glimpse of Silk Weaving at Sualkuchi', Government of Assam.

Cagatay, N. (2000), 'Gender, Poverty and Trade', UNDP report on Trade and Sustainable Human Development.

Census of India (2001), Office of the Registrar General of India, New Delhi.

Durano, Marina F. B. (1999), 'Gender Issues in International Trade', International Gender and Trade Network.

Gammage Sarah, Helene Jorgensen, Eugenia McGill and Marceline White (2002), *Trade Impact Review*, The Coalition for Women's Economic Development and Global Equality, Inc., Global Trade Program, Washington, DC.

UNDP (2006), 'Human Development Report, 2006: Beyond Scarcity: Power, Poverty and the Global Water Crisis', p. 398, Palgrave

Macmillan, New York, ISBN 0-230-50058-7.

IFAD (2003), 'Women: As Agents of Change', Roundtable Discussion Paper for the twenty-Fifth anniversary session of IFAD's Governing Council, February.

Kalima, B. (2002), 'Gender and Debt', African Forum and Network on Debt and Development (AFRODAD), Harare, Zimbabwe, June 27.

Kashyap, S. G. (2000), 'Mahanta lunches special scheme to boost golden muga production in Assam', *Indian Express Newspapers (Bombay) Ltd.*, September 28.

Nageer, F., Abraham, and A. Spieldoch (2003), 'Gender, Sustainable Development, and Trade', International Gender and Trade Network, August.

Pandey, P. (2003), 'Rs. 405 lakh pumped in to revive silk industry', *The Hindu*,

Pathak, G. (2003), 'Assam Weavers in Distress', *The Day After*, June 1-15., Courtesy: http://www.dayafterindia.com/june11/states.html

Silk Export and Import Review (2006), February.

Thakuria, N. (2004), 'Looming Dreams and Reality', SAN- Feature Services, *The Bangladesh Observer*, February 24 (Tuesday).

Williams, M. (2001), 'Imbalances, Inequities and the WTO Mantra', Development Alternatives with Women for a New Era (DAWN) discussion Paper II on the WTO, November.

9

Gender Dynamics in Development Process of India

Kumar Das and Banishree Das

Although gender empowerment has been a buzzword in development circles, the concept has been used in so many different ways by different agents that it remains ambiguous. Conceptualizing power and gender adequately entails understanding its multi dimensional nature, the complex ways in which women experience subordination and the ways in which they negotiate or manage this state of affairs. Ironically all religions make unctuous praises and panegyric worships of women (Geeta, 2002). But the gender gap in terms of different indices such as life expectancy, literacy and earning has in fact increased from sixties to nineties in south Asia and Sub-Saharan Africa. The UNDP has developed a Gender Development Index (GDI) as a tool in order to capture gender inequality. It notes the inequalities between men and women on the same variables that make up the Human Development Index (HDI) related to the overall achievements in that society. It includes three variables: health, education and income. The HDI, however, has been criticized on the ground that by considering only three variables, it fails to take into account important dimensions such as the quality of community life, access to basic amenities and human rights. Important aspects and concerns relevant for women such as safety and security, household allocation of resources, unpaid labour, mobility constraints and lack of sexual and reproductive freedom under patriarchal ideology do not find any place.

It is argued that rising incomes may not ensure improved status for women particularly in a patriarchal society like ours.

Education and income may be high; there may still be greater degree of violence against women. In a society there may not be overt gender disparities in the provision of basic needs, but issues such as dowry, preference of male child over females, may be high. Recognizing the centrality of gender based power imbalances, the UNDP has clearly identified the movement towards gender equality as a political process. UNDP's Gender Empowerment Measure (GEM) attempts to reflect women's political participation, their access to professional positions and earning power. A comparison of GDI and GEM yields interesting results. For example, countries like France and Japan are high in GDI but they lag far behind on the GEM. Some developing countries like China, Cuba and Barbados have high GEM ranking than developed countries like Japan, France and Spain. The GEM is also criticized on the ground that it is again based on three variables.

It is built on a very narrow conception of empowerment. It does not include legal and human rights nor does it reflect cultural constructions of gender identity. Thus, in order to assess the impact of structural reforms on women, the conventional parameters used to measure gender disparity may not be enough. It is, therefore, necessary to consider research methodologies that go beyond the quantitative dimensions in order to address the complexity of these phenomena.

Gender Discrimination

The development process assumes men and women to be abstractly equal, both making rational choices. Gender is not recognized either as an asymmetry or as a system of power relationships. The mainstream economics has rather trivialised the gender issue (Becker 1960). At the most, it addresses the issue of unequal wages among men and women. This myopia is inherent in any patriarchal organization and creation of knowledge. Neo-classical economic theory has concentrated more on wage differentials rather than gender segregation, employing mainly models of perfect competition where wages are equal to the values of worker's marginal product (Macintosh, 1990). The conclusion of such an analysis is that women's economic situation is a result of tastes and choices of women themselves and of employers etc, acquired through both specialization of and socialisation by individuals.

The division of labour by gender within the household in India is stubbornly cultural (Das and Das, 2006). Women as a class are oppressed and subdued by the hegemony of social patriarchy. The gender inequality is very sharp within the rural households. Since the employment options available to the rural women are severely limited and since the opportunities for skill acquisition and job mobility are more limited for the rural female than the male, the work force participation for the poor female in the rural areas means the relentless weariness of heavy workloads and the deprivation of childhood care and schooling for their children (particularly for the girl child). The most serious aspect of gender inequality is the gender gap in literacy level. The highest gender gap is noticed in backward states like Rajasthan followed by Uttar Pradesh, Bihar, Madhya Pradesh and Orissa (Sen, 1990).

The dividing line between productive work and domestic work is not only arbitrary but also it tends to underestimate the women's contribution to domestic work (Agrawal, 1997). The women as a class are saddled with 'multiple burden'. If one takes into account the unpaid work in India, woman in poor households work much longer hours and have no or less leisure time than their male counterparts. In the age of globalization, technology and labour market imperfections have continuously displaced the female workers from high productive activities to low productive activities. It tends to accentuate the concentration of women in domestic works and non-market roles and activities (Das, 1997).

In India, since the beginning of planned development, women have been viewed as a deprived section requiring welfare measures. Indian culture and social ethos have, to a large extent, been influenced by a patriarchal value system. Given the cultural and social background, whether 73rd amendment of the Indian constitution would be able to bring about a significant change in the existing situation leading to empowerment of women is still an open question. As a result of deeply entrenched social attitudes and practices, women by and large have not been independent decision-makers in the country. Their decisions in most cases have been influenced by the wishes and dictates of the male family members. They are always guided by patriarchal social system and therefore are discriminated against in terms of food, cloth, housing, health care and education.

Gender Stereotypes

All religions prescribe, justify and contain the notions of 'ideally masculine' and 'ideally feminine' characters. They claim that man is the norm, the rule and women is a derivation. Man is the measure of humanity. Man possesses the monopoly power to define, interpret, judge. Even social reformers argue that woman needs to be educated so that she continues to function as a good mother. Education must help cultivate women's innate modesty and not instill a desire or ambition in them (Agrawal, 1997). We find many varieties of social stereotypes regarding women in India. Common remarks regarding single mothers are: 'Women are responsible for separation'; They bring separation by 'behaving badly'; They should suffer for their yobbo; 'She has loose character'; 'The termagant and errant wives should suffer their comeuppance'; and so on. But after separation they suffer from predation of men. It is fairly a routine hazard of widows/divorcee ladies. Normally we accept the justification that 'they have money and they earn'. So they suffer from such predations.

However, there is gender discrimination in this phenomenon. The common notion works in the mind of the man that woman should not have left the man despite all adversity. A woman without man to protect her is potentially available for sex and entertainment of other men. She is a 'product' meant for man's consumption and entertainment. She is of the man, for the man and by the man. Children grown up in female-headed households suffer from social stigmatization (Chant, 1999). Common reactions towards lone mothers include imposing isolations through speculative gossips or restricted social contacts. The female neighbours become very jealous and comment on any type of household purchases: jewelry or cloth, etc. They keep distance from lone mothers. It is due to: (i) women themselves are worried about women on their own posing a threat to their marriage (ii) own husband may get suspicious about fraternizing with women who theoretically have more freedom. Solo motherhood is the reflector or rear view mirror for the dynamics of power and dependency. It is largely considered as a social perfidy and recalcitrance. The more difficult and stigmatized solo mother hood is in a society, the greater the barriers against opting out of mental torture of a bad marriage.

The immoral and sexual deviances are linked with reactions to economic circumstances of lone mothers. The upward mobility of a lone mother evokes suspicion about immoral earnings also. They lead a life of social sympathy. Male has created a social atmosphere where the females themselves pity the lone mothers. So, genuine economic prosperity of a lone mother has to be concealed in the society. In order to fend off charges of promiscuity and loose morals, many lone mothers tend to lead extremely restricted social lives. Many lone mothers have good network with the neighbours, but they fear they may lose their sympathy if they were to take up with some other men. Both social stigma and economic disadvantages are mutually reinforcing against the single mothers. These entire manifestations act as powerful deterrents to women's choosing to be free or thinking to be equal to man.

Cultural Artifacts

Women's role, her fertility and her work in the family and society at large are influenced by economic development of the nation. As economic development proceeds, family production for its own use declines. Larger share of goods for family consumption is produced outside the family. This brings changes both in the relation of family members to the outside world and in the relation between family members themselves. But in India, gender discrimination is culturally stubborn. Women remain more burdened with family production. Traditional attitude of the villages, despite paean of modernization, prevails everywhere today. The need for self protection, security and lineage has still remained as a strong incentive for having a cohesive family. Therefore, educated people today (even many doctors) are found to be fathers of 5-7 daughters due to their 'son preference'. Children are socialized to accept their present and future roles without any protests. Boys are encouraged to learn to debate, defy and escape from any responsibility, while girls are taught to obey and remain docile.

Economic development is creating a gap in skill process of man and women and endorsing the revolving doors of occupational segregation. 'High-tech' continuously displaces them to all low-skill and low-paid jobs with ergonomics of casualisation and flexibilisation. Role of schools is not only to teach intellectual skills and impart knowledge but also to indoctrinate pupils with dominant cultural values. Cultural education for girls is full of traditional prejudices. The early socialization of girls by parents and teachers contribute to the development of 'superiority feeling' in boys and 'inferiority feeling' in girls. Machismo, being all pervasive in educational, political, economic and social subsystem, is a real maelstrom for Indian society (Das, 2007)

The Indian mother transmits the notion of correct 'social behavior' of the family to the girls but the boys need not know the name of their own grand fathers. The girl grows in a vertical relation of obedience and command. All adolescent girls are taught to be mellifluent and skilled in domestic spheres involving all repetitive and irksome jobs. But the male does the concentrated bust of activity in certain seasons or weeks of the year and enjoys idleness for long period. The male adults stroll up and down to the town to gossip with friends or to loiter in market places. All these bohemian activities are considered befitting manifestations of the male role. But all duties and tasks of the girls are subsumed in their 'social role' (Karlekar, 1995).

The Indian family, being an undifferentiated unit governed by altruism, is the epitome of gender asymmetries. The right to consume any thing in the house is different for women, regardless of economic status. Any kind of consumption including food is not simply determined by its availability or adequacy. In India, women fast for the welfare of their husbands, while men do not reciprocate. If at all male is fasting that is for spiritual purposes but female fasts for the auspiciousness of the household collectively. The behaviour of women is certainly and commonly bound up with altruism and prioritizing the needs of others. It is the central element in feminine identities. Men eat always before women. Women's eating before the men or male adults of the family is culturally forbidden. Women and girls learn to refuse to take meat, milk, ghee or any rich dishes. They normally eat the residual quantity of food left by the male members.

In formal occasions men and women eat separately. Men eat with the guests. Women eat with the girls and small children. Girls learn and follow the mother to maintain social customs. A Woman never confesses that she is hungry or thirsty. It is considered as non-woman etiquette. Man, while eating, refrains himself from talking and expresses gratification. Male enjoys the 'yum yum' monopoly that seems to live to eat. Man eats slowly with restraints urging the other male co-diners to eat more and more (even in poor families) and take digestives after eating. Women while serving the food carry this modesty to the extremes. Even pregnant and lactating mothers do not get right calorie of food. They suffer from anemia, jaundice and several problems of malnourishment.

Women are progressively weakened by successive pregnancies. Women are admired for working late into their pregnancies. They are expected to take rest only for 2 weeks after the child birth, during which they are given splendid nutritional food. After 3-4 weeks the child is tied to the mother's back. So her food consumption is rigidly determined and so is her workload because it is inseparable from her social role (Maher 1990). Not eating (or fasting) and telling lies that she is not hungry is considered a positive moral values for women but it is neutral (or negative) for men. Girls are indispensable for domestic activities in each family. Therefore, education is a form of consumption from which girls are conspicuously excluded. But son's education is an investment. Thus birth, growth, education or professional achievements of the girls before marriage take place by accident (Das and Das, 2006).

Incidence of Dowry

A host of economic and social structures and processes that reinforce patriarchy devalue and commodify women and promote such horrendous phenomena as dowry. The problem of dowry in India transcends the rural-urban dichotomy. Its incidence cuts across all caste and class boundaries .The prevailing patriarchal myths seek to situate dowry as a girl's share of parental property or as daughter's life insurance policy secured by her parents at the time of her marriage (Mishra, 2000). The structure of acceptance enjoyed by dowry is significant. This explains why some of the victims are not helped by co-villagers. Besides, help and sympathy for the victims of dowry blur gender-based distinction. The attitude of women at the family level and in the official capacity (woman *sarpanch*, woman doctor, woman police, woman BDO, woman teacher, etc) reveals this most unambiguously. Most of dowry deaths and torture are not reported anywhere, because of the fear of social stigma or lack of knowledge about or fear of complexity of long legal process, unless the level of terror and violence becomes a threat to the life of the victim or she dies.

It is unfortunate that most of the dowry victims have been married off in line with patriarchal notions of responsibility by their parents without any attempt to educate them or make them stand on their own feet. This is coupled with a general neglect of a girl's education/career that moulds victims to a stereotyped role associated with reproduction and 'wifely' responsibilities. This reduces them to the position of unpaid maids, veiling a structure of exploitation associated with household labour. We also notice many attempts to argue for festivals, *like durga puja, laxmi puja and kali puja etc*, where women power is worshiped. Women's sub-human status is very often justified by religious fundamentalists by our obsession with our rich tradition. We also draw upon many customs like '*sabitri amabashya'* and the like in order to legitimize predatory demands. This coexists with a perception that commodifies marriage and converts a sacred act into a materialistic exchange.

However, Indians are proud to say that there is love, cohesion, culture, less divorce, and familial harmony inside the house. But this 'pseudo harmony' does not imply a healthy society either. In fact it conceals the disharmony and dominance and represents conflictual cooperation (Agrawal, 1997). The effect of masculinity, which is merely an expression of brute male power with yahoo mentality, has not reduced unfortunately in the era of globalization. Male promiscuity today is being excused, legitimized and celebrated (Das, 2007). On the contrary, beauty, 'chastity and motherhood' are convenient and elaborate fictions which not only convince the women that they are destined to be subordinates to men but also enable them to gladly accept that relations of inequality. Average Indian educated male (even some female social researchers) may simply dismiss all these narrations and arguments as non-issue and dub it as exaggeration of western feminism.

Neo-Housewifisation Process

The urban centres are flourishing with economic activities with large surplus adult men, who leave their wives and children in the villages to take care of their grand parents and property. The propensity to marry among educated Indian urbanites has been falling. So prostitution is flourishing in the urban society. But the same man blames the women as prostitutes. Man makes them either 'good mother' or 'bad prostitutes' in the society. Both represent cultural prejudices against women. Both 'chaste wife' and 'worst prostitute' mirror each other (Das, 2007).These is masculine articulations. The first one connotes life long sexual slavery to one man, while the other sells herself to several men. In either case, femininity is condemned to servitude to male-kind.

The gender relation has not changed much even in towns. It is most oppressive for the rural women. The wife (except in very poor households, where there is no margin of choice) also feels ashamed of working for a wage in the presence of a working husband. She feels good if husband is having enough manliness to keep her as a decorative piece at home as baby-producing machine or care-providing agent. Individually she may not have any compunction. The man-made design is powerful enough to control and suppress her 'feeling of deprivation' or mind to assess her social position as a human-class. It is because she is brought up in the culture of altruism (Karlekar, 1995). It is also very difficult to find a single lady remorsing with yell and yelp or has audacity to face the challenge of any conjugal estrangement. Under cultural pressure woman acts and appears to be happy and jocund. The reduction of number of tasks performed in the family is accompanied by a reduction in the autonomy of the family, which becomes dependent not only on market but on the government and other public institutions. This process has benefited the male and adults, but transformed the housewives to lonely performers of routine manual domestic work confined to the household (Boserup, 1990).

Educated working lady in the metros of India has become smart and free enough comparable to a French lady or any lady of the western society. But it is the travesty of modernity for her. Feminization of jobs is a myth and education is less meaningful (Das, 2007). She has to play several roles as a mother, cook, tutor, tailor, shopper, driver, janitor, gardener, home-nurse in addition to attending guests, old parents, patients in hospital, marriage parties and going to bank, children's school, laundry, temple, etc. This results only in neo-housewifisation, where the modern lady is saddled with multiple burdens (Das, 1997). This freedom of movement involving the remote control of the male does not necessarily imply gender equality or women empowerment in backward states.

Looking Forward

Gender empowerment has been a buzzword in development circles of India, but the concept has remained ambiguous. The gender gap in terms of different indices has increased from sixties to nineties in south Asia. Technology and labour market imperfections have continuously displaced the female workers from high productive activities to low productive activities. The preference for women and girl child workers is most common in the unorganized sector because in such jobs it is relatively easy for the employers to circumvent the laws. The schooling of the girl child is determined more intricately by factors such as caste, religion, family type and size, occupation, kinship pattern, marriage, etc. Marriages of girls without education lead to second stage of bondage in their lives. The whole host of economic and social structures and processes that reinforce patriarchy devalue and commodify women and promote such horrendous phenomena as dowry.

Even today man continues to exercises his ever subtler control on the family production and reproduction system. It is gradually institutionalized at several spheres: work, culture, customs, religion and education. Therefore, liberation of women will not be easy or complete without the destruction of neo-patriarchy which has four levels of control: production, reproduction, socialization and sexuality. It is not enough if girls succeed in the educational ladder or if women's work participation rate increases in the labour market. The social and economic structures today lock production and reproduction together, which perpetrate male dominance and female submission. The liberation of women can only be achieved if the structures in which women are integrated are transformed simultaneously. Modification of any one of them can be offset by a reinforcement of another so that a mere permutation of the form of inequality is ultimately achieved. Thus, a social transformation, which brings real modernity, is warranted for India but not this sort of consumerism.

Economic development process is never gender-neutral. So any prescription based only on 'household bargaining' model of the economists will be inaccurate for backward states. Poverty can not serve as the proxy for subordination of women. Therefore, anti poverty policies can not be expected to necessarily improve the position of women. Until very high level of income is reached, the rise in household income aggravates the gender inequality only. Money is neither necessary nor sufficient for transferring existing asymmetric gender relations. Thus, Gender issue should never be approached with poverty reduction policies. Because this approach believes that women are victims of misdevelopment. Rescuing gender from poverty trap means that we need poverty-independent gender analyses and policies. The gender issue should thus be delinked both from economics and politics.

References

Agarwal, B. (1997), 'Bargaining and Gender Relations: Within and Beyond the Households'. *Feminist Economics*, Vol. 3, No. 1, pp. 1-51.

Becker, G. (1960), 'An Economic Analysis of Fertility', in G Becker (ed) *Demographic and economic Change in Developed Countries*, Princeton University Press, Princeton.

Boserup, E. (1990), 'Economic Change and the role of women', in *Persistent Inequalities: Women and World development,* (ed) Eren Tinker, Chapter-2, Oxford University press, New York.

Chant, S. (1999), 'Women-headed households: Global orthodoxies and Grass root realities', in *Women Globalization and Fragmentation in the Developing World*, (ed) Haleh Afshar and Stephanie Barrientos, Macmillan.

Das, K. (1990), 'Paradox of Poverty and Planning in India', *Economic Quarterly*, Vol. 25, No. 4.

——(1997), 'Asian Profile of Underdevelopment and Poverty', *Asian Profile*, Vol. 25, No. 1, February.

——(2007), 'Status of Women in Indian Society', *Asian Profile*, Vol. 4, No. 3, pp. 234-256.

Das, K. and Banishree Das (2006), '*Technology and Women in the globalization Regime*', Paper presented in World Congress of Economics, held in Helsinki, August.

Geeta, V. (2002), 'God made you different and Nature made us different', *Gender Theorizing Feminism*, Stree Publications, Madras.

Karlekar, M. (1995), 'Search for Women's Voices, Reflections on Field Work, 1968-93', *Economic and Political Weekly*, Vol. 30, No. 17, pp. 30-37.

——(1995), *No Safe Spaces*: Report of a workshop on violence against women, Centre for Women's Development Studies, New Delhi.

Mackintosh, M. (1990), 'Gender and economics: the sexual division of labour and the subordination of women' in *Marriage and the Market* (ed), Kate Young *et al.*, Routledge, London.

Maher, V. (1990), 'Work Consumption and authority with in the Household', in *Of Marriage and the Market* (ed), Kate Young *et al.*, Routledge, London.

Mishra, S. (2000), Economics of Child labour in Orissa, Unpublished Ph. D. Thesis of Utkal University, Bhubaneswar.

Sen, A. K. (1990), 'Gender and Cooperative Conflicts in Persistent Inequalities', *Women and World Development* (ed), Irene Tinker, Oxford University Press, New York.

10

Cultural Perspectives in the Emerging Socio-Economic Milieu

Meera Panigrahi and Sudhakar Panda

Introduction

Economic growth, per se, is not enough. Development planning becomes unidirectional when the objective of higher production is prioritized to the exclusion of social, cultural and ethical aspects of life. As a result, societies tend to experience a distorted pattern of growth and reflect values of life that may be anti-cultural. Growth strategies, whether it is planned growth in a command economy backed by coercion, or profit-driven growth in a market economy, should have multi-dimensional orientations inclusive of a socio-cultural perspective. Preservation and promotion of a society's art, architecture and cultural heritage as also social and moral well-being should form an integral part of the development process. The society, therefore, has to evolve a policy capable of harmonizing its development practices with efficient management of its cultural and human resources, preservation of its beautiful nature and natural landscapes, social values and institutions. This will provide enough scope for the wholesome development of man through his interactions with man, society and nature. Such an approach will pave the path for a holistic development of society, where man finds his peace and proper place. This will ensure what Pattanaik (1997) calls an "Overall social well-being" and not just the "Overall well-being of the societies".

The objective of this paper is to examine, in brief, the development strategies in the centrally planned economies led by the erstwhile Soviet Union and assess their impact on social well-being , on human welfare and above all on humanistic culture. An attempt will also be made to suggest a path of development consistent with culture and humanism.

Socialist Countries

A very distressing event of the last part of the 20th century was the failure of the Russian Revolution of 1917 and the disintegration of Soviet Union. The political regimes and the attempted planned restructuring of the economic system in the centrally planned socialist economies of Poland, Hungary, Czechoslovakia, Yugoslavia, Albania etc. failed. It is interesting to note that the nature and character of the Chinese revolution has undergone significant changes to accommodate new issues and policies greatly divorced from socialist thinking and ideology. The socialist countries have adjusted to change by launching market oriented reforms. They have been moving away from 'authoritarianism in the political system' (Pattanaik, 1997) to different forms of decentralization. How do we explain the failure of the political system to ensure social well-being? How do we explain the process of liberalization and the accompanying institutional changes in several key areas? How do we view the market socialism in China?

These societies placed an overwhelming importance on political ideologies to guide their development process; their socio-political-educational institutions, family and social structures and man-to-man, man-to-woman and man-to-nature and man-to-state relationships. All efforts to develop the state, the economic and the society were conditioned by the dictates issued by the political authority. Social and human relationship, man's inner urges and expressions, feelings and thoughts were made totally subservient to the will to state. Man's craving for his total development, his social political and cultural freedom to live, to think and to write differently were suppressed. Men and women could not be their own natural selves. The vision of Marx of empowering the proletariats to bring about egalitarianism could not be fully realized because its humanistic content suffered depletion under the impact of political authoritarianism.

Such a depletion of Marxian humanism, as Erich Fromm (1965) suggests, was due to misinterpretation of Marx and a communist ideology pouched by Russian leaders whose contempt for individual dignity and humanist values created a fractured culture. Marx was interpreted as a proponent of economistic and hedonistic materialism by many adherents imbued with the spirit of capitalism. Soviet communists conceived of communism in the sprit of capitalism. Their socialism did not produce a society humanly different from capitalism but rather a form of capitalism in which the working class has achieved a higher status (Fromm, 1965).

Marx aimed at liberating men from the pressures of common needs so that they could be fully human. He was concerned with emancipation of man, the overcoming of alienation, restoration of his capacity to relate himself fully to man and to nature through material fulfillment. Marx's philosophy constitutes as Fromm states a spiritual essentialism in secular language because of which its spiritual quality became oppositional to material practice and thinly disguised materialistic philosophy of our age. Marxism which led to the concept of "the economic man" who worked solely for material gain is a devaluation of the real human being for whom producing creatively in a free environment is essential for his spiritual growth. In other words, the backlash of state controlled development perpetrated a restrictive state cultural instead of individual welfare and humanistic culture. The emotional and creative energy of human beings which is at the source of great writings, paintings and new thinking gradually dried up. All these developments invariably resulted in undermining the social-cultural and moral foundations of the socialist societies. In the absence of human freedoms cultural development could hardy flourish. A great socio-cultural vacuum was created. A sort of artificial unity prevailed; the society no longer remained cultured and human; it also lost its internal peace and cohesiveness.

Free Market Economies

The developed capitalist market economies have reached a very high stage of material progress. They are high-tech societies. There is the endless pursuit of wealth which is a functional symbol of power, authority and prestige. There is a cut-throat competition and a never ending expansion of capital base to acquire more and more command over the economy and society. Man is projected as an autonomous, self-reliant, acquisitive and self interested person. In such circumstances, economic life becomes devoid of nobility or the virtues of integrity, honesty and morality. What is more, adoption of scientific methods based on rational interpretation of observable facts in the social and human spheres has resulted in a positivistic stereotype approach to nature and human life, thereby limiting the very concept of humanism.

The ever-growing appetite for growth, prosperity and technical excellence has created unforeseen social, political and economic consequence affecting the inner-growth of individuals. Material well being is accompanied by social evils. One finds that drug addiction, street fighting and gang-warfare's are concomitants of material progress. There is a loss of self identity in the type of utilitarian culture which flourishes in the west and a consistent decline in social morality. The society is no longer loving, caring and sympathetic. No commitment to universal values; to political, social, religious, cultural, and artistic ideals that enable the individual to live, to think, to be honest and to be sincere to himself, and to act on moral convictions. There is less of development of what the American psychologist calls man who is a complex of many selves in one. There is no longer the joy of living. The harmonious development of man's facilities without one-sideness of over-emphasis is subsumed in the struggle for survival in a consumerist ethos. In this way development tends to get divorced from life and culture.

Development of a Humanistic Tradition

Humanism is a philosophy that has influenced the thoughts of all great men who have felt the urge to improve the human condition. It addresses itself to the general and the universal values of life as distinct from the temporal and local. It stresses the importance of the individual human personality and its power to learn from suffering and to rise above circumstances. It aims at creating a cultural climate by perfecting the economic, political, social, religious and artistic foundations of a society to suit the needs of the time and to perfect the human being.

Humanism thus makes the point that men should live by great ideas which can be derived from any source-theology, science, politics or history; infact, all our knowledge should be derived from meaningful human experience. The imbibing of such ideas will help from the mind of the individual. The purpose of humanism is to help cultivate a frame of mind that can evaluate, judge and analyse so that usable elements of culture are preserved or suitably modified to relate to changing social conditions. What is most important for humanistic approach is to relate ideas to society and history in order to see them in their proper perspective. Hence the development of the historic sense or what Lionel Trilling (1950) calls the sense of the past or what H.J. Muller (1943) calls 'the uses of the past', is essential to humanism and development of the society. The historic sense binds us to those aspects of tradition or belief that perfect the internal condition of man, making him morally committed to society and culture.

It is not material welfare alone, but both material and spiritual welfare which contribute to the development of the inner faculties of individuals. The emphasis is not upon technology that brings order comfort, freedom from hunger, wealth and general well-being but upon human values that guide his course in life and aid him in upholding universal truths. It thus not only uses reason for the process of discrimination but also 'seeks to press beyond reason by the use of intuition or imagination' to grasp a higher reality inaccessible to science.

It becomes clear that economic development when fostered in an environment of humanism can give us a whole man, perfect in his moral, social and intellectual life, carefully balancing and harmonizing his intellectual and emotional faculties.

Towards a Humanistic Approach to Economic Development

Culture alone does not have the strength to hold the minds of men in a modern society. Life has been surrendered to technology and there one finds the emergence of a 'one dimensional' human being dangling precariously over a modern wasteland, where there is no hope for life-giving water. Can we have economic development that takes cognizance of these modern developments and can re-model the process of material progress accordingly? Can there be a development process that leads to the development of self and self-realisation?

Scholars from different fields have made an attempt to conceptualise such a development scenario. The humanist psychologist Abrahman Maslow (1964), the social philosopher Rudolf Steiner (1977), the Buddhist monks in Japan, the Anglo German management philosopher Fritz Schumacher (1993) and the Pakistani banker Agha Hassan Abedi (1984) have seen the possibility of humanistic approach to economic development.

Maslow (1964) gives us a hierarchy of needs beginning with "Physiological Needs" (air, water, food, shelter, sleep, sex) followed by "Deficiency Needs" (safety and security), "Growth Needs" (self-esteem, esteem by others, love and belongingness) and the 'Self Actulisation where such fine attributes such as Truth, Beauty, Aliveness, Goodness and Uniqueness etc. find expression in the living of the individual in the society and man develops his full potentialities. Considered in a broader socio-economic-cultural context, Maslow's approach has great relevance to the evolution of the right social structures.

Steiner (1977) is concerned with 'individual self-development in the context of societal evolution'. Steiner develops the concept of threefold commonwealth' the economic socio-political and cultural. According to Steiner, economic, fraternity, political equality and individual freedom can be blended together to have a healthy society. Baigan Ishida who drew his inspiration from the ideas of the Zen priest Shoshan Suzuki thinks that Social order and progress could be brought into conformity and harmony with the cosmos if people followed the precepts of honesty, self-restraint and order. The inner heart (the true heart of man) and the natural order (the cosmos) are one and the same. Schumacher (1993), the writer of small is Beautiful developed a new type of economic thinking where people mattered more than economics and economic development became compatible with the human being. Aga Hasan Abedi of Pakistan , the founder of the Bank of credit and Commerce (BCC) in Pakistan makes an attempt to relate the laws of nature (The Totality Principle, The Latency Principle, This Flow Principle and integrity Principle to development and highlights the inter-dependence of man and nature. A more broad based approach emerges with Pattanaik's concept of "overall social will being and well being of people" with its economic, social, political, intellectual and aesthetic dimensions (Pattanaik, 1997).

The Middle Path

It may be observed that in all these writings the focus is upon man as man and the development of man in social context which facilitates the development of his total personality. The development of social policy and administration should develop the right environment for both the utilitarian and ethical, cultural aspects of the human personality. No aspect of social policy is to be given exaggerated importance at the cost of wholesome and balanced development of a social order where economics, politics, history, literature, art and other creative expression of man flourish. In such a milieu man moves to a higher realm of thinking and divinity and stays free from the bestial levels by exercising moral restraints upon his wild impulses.

He has to recognize the middle position in the scheme of nature by bringing about a dynamic blending of moral and material development. If we can follow the golden mean which is characteristic attitude appearing in almost every system of Greek Philosophy we can have balanced development and healthy cultural ethics. The golden mean preached the motto of measure and harmony as against excess and disproportionateness and was a way of checking violence and impulsiveness of character that characterize modern civilisation.

Will Duran the noted philosopher says that Aristotle found the middle path, the golden mean, the real guide to excellence. He also finds that Plato had the same thing in mind when he called virtue with knowledge. The Seven Wise Men had established the tradition (of the middle path) by engraving on the temple of Apollo at Delphi, the motto medenagan "nothing in excess" (Durant 1967:75, 77)

Why the Middle Path?

Given the costs and undesirable effects of growth, reformation in economic development to ensure humanistic progress will depend to large extent, on this golden mean or the middle path. Viewed from the perspective of post-modern developments, this would entail a slower rate of growth in GNP and discriminate use of technological methods. Considering the reestablishment of values that will follow the pursuit of this middle path, foregoing high development and affluence is but a small price to pay. This would mean added emphasis on synchronizing growth policies in the fields of education, health, environment along with production of cultural goods of high order (books, T.V. serials, music, dance, drama, art, see Pattnaik's Cultural and Human Development – 1997). We may look forward to a society which is free from poverty and hunger and from politicalisation of religion and social issues. Hence, culture-directed policies in homogenous mass consumer society will put a brake on the rate of self-consumption that characterizes post-modern culture and free us from the monotony of an increasing standardization of tastes and desires.

Can we follow this middle path which Buddha, whom we accept as aņ avatar (reincarnation) advocated? A middle path may help us in transcending the limits and excesses of materialization and building a society increasingly devoted to the balanced and wholesome development of the human being. Such a social reality can be established if culture becomes both the context for development as well as the missing factor in policies of development (Arizpe 1997).

References

Abedi, A. B. (1984), *Real Management*, BCC Internal Publication.

Arizpe, L. (1997), Foreward on *'Cultural and Development'*, UNRISED-UNESCO Series of Occasional Papers.

Durrant, W. (1967), *The Story of Philosophy,* Washington Square Press, New York.

Fromm, E. (ed) (1965), *Socialist Humanism*, Garden City, NY: Doubleday.

Maslow, A. (1964), *Motivation and Personality*, Harper and Row.

Muller, H. J. (1943), Science and Criticism: *The Humanistic Tradition in Contemporary Thought*, New Haven, Yale UP.

Pattanaik, P. K. (1997), 'Culture and Human Development', UNRISD–UNSECO Series of Occasional Papers.

Schumacher, E. F. (1993), *Small is Beautiful,* Vintage, UK.

Steiner, R. (1977), *Social Renewal*, (Steiner Press).

Trilling, Lionel (1950), *The Liberal Imagination*, Secker and Warbury, London.

11

Child Labour in India: Trends, Determinants and Policy Interventions

Saundarjya Borbora and Arghya Mukherjee

Introduction

Child labour is a major social problem in most of the developing countries including India and in the present era of globalization, it has emerged as a major international issue affecting the economic relations amongst countries. The term child labour has been defined differently by different organizations and in different countries and the term 'child work' and 'child labour' are often used interchangeably. Often these led to confusion and lost its focus on real priorities. Francis Blachard (1983), the former Director General of the ILO, has defined child labour as that which includes "children prematurely leading adult lives, working long hours for low wages under conditions damaging to their health and to their physical and mental development, sometimes separated from their families, frequently deprived of meaningful education and training opportunities that could open up for them a better future".

According to the Encyclopedia of Social Sciences, "when the business of wage earning or of participation in itself or family support conflicts directly or indirectly with the business of growth and education, the result is the child labour". Therefore, from these, broadly, it may be understood that child labour is any work within or outside the family, which affect the child's ability to participate in leisure, play and education and which impairs health and development of children. Usually, child labour stands for participation of children below 14 years of age in the labour force.

In India, the problem of child labour is complex. A large body of studies on child labour exists both on theoretical and analytical aspects. Basu (1999) reviews early theoretical ideas, bargaining models and models with multiple equilibria. Basu and Van (1998) demonstrated equlibia with child labour at low wages while the other has higher wages but no child labour in labour market. Parsons and Goldin (1989) deal with the issue of investment in education and availability of efficient capital market. Grootaert and Kanbur (1995) model child labour as a rational time allocation decision made jointly by children and their families. There are also a number of empirical studies providing various aspects of child labour in India. Mention may be made of some like Myron Weiner (1991), D.P. Chaudhri (1997), M. Swaminathan (1998) and G. K. Lieten (2000).

This chapter tries to focus on some of the aspects of child labour in India like the dimensions of child labour, gender variations and analyse some of the determinants of child labour. On the basis of the analysis and discussion, some policy prescription will be enumerated which may help in reducing the problem of child labour in the country.

Magnitude of Child Labour in India

The magnitude of child labour is alarming in India. Because of number of limitations such as presence of informal and unorganized labour market, it is difficult to provide the exact estimate of the magnitude of child labour. However, various agencies tried to estimate the extent of child labour in India. According to 1971, 1981 and 1991 census of India, the number of working children accounted for 10.74 million, 13.60 million and 11.28 million respectively. The ILO estimated child labour at 15.10 million in 1975 and 23.17 million in 1996. NSSO, India estimated child labour at 17.60 million during 1987-88 and 13.50 million during 1993-94. The ORG estimated the number of working children at 44 million. The Planning Commission of India put it at 17.36 million in 1983. These are also tabulated in Table 11.1.

Table 11.1: Trend and Magnitude of Child Labour in India (million)

Data source	Year	Magnitude of Child Labour
Census of India	1971	10.74
	1981	13.60
	1991	11.29
ILO	1975	15.10
	1996	23.17
NSSO, India	1987-88	17.60
	1993-94	13.50
Planning Commission (GOI)	1983	17.36
ORG, Baroda	1983	44.00

Source: as cited in Sekar, Helan R., Child Labour Legislation in India, V.V.Giri National Labour Institute, Noida, 1997, p. 20.

Although the figures from different sources are not the same, it surely depicts that child labour is a major problem that needs to be tackled at various levels, be it in the government, society, industry and other economic sectors. The following section provides some inputs about various dimension of child labour in India.

Dimensions of Child Labour in India

NSS data as above mentioned the existence of child labour of 13.50 million in 1993-94. Table 11.2 provides estimates of incidence of child labour from various sources. According to NSS 1993-94, the estimates of the incidence of child labour is about 6.2 per cent, while census gives 5.4 per cent in the year 1991. In rural areas, NSS estimates are higher than those of census and NCAER. The percentages of child labour in rural areas are two to three times higher than those exist in urban areas. There is no much difference between incidence of child labour for boys and girls according to the sources.

Table 11.2: Age-group-wise Incidence of Child Labour in India (5-14 Age-groups)

	Census,1991	NSS, 1993-94	NCAER,1994
Total	5.4	6.2	-
Rural	6.4	7.2	4.3
Urban	2.0	3.1	-
Boys	5.7	6.3	-
Girls	5.1	6.0	-

Source: Census 1991; NSS on employment and Unemployment, 50th Round; NCAER Human Development Survey, 1994.

The NSS data over a period 1977-78 to 1993-94 shows that the incidence of child labour has been declining in both rural and urban areas, which is shown in Table 11.3. In rural areas, the percentage of child labour for boys was higher than the girls till 1987-88, while in 1993-94 it is same. In case of urban areas, percentage of boys was always higher than that of girls.

Table 11.3: Trends in Incidence of Child Labour in India (5-14 Age-groups)

	Rural Boys	Rural Girls	Rural Total	Urban Boys	Urban Girls	Urban Total
1977-78	14.4	11.6	13.1	6.1	4.4	5.3
1983	13.5	12.5	13.0	6.1	3.8	5.0
1987-88	10.1	9.6	9.9	4.4	3.3	3.9
1993-94	7.1	7.2	7.1	3.6	2.5	3.1

Source: 1. Computed from NSS 50th Round data for 1993-94. 2. Visaria et. al (1993) for 1977-78, 1983 and 1987-88.

In India, child labour is concentrated in agriculture. Cultivators and agricultural labourers constitute approximately 78 per cent for boys and 83 per cent for girls. Manufacturing in household industries comes second which constitutes 20 per cent boys and 13 per cent girls. (Census, 1991). Some of the sectors where child exploitation are concentrated are, "power loom industry in Bhiwandi (Maharashtra), match industry of Sivkasi (Tamil Nadu), gem-polishing in Jaipur (Rajasthan), shellac industry in Bihar and Madhya Pradesh, the carpet industry of palamau, Varanasi and Mirzapur, the lock industry in Aligarh, pottery in Khurja and glass factories in Firozabad (all in Uttar Pradesh) and the bidi manufacturers, brick kilns, plantations, tea shops and middle class houses all over the country." (Lieten, 2000)

There are also regional disparities in the incidence of child labour. Table 11.4 provides the percentages of child labour across the states and Table 11.5 provides the rank of these states. For some states ranks differ depending on the source of data.

The work participation rates for children are higher for PSS category data by NSS. The NSS principal and subsidiary numbers for rural areas show that Andhra Pradesh accounts the highest incidence of child labour (17.8 per cent), whereas Kerala (0.76 per cent) reports the lowest. These two states have same ranks for urban areas. The disparities are much higher in rural areas as compared to urban areas. It is also interesting to note that some backward states like Bihar, Uttar Pradesh, Madhya Pradesh and Orissa have lower incidence of child labour compared to some southern states. Because of different sources, data may not be comparable as, to some extent, it depends on methodologies adopted for data collection.

Determinants of Child Labour

There are numerous demographic, cultural, social and economic factors responsible for the prevalence of child labour in India. A comprehensive analysis of child labour in India is not possible in this chapter due to paucity of data. Hence, only five dominant variables are chosen for analysis, which are expected to provide a rough idea as to what factors are likely to affect the prevalence of child labour in India. The data on these variables are collected from different secondary sources viz. CMIE, Census of India and other published reports and journals for major sixteen

Table 11.4: Incidence of Child Labour across Indian States (5-14 Age-groups)

	Rural				Urban		
	Census 1991	NSS 1993-94 PSS	NSS 1993-94 PS	NCAER 1994	Census 1991	NSS 1993-94 PSS	NSS 1993-94 PS
Andhra Pradesh	125	17.8	15.3	9.0	3.1	6.8	5.7
Assam	-	2.6	1.7	2.6	-	3.8	3.6
Bihar	4.4	3.7	3.2	3.9	1.6	1.3	1.2
Gujarat	7.1	4.1	2.8	6.2	1.7	2.0	1.4
Haryana	3.0	2.6	1.3	1.9	1.1	2.4	1.9
Himachal Pradesh	4.8	13.6	3.2	0.8	1.3	2.4	1.5
Jammu&Kashmir	-	5.6	3.3	-	-	1.1	0.8
Karnataka	111	13.9	10.7	7.4	3.5	4.3	4.0
Kerala	0.6	0.8	0.5	0.4	0.5	o.6	0.5
Madhya Pradesh	9.9	8.4	6.4	3.5	1.8	1.5	1.1
Maharashtra	8.1	6.5	5.3	8.0	1.6	2.1	1.8
Orissa	6.5	7.4	5.5	5.1	1.9	2.8	2.2
Punjab	3.6	2.7	2.1	3.4	1.6	1.7	1.4
Rajasthan	7.8	12.2	11.4	1.2	1.7	3.2	2.6

Contd...

Tamil Nadu	5.9	10.4	9.3	5.6	2.6	5.2	4.6
Uttar Pradesh	4.2	5.0	3.4	1.5	2.3	3.2	2.2
West Bengal	4.9	5.1	3.5	6.7	1.9	3.8	2.9
All India	6.4	7.2	5.8	4.3	2.0	3.1	2.5

Note: PS-Principal Status; PSS- Principal and Subsidiary Status

Source: Census, 1991; NSS 50th Round on employment and unemployment; Duraisamy, M (2000)

Table 11.5: Ranking of Indian States Based on Incidence of Child Labour (5-14 Age-group)

	Rural				Urban		
	Census 1991	NSS 1993-94 PSS	NSS 1993-94 PS	NCAER 1994	Census 1991	NSS 1993-94 PSS	NSS 1993-94 PS
Andhra Pradesh	15	17	17	16	14	17	17
Assam	-	3	3	6	-	13	14
Bihar	5	5	6	9	4	3	4
Gujarat	10	6	5	12	7	6	5
Haryana	2	2	2	5	2	8	9
Himachal Pradesh	6	15	7	2	3	9	7
Jammn & Kashmir	-	9	8	-	-	2	2
Karnataka	14	16	15	14	15	15	15
Kerala	1	1	1	1	1	1	1
Madhya Pradesh	13	12	13	8	9	4	3
Maharashtra	12	10	11	15	5	7	8
Orissa	9	11	12	10	10	10	10
Punjab	3	4	4	7	6	5	6
Rajasthan	11	14	16	3	8	11	12

Contd...

Tamil Nadu	0	13	14	11	13	16	16
Uttar Pradesh	4	7	9	4	12	12	11
West Bengal	7	8	10	13	11	14	13

Note: PS-Principal Status; PSS- Principal and Subsidiary Status Ranks in Ascending order for incidence of child labour.

Source: Census, 1991; NSS 50th Round on Employment and Unemployment; Duraisamy, M (2000) for NCAER data.

states for the year 2001. The variables are – SDP per capita, School dropout rate, literacy rate, persons below poverty line and urbanization.

State domestic product per capita is used as a proxy for index of economic development in the state. It is assumed that higher the level of SDP per capita, the lower will be the percentage of child labour in total population. This is logical as with economic development and rise in incomes, parents are less likely to send their children to work for supplementing family income. Secondly, with rising incomes it is expected that there is greater awareness among parents about the need to educate children and view education as an investment in human capital.

Dropout rate from school for boys and girls increases the number and percentage of child labour. An important reason for this is the high opportunity cost of time of children for foregone work or other productive activities. Another reason is perspective uncertainty about the returns from investment in schooling. Even free education often involves direct costs to the household in the form of uniform, transport, books etc. that make sending children to school an unattractive option.

Literacy rate is a universally accepted variable used to explain the difference in child employment ratio in different regions. Poverty compels the poor households to depend on child labour and their incomes to supplement their family income. And the expected relationship between the percentage of population below the poverty line and percentage of working children to population is positive.

Urbanization can be another factor, which determines the extent of child labour in a country. The rapid urbanization has opened up new avenues for employment of poor children like working in teashops, garages, domestic servant etc. A large proportion of children in urban India are engaged in un-organized sector, with poor working condition and exploitative wage rates. However urbanization has some positive consequences for child labour. It may lead to lower poverty levels, higher literacy levels, lower population per household and high proportion of children going to school. Hence, urbanization may or may not have any direct relation with incidence of child labour it is assumed that there is a negative relationship between percentage of child labour and urbanization.

Some other factors, which have an important bearing on child labour, could not be included as they are subjective in nature and difficult to quantify.

All the above stated a – priori hypothesis have been tested with the help of a multivariate regression mode. The regression equation used and computed is as:

$$Y = \alpha + \beta_1 X_1 + \beta_2 X_2 + \beta_3 X_3 + \beta_4 X_4 + \beta_5 X_5 + U$$

where Y is the dependent variable representing child labour. The explanatory variables are- percentage of people below poverty line (X_1), percentage of drop out rate (X_2), percentage of literacy rate (X_3), per capita state domestic product (X_4) and percentage of urbanization rate (X_5). U is the random disturbance term.

It was hypothesized that

$\beta_1 > 0$, $\beta_2 > 0$, $\beta_3 < 0$, $\beta_4 < 0$ and $\beta_5 < 0$

Table 11.6: Results of Multiple Regression Analysis

Variables	Estimated coefficients	Standard error of coefficients	t-value
1	2	3	4
Constants	6.6	3.085	2.140
X_1	-.002079	.021	-.101
X_2	-.005008	.020	-.245
X_3	-.06642	.030	-2.194***
X_4	-.00007364	0	-.879
X_5	.01551	.027	.581
R-square	.621		
F	3.273		

Note: 1*** significant at 10 per cent level. 2. Degrees of freedom F (5, 10)

Regression result is tabulated in Table 11.6, which shows that all the explanatory variables explain about 62.1 per cent of the variation in percentage of child labour in total population. However, except the slope coefficient of literacy rate, neither of the slope coefficients is individually statistically significant. The percentages of people below the poverty line and dropout rate are insignificant and have negative signs. A priori one will expect a positive relationship between percentage of child labour in total population and persons below the poverty line and between percentages of child labour in total population and dropout rate. Although most of the variables are insignificant, if we test the hypothesis all the coefficients are zero, F statistic is significant i.e. rejection of the hypothesis. It implies that variables are highly correlated and there exists the problem of multicollinearity. Therefore in the present analysis the influence of each variable on child labour is considered separately. The regression results are provided in Table 11.7.

The table shows that for percentage of child labour to total population, variables dropout rate and literacy rate are significant at 1 per cent level of significance, whereas SDP per capita and percentage of people below the poverty line are significant at the 5 per cent level. The estimated relationship of urbanization is as hypothesized in sign, though not significant.

Table 11.7: Regression Results

Constants	Regression coefficients	R-square	t-values	Explanatory variables
1	2	3	4	5
.649	.003491	.252	2.174**	X_1
.437	.03025	.394	3.017*	X_2
6.174	-.06980	.581	-4.403*	X_3
2.664	-.0001062	.286	-2.365**	X_4
2.160	-.02698	.104	1.276	X_5

Note: 1.* 1per cent level of significance. 2. **5 per cent level of significance

Policy Issues

It is essential to adopt policies to reduce child labour over time and with ultimate objective of elimination. But formulation of these policies is very complex since many a time it is seen that there is existence of child labour working in their own families. Some of the policies that may help to reduce the problem of child labour in India are discussed below.

Economic Development, Poverty and Child Labour: Policies for economic development and reduction of poverty will certainly help reduce child labour. Increases in adult wages/income are important to reduce supply of child labour. But studies have shown that aggregate economic growth alone is not a sufficient condition for reduction of child labour. (Swaminathan, 1998)

Impact of Globalization: Globalization and liberalization has opened up the Indian economy and a lot of focus is given to the export sector, which may have an impact on child labour. Globalization may influence the pattern and size of public expenditure on education. Budgetary allocations to education are gain influenced by states' success in the mobilization of resources through tax and non-tax revenues given the prioritization of spending on education.

Ensuring Compulsory Education of Children: Compulsory education for children is a necessary condition for reducing child labour. In narrow sense, it is obligatory on the part of parents to send their children to school. But in a broad sense compulsory education may be interpreted as "(a) a compulsion on the state to provide adequate schooling facilities to all children, and (b) subject to that, an obligation of the parental community to send all children to school. Thus, understood compulsory education in a broad notion" (Dreze, 1997). It is to be noted that non-coercive means can be used for promoting compulsory education. The girl child is going to be particularly benefited from this policy (Sinha, 1994).

Role of the Government: The government has an important role to play in implementing different policies and should have concern for eradication of child labour in India. Besides, specific incentives may be provided to different sections of the society so that education does not become a burden to the families. Some of these may be mid-day meal, free education, which may include books and uniforms and credit availability for education. Some positive steps have been taken in the recent years in that direction.

Conclusion

The paper has shown that a multi-pronged strategy is necessary in order to deal with the problem of child labour in India. There is a necessity to improve the quality of schooling, economic growth, adult wages/incomes, and poverty reduction etc. The problem of child labour is multi-dimensional and therefore it requires complementary strategies and involvement of all sections in the society. Given the socio-political urgency to solve the problem, a shift in public policy may be attempted to make it more inclusive and purposeful.

References

Basu, K. (1999), 'Child Labour: Causes, Consequences and Cure, with Remarks in international Labour standards', *Journal of Economic Literature*, Vol. 37, No. 3, pp. 1083-1119.

Basu, K. and P. H. Van (1998), 'The Economics of Child Labour' *American Economic Review,* Vol. 88, No. 3, pp. 412-427.

Blanchard, F. (1983), 'Introduction', in ILO: Report of the Director-General, International Labour Conference, 69th Session, 1983, Geneva.

Chaudhri, D. P. (1997), 'A Policy Perspective on Child Labour in India with Pervasive Gender and Urban Bias in School Education', *The Indian Journal of Labour Economics,* Vol. 30, No. 4, October-December.

Chaudhri, D. P. (2002), 'Child Labour in South Asia: Domestic and International Initiatives Including ILO and WTO', *The Indian Journal of Labour Economics*, Vol. 45, No. 3, July-September.

Chandrasekhar, C. P. (1997), 'The Economic Consequence of the Abolition of Child Labour: An Indian Case Study', *The Journal of Peasant Studies*, Vol. 24, No. 3.

Dev, M. S. (2001), 'Child Labour in India: Dimensions, Determinants and Policies', in *Economics of Child Labour,* (ed.) K.P. Kanan, pp-1-37, Deep & Deep Publications Pvt. Ltd., New Delhi.

Duraisamy, M. (2000), 'Child Schooling and Child Work in India', World Conference Econometric Society, C-13-8: Household Economics, 16 August, Seattle, USA.

Dreze, J. (1997), 'Primary priorities, Lesson in Compulsory Education', *Times of India,* 15 October.

Grootaert, C. and R. Kanbur (1995), 'Child Labour: An Economic Perspective', *International Labour Review,* Vol. 134, No. 2, pp. 187-204.

Kaur, A. and K. Kaur (2003), 'Child Labour in India: Causes and Implications', in *Problems of Child Labour in India* (eds) R.K. Sen and A. Dasgupta, pp. 3-17, Deep & Deep Publications Pvt. Ltd., New Delhi.

Lieten, G. K. (2000), 'Children, Work and Education', *Economic and Political Weekly,* Vol. 35, Nos. 24 and 25.

Lieten, G. K. (2002), 'Child Labour and Poverty: The Poverty of Analysis', *The Indian Journal of Labour Economics,* Vol. 45, No. 3, July-September.

National Sample Survey Organization (1993-94), *Employment & Unemployment,* NSS 50th Round, Ministry of Statistic and Programme Implementation, Government of India, New Delhi.

Parsons, D. O. and C. Goldin (1989), 'Parental Altruism and Self-Interest: Child Labour Among Late Nineteenth-Century American Families', *Economic Inquiry,* Vol. 27, pp. 637-60.

Sekar, H. R. (1997), 'Child Labour Legislation in India', V. V. Giri National Labour Institute, Noida, p. 20.

Sinha, S. (1994), 'Child Labour and Compulsory Education', *The Child and the Law,* UNICEF, New Delhi.

Swaminathan, M. (1998), 'Economic Growth and Persistence of Child Labour: Evidence from an Indian city', *World Development,* Vol. 26, No. 8, pp. 1513-1528.

Visaria, P. A. Gumber and L. Visaria (1993), 'Literacy and Primary Education in India 1980-81 to 1991', *Journal of Educational Planning and Administration,* Vol. 7, No. 1, pp. 13-62, January.

Weiner, M. (1991), *The Child and the State in India,* Oxford University Press, Delhi.

Weiner, M. (1996), 'Child Labour in India – Compulsory Primary Education on the Political Agenda', *Economic and Political Weekly,* Vol. 31, pp. 45-46.

12

Pattern of Internal Migration in Karnataka

Mihir Kumar Mahapatra

Introduction

To sustain higher growth with economic development, an improvement in rate of savings and investment and smoothening up of distribution of income have been emphasized in the development theory. Nevertheless, physical capital alone may not necessarily ensure a quantum jump in growth of GDP along with decline in regional disparities unless human capital is assigned a pivotal role. Of late, with the growth of information technology and service sector, workers' intellectual capability are becoming no less important than the quality of machines installed, or the quality of raw materials processed, or any combination of the two (Chadha, 2004). In the absence of adequate provision for development of human entity and opportunities to grow, migration of workers from a backward region to the developed one along with the emergence of 'jobless growth' may not be ruled out. This may not necessarily ensure smoothening of regional disparity. Rather, aggravation of persisting regional disparity can be a normal phenomenon.

Against the above backdrop, the present study broadly makes an attempt to examine the pattern of migration in Karnataka by taking into account 1991 census figures. In this context, the rationale of migration as well as direction and magnitude of inter-district migration have been examined. It needs to be mentioned here that the present study has emphasized only on economic aspects while examining the rationale of migration, though other factors play a role in this direction. Another shortcoming of the present exercise is the failure to assign adequate importance to female migration that is mostly on account of marriage.

Sources of Data on Migration: A Critical Evaluation

Decennial Census of India and the National Sample Survey Organization (NSSO) are the two major sources that provide information on migration. As regards Census of India, during 1881-1961, information about 'place of birth' was collected and reported by the Registrar General of India. It may be mentioned here that till 1931 it was difficult to examine the process of migration as information on internal migration provided in the Census reports were not adequate. Those reports broadly provided information on crossing of provincial/state/agency boundaries. In 1941, information on the above-said aspects was not collected on account of World War II. It was only in 1951 when data on internal migration, inter-district and intra-district migration were available. In the subsequent census report (1961), apart from the available information on 'birth place', statistics on rural/urban classification of the migrants and 'duration of residence' at the 'place of enumeration' were provided.

However, the concept of 'last residence' was introduced in 1971, while reasons for migration according to place of 'last residence' were incorporated in 1981 census reports. It is to be noted here that 'last residence' is applicable if the person is outside the village or town of enumeration and not in another house or somewhere in the same locality. This can not be applicable if the concerned individual is on tour and therefore, shifts from one place to another (Narasimhan and Chandra, 1998). Therefore, the information about migration is almost on the basis of 'place of last residence' since 1981 except for few that reflect persons born in one district but enumerated in other district, i.e., inter-district out-migration and in-migration.

As regards Census of India definition, migrants are those whose 'places of birth' are different from places of enumeration. In other words, if a person is born at a place other than the 'place of birth' then he/she can be treated as a migrant. But the definition based on 'place of birth' fails to capture multiple movement of a person. If a person migrates for certain duration and comes back to the 'place of birth' at the time of enumeration, then he/she may not be treated as a migrant (Narasimhan and Chandra, 1998). Taking into account certain traditions and customs it can also be argued that women may go to their native places at the time of delivery of baby and in that case the 'place of birth' can be different from 'place of enumeration'. Considering this definition, one can argue that the concerned person (lady) is a migrant. However, it is not assigned adequate importance precisely because this sort of phenomenon is confined mostly to upper caste people especially during the first birth and is not a universal phenomenon (Visaria and Kothari, 1985).

Another major source of information is the NSSO. As part of employment and unemployment status, the NSSO has been providing information on migration since the 9th round (1955). During the period 9th-12th round, the information on migration was confined to labour force, while detailed information on internal migration has been provided since the 13th round of NSSO survey. The NSSO defines 'migrant' as a person whose village/town of enumeration is different from his/her last usual place of residence. In this case, usual place of residence is defined as a place where he/she has stayed for at least six months. [1] However, the figures available in all the rounds except 38th (1983) and 43rd (1987-88) rounds can not be compared with census figures either because of poor coverage, i.e., confining to a specific population group or due to differences in definition (James, 2000). [2] Added to this, NSSO survey may not necessarily capture the extent of migration on account of the missing households when all the members have left the village. No doubt, the neighbours can provide the information but they may not be necessarily willing to reveal the information or they might be unaware of it (Visaria and Gumber, 1990).

Migration of Workers: Theoretical Considerations

Migration is not determined by economic factors alone, rather social, cultural, political and ecological factors play a vital role in determining the decision to migrate. The pace of migration has accelerated in recent years on account of rapid improvement in infrastructure, though the process of migration was in place since time immemorial. Usually rural-urban migration is on account of disparities in the provision of infrastructure, basic services and employment opportunities. The development of certain regions through rapid industrialization and urbanization, growth of mega-cities, low productivity of agriculture in some of the regions and decline in absorption capacity of agriculture are some of the aspects that drive the workers to migrate from backward regions to the developed ones. Therefore, the volume of migration within a territory varies directly with the diversity of the area (Lee, 1966).

In examining the rationale migration and consequences of migration, different schools of thought put forth diverse views. For instance, Lewis (1954) in the dual economy model argues that migration from rural to urban areas is the process by which surplus agricultural labour is withdrawn from the rural areas to more productive urban industrial sectors. The marginal productivity of labour in the subsistence sector is either zero or very low and therefore prevalence of low wage is inevitable. In contrast, both marginal productivity and wage rate are relatively high in the modern sector and there is scope for employment in the urban modern sector. This provides an incentive to migrate and the labourers can also assist in improving capital formation in the cities. Ranis and Fei (1961) argue that migration can bring wage equality between a traditional labour surplus agriculture and modern industrial sector. There is scope to withdraw a major portion of the surplus labour force from the traditional agriculture to modern urban industrial sector without incurring any loss to the former.

However, migration may not necessarily be unidirectional, i.e., from rural to urban area. Based on the comparative advantage of the place of destination over the place of origin, a reverse flow of migration can not be ruled out. In addition, intra-rural mobility may also be feasible.

In the Neo-classical framework, decision to move is considered as rational. For instance, Todaro (1976) argues that migration is in response to the urban-rural differences in 'expected' rather than 'actual' earnings. Considering the available opportunities, the migrants chose the one that can maximize 'expected' gains rather than 'actual' earnings from migration. On the whole, migration can be primarily on account of 'push' or 'pull' factors, if not both. Alternatively, it is rational to examine whether the circumstances compel the migrants to leave their native place or persistence of relatively higher wage in the urban pockets attracts them to cities. Overall, the Neo-Classical theory emphasizes on pull aspect while examining the forces behind migration, though other theories assign importance on push factors (James, 2000).

Rationale of Migration

The decision to migrate is influenced by various factors that differ across space and over time. In a study conducted in the city of Raichur (Karnataka) in 1982-83, it was argued that larger proportion of young, unmarried, unemployed men with lower level of educational attainment migrated to the city (Joshi, 1989). A majority of them were from middle-class families of Karnataka especially from the district itself and had been absorbed in white-collar professions, professional and technical occupations. Considering the reasons for migration, it was observed that 54 per cent of the respondents assigned voluntary reasons as the determining factor while 46 per cent argued that migration was inevitable (push factor). [3] Among the voluntary reasons, scope for better education, desire to build career by achieving excellence in the chosen discipline, provision of good infrastructure and promising future prospects, discontentment in the previous place and seeking employment opportunities were some of the crucial aspects that were prioritized.

In the present context, reasons for migration to cities are taken into account to draw inferences about the proximate determinants of migration. Among the factors considered for migration to cities by the Census of India, marriages followed by family movements have been prioritized by the respondents excluding other factors. An almost similar trend was noticed in a decade earlier (1981). But in the present analysis, marriage can not be assigned a pivotal role to examine the rationale of migration. In addition, the association between marriage and family movement may not be strictly established as in the urban area of the state, marriage is not emphasized to a great extent in comparison to the rural area.

Among the economic factors, employment is one of the crucial factors as 11 per cent of the migrants in the state emphasizes on this aspect. This is much higher in urban areas (20 per cent) and in the developed regions of the state. For instance, on an average around 25 per cent of the migrants in southern part of Karnataka cited employment as the reason for migration. [4]

It is often argued that there has been a positive correlation between formal schooling and increased tendency for migration. In contrast, in the absence of adequate provision for education in the rural areas, acceleration of rural-urban migration can not be ruled out. Only 3 per cent of the total migrants emphasize on education as the reason for migration to cities, though in both level of literacy and educational attainment, their performance is not worth reckoning. [5]

On the whole, the factors taken into consideration in the Census report are not exhaustive. In addition, the factors taken into account reflects migration to various cities, not migration as a whole (inter-district, intra-district, inter-state, intra-state etc). Taking cognizance of the above shortcomings and to strengthen the present analysis, nine more economic factors at the district level have been considered. [6] The regression coefficients of the double log model reveals positive elasticity of gross migration with respect to number of towns, density of population, poverty ratio, adult literacy rate, average size of agricultural land holding, net area irrigated and net area. In fact, some of the major factors that are directly associated with gross migration and that influence the process of migration, to a large extent, include number of towns in a district, adult literacy rate, net area sown and density of population. Higher level of urbanization as reflected by growth of town accelerates process of migration and migrants prefer to rush to the districts having higher density of population.

On the contrary, low per capita income and to some extent scanty rain fall seem to compel the people to migrate, though the degree of association of the latter with migration is relatively low as compared to the former. Overall, negative elasticity of migration with respect to per capita income reflects role of 'push factor' in deciding whether to migrate or not. In this context, positive association between the percentage of people living below the poverty line and the extent of migration also mirror the same trend. Overall, agriculture does not seem to be a major determining factor except the extent of rain fall which influences the rate of migration to some extent.

Pattern of Migration in Karnataka

Inter-District Migration in Karnataka: The movement of people (inmigration and outmigration) across the districts in the state provides interesting observations. [7] In a relatively underdeveloped region (Northern Karnataka), outmigration outweighs inmigration with a high margin for almost all the districts barring Belgaum and Uttar Kannada. In contrast, extent of outmigration from the southern region as a whole is lagging behind immigration, though a reverse trend is noticed in majority of the districts in this region. This is partly because; in the southern region, Bangalore determines to a large extent the process of migration. As per census 1991, around 6.57 lakh people have been migrated to Bangalore while around 2 lakh people have outmigrated from this district. As a result, there has been net migration of about 4.5 lakh to the district. Among the migrants, proportion of female is much higher than that of male in both regions, partly may be due to marriages.

No doubt, outmigration in absolute term (12.1 lakh) is higher than inmigration (11.35 lakh) in the northern region as a whole in 1991 but migration as proportion of total population is lower in the underdeveloped region (northern region) as compared to the developed region (southern region). For instance, migrants as percentage of total population are around 8 per cent in southern region of Karnataka, while they are lower at 6 per cent in northern region in 1991. The rate of migration in southern region is even higher than the state average during the above-said period. Besides, as noticed outmigration is more than inmigration in majority of the districts in the southern region (7 out of 12 districts). Therefore, it reflects that level of development and extent of mobility are positively associated, *ceteris paribus*.

As usual, proportionately higher female migrants are noticed in both the regions as compared to their male counterparts. Female inmigration is more than their outmigration in the developed southern region. The difference is pronounced in Bangalore. In contrast, female outmigration is much higher than female inmigration in Dakshina Kannada.

Migration across Regions

It is interesting to learn that inter-district migration is almost region specific barring few cases such as Bellary and Chitradurga. In other words, majority of the people who have migrated to a particular district in a specific region belongs to some other districts in the same region. For instance, 87 per cent of the people have migrated to Belgaum (a district in the northern region) in 1991 are from the northern region and the remaining around 13 per cent have migrated from the southern region. An almost similar trend is noticed in the southern region. Around 89 per cent of total population migrated to Bangalore are from the southern region. In addition, no drastic change in this pattern is noticed over time, i.e., during 1981-1991. North Karnataka region has contributed 90 per cent and 87 per cent of the total immigrants to Belgaum in 1981 and 1991 respectively. However, inter-district migration is not only confined to the region itself but also to the adjacent districts, i.e., districts surrounding a particular district. Around 76 per cent of the population migrated to Belgaum in 1991 are from Bijapur and Dharwad having respective share of 42 per cent and 34 per cent. But in 1981, a relatively lower proportion (61 per cent) of the people migrated to Belagum are from Bijapur (37 per cent) and Dharwad (24 per cent).

Inter-Censal Inter-District Net Migration

Decadal inter-district migration of population is a crude indicator that reflects net migration of people by taking into account total population survived who migrated a decade ago. It also reflects direction of movement of people over time so as to locate the trend and pattern of migration, i.e., whether flow of migration is from the developed to under developed region or vice-versa. Based on place of birth figures for 1981 and 1991, an indirect estimate of inter-censal net migration can be computed. [8]

Net Migration = (In Mig $_{t+10}$ - Out Mig $_{t+10}$) - (S_i In Mig $_t$ - S_o Out Mig $_t$)

where Mig. t+10: In Migration in 1991, Out Mig t+10: Out Migration in 1991

In Mig t: In-migration in 1981, Out Mig t: Out-migration in 1981, Si: Survival ratio of in-migrants and So: Survival ratio of out-migrants.

In this case we have assumed that the survival ratio of inmigrants and outmigrants is the same, though it may not be technically correct. [9]

Over a decade, inmigration has outweighed outmigration in Bangalore substantially as net migration of people to Bangalore (undivided) turns out to be around 3.5 lakh. In contrast, out-migration is higher than in-migration in Dakshina Kannada in the northern region followed by Tumkur, Kolar and Mysore in the southern region. In the northern region, though outmigration has outweighed inmigration for a majority of the districts, yet it is not so pronounced barring Bijapur. In the entire state, people are keen to move to Bangalore and the desire to move is noticed mostly from some of the above-said districts especially from the southern region. In other words, migration is mostly confined to urban centres of the state. This is in contrast to the direction of life time inter-district region specific migration.

Summary and Conclusions

The present study brings out some interesting observations. One of the crucial economic factors that motivate people to rush to various cities is to explore employment opportunities available in the city. Apart from inadequate employment opportunities available in various districts, higher level of poverty ratio and low level of per capita income also compel the people to migrate. The role of 'push' factor in the process of migration is also evident from proportionately higher number of inter-district outmigrants as compared to inmigrants in the underdeveloped northern region in 1991. In contrast, outmigration is lagging behind inmigration in the southern region in absolute terms.

It is often argued that migration is unidirectional, i.e. from under developed region to developed region. But the present analysis reveals that migration is almost confined to a specific region, i.e., majority of the people in both the underdeveloped and developed region migrate to some of the adjacent districts in the same region. Besides, it is interesting to note that people in the developed southern region are relatively more mobile than that of northern region suggesting positive association between level of development and desire to migrate, *ceteris paribus*. Overall, it suggests that migration is not necessarily either due to 'push' or 'pull' factor as the former can be a dominant factor in the underdeveloped northern region while the latter can be assigned adequate weight in the developed region.

The pattern of migration over a decade reveals that large numbers of people prefer to migrate to Bangalore district partly because of the city life in Bangalore. At the other end, relatively more people have migrated from some of the districts of southern region, namely, Dakshina Kannada, Tumkur, Mysore and Kolar. On the whole, the present analysis suggests that there is an urgent need to make sincere efforts to develop the northern region of the state and bring down regional disparity between the regions through introduction of various policy measures.

Notes

1. NSSO 38th (1983) and 43rd (1987-88) rounds.

2. 'In the 9th, 11th and 12th rounds of NSS survey, the information on migration was collected for the labour force while from 13th to 22nd round the definition of migration was limited to the movement during the last one year, which makes it difficult to compare with census figures on life-time migration (James, 2000)'

3. Involuntary reasons include dependents following the earning member, family problem especially death of the head of the household and employee's appointment/ transfer to the city etc.

4. To examine the degree of association between the level of development and reasons for migration, average figure for the region has been estimated though it may not be considered technically sound.

5. Not shown in the table.

6. The figures for almost all the determining factors are for 1991 barring rain fall. In case of rain fall, normal rain fall figures during 1901-70 have been taken into account.

7. As defined in the UN Manual VI (1970) and quoted in Registrar General of India (1989), migration is a move from one migration-defining area to another (or a move of some specified minimum distance) that was made during a given migration interval and that involved a change of residence. A migrant is a person who has changed his/her usual place of residence from one migration-defining area to another (or who moved from specified minimum distance) at least once during the migration interval.

'A person whose area of residence at the census or survey date differs from his area of birth is called the 'life time migrant'. The number of such persons in a population is commonly referred to as 'life time migration. Every move is an 'out-migration' with respect to the area of origin and 'in-migration' with respect to the area of destination. Every migrant is an 'out-migrant' with respect to the area of departure and an 'in-migrant' with respect to the area of arrival. ..... The term net-migration refers to the balance of movements in opposing directions, with reference to a specific area and hence, it is the difference between in-migration and out-migration. If in-migration exceeds outmigration, the net gain to the area is classified as net-inmigration and takes a positive sign. In the opposite case, there has been net out-migration which takes a negative sign (Registrar General of India, 1989)'.

8. For detail discussion, see United Nations (1970) and James (2000).

9. It is on account of non-availability of figures.

References

Chadha, G. K. (2004), 'Human Capital Base of Indian Labour Market: Identifying Worry Spots', *The Indian Journal of Labour Economics*, Vol. 47, No. 1, P. 3-47.

Gill, S. S. (1998), 'Migration of Labour in India', *Indian Journal of Labour Economics*, Vol. 41, No. 4.

Government of Karnataka (1999), *Human Development in Karnataka, 1999*, Planning Department, Government of Karnataka.

James, K. S. (2000*)*, 'Internal Migration in Andhra Pradesh, A Quantitative Analysis',

Working Paper No. 38, Centre For Economic and Social Studies, Hyderabad.

Joshi, K. G. (1989), *Migration and Mobility: A Sociological Study of Urban Karnataka*, Himalaya Publishing House, Mumbai.

Lee, E. S. (1966), 'A Theory of Migration', *Demography*, Vol. 3 No. 1, pp. 47-57.

Lewis, W. A. (1954), 'Economic Development with Unlimited Supply of Labour', *The Manchester School of Economics and Social Studies*, pp. 5447-5454.

Narasimhan, R. L. and H. Chandra (1998), 'Sources of Data on Migration and Recent Trends', *Indian Journal of Labour Economics*, Vol. 41, No. 4.

Ranis, G., and J. C. H. Fei (1961), 'A Theory of Economic Development', *American Economic Review,* Vol. 51, pp. 533-565.

Registrar General of India (1989), *Geographic Distribution of Internal Migration in India 1971-81, Census of India.*

Registrar General of India (1998*), Census of India, Karnataka Series,* Census Commissioner and Registrar General of India.

Sjaastad, L. A. (1962), 'The Costs and Returns of Human Migration', *Journal of Political Economy*, Vol. 70, No. 5.

Srivastava, R. (1998), 'Migration and Labour Market in India', *The Indian Journal of Labour Economics*, Vol. 41, No. 4. pp. 583-616.

Todaro, M. P. (1969), 'A Model of Labour Migration and Urban Unemployment in Less Developed Countries', *The American Economic Review*, Vol. 59, pp. 138-148.

Todaro, M. P. (1976), *Internal Migration in Developing Countries*, International Labour Office, Geneva.

United Nations (1970), 'Manual VI: Methods of Measuring Internal Migration'; Population Studies No.47, Department of Economic and Social Affairs, United Nations, New York.

Visaria, P. and A. Gumber (1990), 'Internal Migration in India: A review of the National Sample Survey Data', Working Paper No.32, The Gujarat Institute of Area Planning, Ahmedabad.

Visaria, P. and D. Kothari (1985), 'Data Base for the Study of Migration and Urbanization in India: A critical Analysis', Working Paper No.2, The Gujarat Institute of Area Planning, Ahmedabad.

Part III: Management of Natural Resources and Environmental Protection

13

Natural Resources, Sustainable Development and Disadvantaged People

Damodar Suar, Himadri Sinha and Laxmi Bilash Hota

Introduction

The World Commission Report on 'our common future' (Brundtland 1987) formed the basis for the United Nations Conference on Environment and Development in Rio de Janeiro in 1992. The conference brought into sharp focus that the natural system was overburdened with current human activities. The first principle of the Rio Declaration stressed that human beings were entitled to a healthy and productive life in harmony with nature (UN, 1993). The resulting Agenda 21 took this principle of sustainable development (SD) further. Despite ongoing efforts, the United Nations General Assembly expressed concern over continuing deterioration of the environment and called for Johannesburg World Summit in 2002 to focus on the status of Agenda 21. There was a gradual shift in thinking from Rio to Johannesburg. The first shift was that unlike Agenda 21, Johannesburg summit recognized poverty as the running theme linked to multiple dimensions from access to energy, water and sanitation to equitable distribution of benefits of biodiversity. Second, the summit emphasized on the integration of social, economic and environmental needs of people for SD. Third, it called for business group participation in financing SD projects.

SD has three aspects. First, SD meets the socio-economic needs of the present generation. Second, it incorporates the optimum use, improvement, and renewal of natural resources for ensuring the living standards of future generations. Third, SD calls for preservation of cultural plurality, continuation of eco-friendly institutions, and people's participation in development. What are the operational substances from such descriptions? First, awareness and values about the man-nature balance, anti-materialism, optimum consumption, community participation in resource conservation, and socio-economic equality amongst all can upset the overuse and non-conservation of natural resources. Second, a society or a community that uses and conserves the surrounding natural resources is sustainable one. In the context of forest-dependent communities of *Kondh* community of Phulbani district in Orissa, SD is the attainment of a decent livelihood through the use and conservation of forest resources.

Improving eco-efficiency remains an essential element of SD. This is because 'our common future' identifies three interconnected principles: (a) environmental efficiency, (b) intra- and inter-generational social justice, and (c) participation in decision-making. Moreover, eco-efficient growth in the long-run can meet the earth's limits (Jansen, 2003). With this backdrop, the study discusses how natural resources can be used and conserved for SD of the disadvantaged people-- poor, scheduled castes, scheduled tribes, and women.

Natural Resources

People seek to manage natural resources for two reasons. First, management of natural resources improves their conditions of livelihood. Second, environmental degradation is threatening, either to life sustaining processes through deforestation, fuel shortage, etc. or to people's aesthetic value. Though related, the first reason predominates in development parlance and the second in conservationist stance.

The nature of resource has a bearing on its management. Trees are fixed to a given land base and can be privatized or remain in commons. Fishes are mobile and cannot be confined in water bodies except state or private aquaculture. It is the nature of the resource that determines the regime in which it exists. Natural resources can be held under any one of the four property rights regimes: (a) open access, (b) common property, (c) private property, and (d) state property. In practice, natural resources are rarely managed by one of these alone. Open access regime entails the absence of property rights. People capture and use natural resources opportunistically but do not manage them. It is neither a property rights regime nor a management regime.

Under common property regime, an identifiable group uses the resource and such arrangements are either *de facto* or *de jure*. There exist rules concerning who may use the resource and how the resource should be used. Proponents of privatized natural resource management have suggested that market dynamics coupled with long-term security tenure provide the best ingredients for efficient management. Supporters of property controlled by state (sites licensed for mineral exploitation, national parks, etc) rest their argument on equity consideration and collective societal interest in common pool resources. The last two types of resources may belong to specific owners but people manage them. Large-scale privatization of common pool resources has often resulted in people's agitation.

A case in point is the agitation of fishermen and peasants in coastal Tamil Nadu. When 1,500 acres of cultivable land were encroached upon for shrimp farming by 10 major companies, it led to the socio-economic and ecological degradation in the region. The ground water of the area became saline, and women had to commute long distance to fetch water. The fish vendors were restricted from using the traditional pathway along the coastline, and the villagers lost access to fuel, fodder and drying yards for fishnets. Consequently, people's agitation intensified. Possibly, the agitation would pacify with a policy to (a) prevent environmental degradation, and (b) ensure livelihood to peasants and fishermen (Bob, 1998).

How Can Eco-efficiency be Achieved?

Improvement in eco-efficiency to fulfill the needs of present and future generations requires mutually reinforcing cooperation among society, institution, technology, and network with development-oriented institutions.

- Society refers to justifying nature, conditions and volume of social needs to be fulfilled: sufficiency.
- Institution refers to organizational arrangements to fulfill needs: effectiveness.
- Technology provides the means to fulfill needs: efficiency.
- Network refers to functional relationship with institutions that helps acquiring knowledge and support: catalysts.

Society: Sambandh, a grassroots NGO, has been working in Mayurbhanj district of Orissa. Its personnel after field visits and discussions in 39 villages of Karanjia and Jashipur blocks realized that the rainfall in the area was moderate and crop failure was frequent. The problem was discussed with villagers and resource management exercise was conducted. Villagers were trained on cash crop cultivation, soil conservation, watershed development, community forestry, and group activities. With the active participation of villagers, a check dam was constructed in Dhalabani *Gram Panchayat* and land resources were identified for use (Sambandh, 2001). The means to satisfy the villagers' needs were rationalized through discussion, training, appropriate technology and institutional arrangement of villagers.

In Orissa, National Tree Growers' Cooperative Federation Limited (NTGCFL) identified villages that had rich forest cover earlier. Subsistence economy, absence of rights over forest resources and lack of understanding of ecological disaster led to rampant forest destruction. NTGCFL, however, found that people's zeal for protecting the forest was not completely eroded. They showed little interest in protecting pure strand of Sal or Teak, which had no tangible benefit other than timber. NTGCFL continued its effort for bringing awareness through village meetings, documentary films, and encouraging progressive individuals to take up the leadership. Instead of imposing a blue print, NTGCFL facilitated the villagers to decide and develop their own plan to harness the diverse stock of local knowledge. Villagers opted for conservation of mixed forest consisting of trees and plants that met their multifarious needs. NTGCFL succeeded in getting these activities registered under the cooperative societies act and villagers got legal rights over forest produce. By 2001, 120 societies were promoted in Angul and Dhenkanal districts. NTGCFL enabled the communities to use local knowledge and skills, and to develop rules, norms and institutions for use and conservation of forest resources.

First, communities or societies can use and conserve natural resources when they are made aware about the benefits of conservation. Being aware about livelihood security through resource conservation, the forest dwellers of Angul and Dhenkanal who were destroyers of forest turned into preservers of forest. Second, people seek to manage the resources when benefits of management are perceived to exceed its cost. For villagers of Karanjia and Jashipur, the benefits increased land-based income. The real and immediate benefits to villagers of Angul and Dhenkanal districts were collection of non-timber forest produce and fuel wood. Villagers were assured of long-term financial benefits from timber sale in future. Third, the local communities need to be identified with certain resources so that they can conserve those resources.

In above cases, people managed the land and forest resources when (a) resource-base had well-defined boundaries for each village, (b) they had local right over resources, (c) local priorities were addressed, (d) local institutions were recognized, (e) time-tested indigenous technology was adopted, and (f) they had past successful experiences in managing resources (Balland and Platteau, 1996; Ostrom, 1990). NGOs only facilitated. Fourth, trust, interdependency and homogeneity of identities or social capital among people are crucial for resource conservation. The homogeneity of identities promoted projects' success in each tribal village of Karanjia and Jashipur blocks and in each village of Angul and Dhenkanal districts where at least 75 per cent of the population belonged to a specific caste/tribe. Otherwise, conflict and free-riding might destroy resources.

Institution: In 1990, people of Chichkali village in Raipur district organized themselves to utilize the water flowing through the nearby area. The area was frequently hit by drought, and a need was felt for irrigation facilities. Shree Sharma, headmaster of the local primary school, impressed upon the villagers that they could change the situation provided they unite. Villagers getting organized informally constructed a canal, installed few motors, and irrigated nearly 80 hectares of land in the first year. They approached the local (government) authorities in 1993 and were able to get a similar scheme sanctioned (Naidu, 1993). Leadership, informal village institution, priority to local needs and adoption of local technology has facilitated development.

Khaksi Toli is a tribal hamlet in Bero Block of Ranchi district in Jharkhand. In late fifties, villagers under the leadership of Sri Simon Oraon started protecting the forest on 40 hectares of land. With subsistence level of rain-fed agriculture, Simon realized that forest protection alone might not offer a viable source of livelihood. He took up water harvesting work. A small dam was constructed to store water at the higher elevation which was then connected with three tanks in a series at the downstream. Dam water was used for ground water recharge and surface irrigation. Multiple cropping became possible and agricultural production increased. Villagers took up fisheries in all tanks. Later on, Simon persuaded the district administration and with its help, a village cooperative was formed. The cooperative received assistance under tribal sub-plan. Today, Khaksi Toli has a watershed and forest protection body to meet the livelihood demands of tribals.

First, in the above cases, local leaders have taken the initiative, organized people, capitalized on local knowledge, adopted indigenous technology and conserved natural resources. Second, equitable distribution of benefits through democratic institutions has energized people to conserve resources. Empirical evidences confirmed that more the freedom to institutional members in forming their rules, institutions and resolving conflicts, more was the constituents' participation in forest conservation (Sinha, 2003).

Ratnakiri is the northeastern province of Cambodia with dense forest, fertile soil and low population density. The livelihood of people depends on swidden agriculture and collection of fruits, vegetables, medicinal plants, fibres, and building materials from the forest. Swidden agriculture is a form of rotation cropping that regenerates natural forest in a period of 10-15 years. Old forests are not cleared and moderate terracing checks the soil erosion. Although it did not require any external input except human labour, its productivity was lower than modern cultivation. For generations, people cultivated the land over which they had customary rights.

Situation changed since 1993 when Ban Lung people, the business community from the provincial centre, emboldened by economic liberalization began to stake claims on these lands. They put signpost for proposed modern farm in all around the traditional land. Local communities took unified action against these encroachments. But absence of legal rights over land was their biggest obstacle. Understanding their helplessness, few local and international NGOs came forward and mobilized a mass movement. Impressed by this, King Nordom Sihanouk in 2001 took an initiative to persuade the Cambodian government to pass an act to legalize the rights of indigenous people over mountainous land, forest and river, and to stop transfer of land to outsiders who were not acquainted with traditional land and water management.

This law stopped the conversion 20,000 hectares of upland forest into oil palm farm and many such projects initiated by Ban Lung communities. According to an estimate, land transfer would have displaced 4,500 locals, disturbed the whole landscape by doubling soil erosion and increasing silt in the river. Furthermore, the law also stalled the introduction of external input-based agriculture that could cause permanent loss of regenerating forest (NTFP Project, 2002). Hence, SD can be achieved through legitimizing the eco-friendly communal entitlements and practices.

Technology: Historical evidence confirmed that many parts of Gujarat had 47 years of drought during last 99 years. By 1987, around 12,000 villages had severe drinking water crisis that crippled human and animal lives. Government implemented a series of cooperative irrigation and watershed programmes to tide over the crisis. Such projects mostly benefited large farmers. Swadhyay Parivar is an informal family-based organization inspired by a religious group. Associates of the parivar initiated a unique well recharging approach to mitigate the crisis. In this technique, surface runoff during rains from fields was collected into a tank measuring 5 x 4 x 6 feet at various points. Muddy water was allowed to settle down and once the mud was settled, the clean water was drained through a pipe into the near by well. Pits were cleaned at regular intervals. By 1996, a total of 59,617 wells were recharged in Junagarh, Amreli, Jamnagar, Kutch, Rajkot, and Surendarnagar districts (Hathi, 2001). This approach responded to water crisis, increased ground water, facilitated vegetative growth, and encouraged villagers to grow tree temples (devotional forestry) and orchards in wastelands.

Reasons for such success are that people (a) are awakened collectively to replenish the mother earth through religious teachings, and (b) have adopted low cost and simple technology what they are capable of comprehending and handling.

Network: Different stakeholders, state, NGOs and communities, are involved in management of natural resources. One alone does not possess the resources to promote SD. Development networks, within and across these sectors, can further the prosperity of bottom line.

Village Relegaon Siddhi, a semi-arid village in Maharastra, has demonstrated the power of community-based partnership and networking. The project was water harvesting through community initiatives. Based on the success of the water-harvesting project, other developmental activities were realized such as women's empowerment, enrolment of girl children, etc. The development partners included the block administration, NGOs, schools, parent-teacher association, media and local foresters.

Five hundred semi-arid villages situated in the Aravalli hills of Rajasthan's Alwar district had begun to revive the local traditions of water harvesting under the leadership of a local

NGO. The restoration of the depleted ground water resources led the local farmers to withstand consecutive drought years. It resulted in arresting migration. In all these endeavours, Alwar villagers had network and extensions with local collectorate, research institutions and environmental activists. Inspirational leader Sri Rajendra Singh of Alwar villagers and Sri Anna Hazare of Relegaon Siddhi have made efforts to replicate similar projects in other dry parts of the country through NGOs and self-help groups.

First, benefits of networking and partnership are maximized when partners pursue a common goal. They focus on fulfilling their responsibilities in a most effective and efficient way. While the parent-teacher association and schools looked after enrolment of girls, NGOs looked into empowerment of women, and local foresters into plantation. That made holistic development possible in Relegaon Siddhi. Second, all developmental projects face threats to success. When partners share their expertise and experiences, each partner takes advantage of others without compromising its own essence. Moreover, partners' varied skill sets, contacts, spheres of influence, and prior experience in combination respond to both internal (design) and external (contextual) threats to mitigate risk. Third, partners' activities around a common goal build social capital. Lastly, partners' success in development projects creates confidence to extend and replicate the project in other similar areas.

Conclusion

With the demand for rapid socio-economic development, complete non-violence on nature is impossible. Use and conservation of natural resources simultaneously can help attaining well-being of people on a sustainable basis. Interrelated changes in above-mentioned four dimensions with the principles can ensure continuous maintenance of natural resources and SD of disadvantaged people.

SD demands a rich mix of societal justice, institutional governance, technology and networking. But, local actions always are not sufficient. As Johannesburg summit points out, global action is required to protect the rights of the poor, reduce the wasteful consumption of the rich, and ensure the equitable distribution of benefits of biodiversity. The findings of the study are based on a set of case studies that may be contradicted by another set of studies. Deriving principles from well-known cases add credence to our findings.

References

Balland, J. M. and J. P. Platteau (1996), *Halting Degradation of Natural Resources: Is there a Role for Rural Communities?* , FAO and Claredon Press, Oxford.

Bob, S. (1998), 'Tragedy of Commons', *Journal of Rural Development*, 17(1), 25-35.

Brundtland, G. H. (1987), *World Commission on Environment and Development: Our Common Future*, Oxford University Press, Oxford.

Hathi, T. R. (2001), 'Water Crisis and Indigenous Approach Towards Resource Utilisation' in G S Monga (ed), *Environment and Development*, Deep & Deep Publications, New Delhi, 270-82.

Jansen, L. (2003): 'The Challenges of Sustainable Development', *Journal of Cleaner Production*, 11(1), 231-45.

Naidu, B. R. (1993), *A Report on Watershed Programme*, DRDA report, Raipur.

NTFP Project (2002), *Community Land Use Planning: A Case Study from Krola Village, Ratnakari, Cambodia*, Non-Timber Forest Produce Project: Ratnakari.

Ostrom, E. (1990), *Governing the Commons: The Evolution of Institutions for Collective Action*, Cambridge University Press, Cambridge.

Sambandh (2001), *Annual Report 2000-2001*, Sambandh, Bhubaneswar.

Sinha, H. (2003), *'Some Determinants of People's Participation in Community Based Forest management*", Unpublished Doctoral Dissertation, Indian Institute of Technology, Kharagpur.

United Nations (1993): *Agenda 21*, United Nations, New York.

14

Joint Forest Management (JFM) Forests in Andhra Pradesh

Bhagirath Behera

Introduction

Devolution of resource management and access rights to local communities has become an important policy tool for many developing countries. Over the last two decades, a profound change has been witnessed in the area of natural resource management especially in the forestry sector, with countries at least partially devolving rights and responsibilities over their natural resources to the users (Edmonds, 2002; Larson and Ribot, 2004), with the hope that forest resources will be better conserved and at the same time livelihood systems of forest-dependent people will be improved. The apparent change in policy from the traditional state-managed top-down approach to the community level is fueled by the recognition of the limits of government agencies in managing resources at the local level, which has resulted in massive degradation of natural resources and of local people's livelihood systems. International and national donor agencies are also heavily involved in promoting these policy reforms believing that they can achieve both the objectives of conservation and of poverty reduction and development. The power to local communities has been strengthened either through power-sharing arrangements with the state, more legal access to natural resources, or decentralization within government institutions that ensure more power to local communities.

India has been at the forefront of devolving natural resource management to the local-community level, particularly in the forestry sector, for more than a decade. Its 1988 forest policy was a landmark, because for the first time it recognized the importance of community involvement in forest management for achieving improvements in community livelihood and the protection of forest resources. In a follow-up document issued in 1990, the central government issued guidelines to all the state governments to implement 'Joint Forest Management Systems' by devolving everyday forest use and management rights to the community. Accordingly, almost all the states have formally resolved to implement JFM, making it one of the largest of such programs in the world (Kumar, 2002; Behera and Engel, 2006).

The overall empirical evidence on the outcomes of JFM in India shows mixed results. Some studies have shown improvements in outcomes such as increased yield of timber and non-timber forest products (NTFPs), fuel wood, and fodder (Joshi, 1999; Khare et al., 2000; Ballabh et al., 2002). Others indicate a lack of control and management of forest by the communities, despite the fact that communities have *de jure* rights over the forests (Bulte and Engel, 2004). It is also argued that the differences in outcomes of JFM may partly be due to the fact that the degree to which specific rights and benefits were actually devolved from the forest department to the local communities differs significantly across states (Damodaran and Engel, 2003, Sarin, 2002, Ballabh, et.al, 2002, Agrawal and Ostrom, 2002).

Equity in the distribution of benefits from the JFM forests between different sections of participant households within a community is an important issue that is likely to affect the sustainability of JFM institutions (Behera and Engel, 2006a). Which people within communities actually benefit most from the JFM program? Are forest dependent and marginalized people, who should benefit from the JFM program, actually better off than before JFM was introduced? Often, it is found that given a share in total benefits from the final harvest of timber, community rules favour long-term increased timber benefits through forest closure and plantation of slower growing high-value species. As a consequence, poor forest-dependent households are marginalized as they suffer from the reduced availability of and access to non timber forest products (NTFPs) (Kumar, 2002). Similar observations are also made by several other studies which have documented that under the strict rules of JFM, poor people are deprived of their genuine rights to access non-timber forest produce (Sarin, 1996, 1999; Agarwal, 2001).

Households, both poor and rich, depend on JFM forests to collect a variety of forest products to meet their daily subsistence needs. The collection of forest produce ranges from firewood for domestic energy requirements, fodder for animals, timber for house construction and agricultural implements, and a large number of NTFPs for different uses such as edible (fruits, plants, flowers, roots, herbs etc.) and non edible (thatched grasses, leaves, fruits, flowers, herbs etc.) products. Firewood collection and grazing are the two main activities which contribute to forest degradation in the event of people adopting an unsustainable use of forests for these activities (Trossero, 2002; Heltberg, 2001). For instance, when people indulge in cutting green branches of live trees instead of dry or fallen wood and leaves for firewood without replanting new trees, this behavior leads to forest degradation. Grazing, on the other hand, can be detrimental to the growth of forests if sustainable grazing practices are not followed (i.e. allowing the grazed forests for natural regrowth by leaving it ungrazed for few months or years).

Human and livestock population in an area is not linearly associated with forest degradation. The forest degradation can be halted or reversed by introducing institutions that can adopt sustainable forest use policies in the local communities. This was exactly the policy objective when JFM institution was adopted in the villages that are located in and around forests: to contain the use of forests and at the same time replants and manage the forests in such a way that leads to halting forest degradation and consequently a natural regrowth of forests.

The objective of this paper is to examine the determinants of distribution of benefits from the JFM forests among different sections of participant households. The chapter is based on an in-depth study conducted in 55 FPCs in the Indian state of Andhra

Pradesh. Both qualitative and quantitative approaches were used to elicit information. Qualitative methods include focus group discussions among different groups of FPC members such as women, poor and lower caste groups, and peer group discussions. Quantitative information was collected through community-level and household-level structured questionnaires.

In this chapter two major forest uses are considered for analysis: firewood collection and grazing. First, firewood collection and grazing practice in the JFM villages are described using descriptive statistics for an understanding of whether the JFM institution, in any way, has helped to change people's forest use patterns. Second, factors that determine the use of JFM forests for firewood collection and grazing practices by the participant households in the communities are determined using econometric models.

Use of JFM Forests for Firewood Collection

People collect firewood for different uses, namely cooking, and heating homes and water. Apart from that the vast majority of poor people depend exclusively on the sale of firewood in the local market for their daily living. Under the JFM, rules are formulated for the users to restrict the collection of firewood in the protected forests. Table 14.1 presents the statistics on the change of pattern (sources) of firewood collection by FPC members due to the adoption of JFM. The information was collected by asking the members to rank the sources of their firewood collection as first and second most important sources before and after the JFM program. As can be seen from the table, out of 655 households 71 per cent used current JFM forests as their most important source of firewood before the JFM program started in the village, while after JFM around 55 per cent households used these forests as their most important source of firewood, indicating a decline of 16 per cent. This may be attributed to the restrictive rules that are imposed on the users after JFM. However, a shift from the JFM forests to other forests can be observed from the table in the category of first most important source. Around 18 per cent of households reported shifting their firewood collection from the JFM forest to other forests (i.e. before JFM 17 per cent used other forests, while after JFM 35 per cent people are using other forests for firewood collection).

Table 14.1: Changes in Sources of Fuel Wood Collection of Households before and after JFM (in Percentage)

	Before FPC		After FPC	
Sources of fuel wood collection	Most important	Second most important	Most important	Second most important
From private land	2	10	4	13
Village common land	10	40	5	23
JFM forests	71	8	55	34
Other forests	17	34	35	22
Crop residues	0.2	8	0.3	6
Animal dung	0.0	0.4	0.0	0.4
Bought from the market	0.2	0.2	0.2	0.2
Other (Gas)	0.0	0	0.5	2
N	655	448	655	503

It can be said that the average volume of firewood consumption may not have gone down because of rules framed after the adoption of JFM program, as the data show the pressure has shifted from the JFM forests to other forests (non-JFM forests). Hence to reduce the pressure from the forests complementary policies should be adopted that reduce demand for firewood.

Determinants of Firewood Collection

Table 14.2 presents the results of determinants of household dependency on forest for firewood collection. The dependent variable is annual firewood collection from JFM forests.

Table 14.2: Determinants of Household Dependency on Forests for Fuel Wood Collection

Fuel wood collected from JFM forests	Coef.	Robust Std. Err.	t-value	P-value
Number of trees owned	-0.011	0.003	-3.15	0.00
Per capita forest area	6.618	2.813	2.35	0.02
Land size	-3.305	2.582	-1.28	0.20
Household size	7.541	1.190	6.33	0.00
Number of improved stoves	-5.091	3.360	-1.52	0.13
Distance to the JFM forests	-7.907	2.309	-3.42	0.00
_cons	53.170	8.216	6.47	0.00
Number of observations	660	-	-	-
F(6, 653)	12.76	-	-	-
Prob > F	0.0000	-	-	-
Root MSE	58.069	-	-	-

All the explanatory variables show the expected signs. Number of trees owned is negatively related to firewood collection and significant at the 1 per cent level, meaning that households owning more trees in their own land are less likely to depend on the forests for firewood. This has a very important policy implication for reducing pressure on the forests. People living in and around the forests should be encouraged to plant trees on their own land. Although several efforts in this regard have been made by the government, they were hardly successful in achieving the desired objectives. For instance in the 1970s and 1980s, the Indian government had introduced a social forestry program which was aimed at encouraging people to plant trees in private and village common land especially for firewood. The program was a failure because of a lack of participation and faulty implementation (Saxena, 1999). Per capita forest area, which indicates the scarcity of forest resources, shows a negative relationship with firewood collection and is significant at the 1 per cent level. This indicates that firewood collection falls when the forest resource is scarce and increases with the availability of abundance resources.

Household land holding size is negatively related with collection of firewood, although not significant. Households with greater landholdings may rely less on forests for firewood because they may use crop residues as a substitute. The coefficient on household size is positive and significant at the 1 per cent level, implying that large households collect more firewood from the forests. This is because large households may consume more firewood in activities like cooking, heating water etc. Moreover, large households collect more firewood as they have the advantage of having more manpower to do so. The number of improved stoves is negatively related to the firewood collection and it is close to the 10 per cent significance level, indicating that households having improved stoves are less likely to collect firewood from the forests, as improved stoves consume less fuel compared to the ordinary stoves. This also has very important policy implications for the conservation of forests. During the implementation of the JFM program, there was a provision under community development to provide improved stoves to the member households, which was aimed at reducing the pressure on forests. It seems that this might work well in the direction of achieving the objective of forest conservation by reducing usage pressure. However, it was seen that the distribution of such improved stove did not cover all the households in the community. The Forest Department did not give adequate priority to this important aspect of forest management, but instead focused on trivial things like distribution of televisions, and video recorders which are less important for the people.

As expected, distance to JFM forests shows a negative association with firewood collection and is significant at the 1 per cent level or better, meaning that households that are located close to JFM forests tend to collect more compared to those households located far from JFM forests.

Use of JFM Forests for Grazing

Table 14.3 presents average months of grazing by different sources. Out of 660 households 269 (41 per cent) households are reported to have grazed their cattle in the JFM forests on average for about two months a year. It appears that households tend to graze their cattle more or less equal amount of time in both other forests and JFM forests, as the table indicates that out of 660 households, 234 (35 per cent) households have used other forests for grazing on average for 2 months a year. Similarly, village common land and private lands are also used with an average of 1 month each for grazing purposes.

Instead of taking cattle out for grazing, they can be stall fed at home by collecting fodders from forests and village common land such as grasses, green leaves, etc. Farmers can also use crop residues such as paddy straw from their own private land. Table 14.4 presents the information related to the number of months spent stall feeding cattle from different sources. Only 37 households (6 per cent) out of 660 reported having stall fed their cattle by collecting grasses from the JFM forests, spending on average 0.16 month. The reason for less people using JFM forests for stall feeding is that JFM forests are generally degraded forests and do not contain green grass in abundance for stall feeding. This is similar in other forests, where reported by 28 households to be used as a source of stall feeding. Our experience from the field indicates that people often use forests (both JFM and other) during the rainy season, when they cannot take out cattle to graze due to sometimes uninterrupted rain. Furthermore, people collect

Table 14.3: Sources of Livestock Grazing (in Months)

Grazing in (months)	Total households	Number of households grazed	Mean	Std. Dev.	Min	Max
In JFM forests	660	269	2.13333	3.061402	0	12
In other forests	660	234	2.15303	3.448195	0	12
In village common land	660	188	1.19848	2.340187	0	12
In own land	660	166	1.07727	2.218374	0	12

Table 14.4: Sources of Stall Feeding (in Months)

Stall feeding (in months)	Total households	Number of households grazed	Mean	Std. Dev.	Min	Max
In JFM forest	660	37	0.157576	0.715758	0	6
In other forest	660	28	0.130303	0.725426	0	10
In own-land	660	201	1.151515	1.959703	0	12
In village common land	660	64	0.268182	1.021418	0	12

grass from the forests for stall feeding in the night especially during rainy season when grasses are available in abundance compared to other seasons.

As the table shows, a large proportion of households (201 out of 660) use their own land for stall feeding, and some of them even used it during the whole year. It was found that landed households sometimes preferred to keep their cattle at home and feed them with grasses and other crop residues from their own land. Stall feeding is directly linked to land ownership and number of cattle to be fed. If the farmers have few cattle and a relatively large size of land allotted for the cultivation of grass, they would prefer to keep their cattle at home. However, it is also found that landed households living in forest areas where only timber tree species are grown are seen growing grass in their own land for cattle, especially when cow and buffaloes are raised for milk business.

Determinants of grazing in JFM forests

Table 14.5 presents the results of an OLS regression of grazing dependency on various explanatory variables. Livestock units is positive and significant at the 5 per cent level, indicating that the use of the JFM forests for grazing increases with the increase in the number of livestock being held. Households with greater livestock holdings normally belong to richer sections of society. The fact that richer households depend more on JFM for grazing is further confirmed by the results of the land size variable, which is positive and significant at the 1 per cent level. The coefficient on caste indicates that higher caste households are more dependent on the JFM forests for grazing, which may again related to ownership of livestock. Per capita forest area is negatively related to grazing in the JFM forests, meaning that as per person availability of forest area decreases, more people tend to depend on JFM forest for grazing. Household size is positively related but not significant. Distance to JFM forest is negatively related to the grazing and significant at the 1 per cent level, indicates that the use of JFM forests for grazing increases as the distance to the forest declines.

The descriptive statistics and the econometric results of the determinants of grazing clearly indicate that poorer section people are relatively excluded from the benefits of grazing in the protected forests. This is partly due to the grazing policy of the forest department adopted in the JFM forests, which do not allow goats in the forests for grazing as goats are more harmful for forest growth. Unfortunately, goats are typically raised by poorer and lower caste people. The forest department persuaded the goat owners to sell off their goats and in return the goat owners were promised other hybrid small ruminants such as sheep, which are considered less harmful for forests. Empirical studies (Mukherjee et al, 2004) and our field experience indicate that these poor people have in fact sold their goats and in return did not receive the hybrid species of sheep as promised by the forest department.

Table 14.5: Determinants of Household Use of Forests for Grazing

Grazing	Coef.	Robust Std. Err.	t-value	P-value
Livestock units	0.099	0.019	5.320	0.000
Per capita forest area	-0.313	0.082	-3.820	0.000
Land size	0.391	0.129	3.030	0.003
Household size	0.113	0.072	1.570	0.117
Distance to JFM forests	-0.509	0.100	-5.060	0.000
_cons	1.778	0.467	3.810	0.000
Number of obs	660			
F (5, 654)	24.7			
Prob > F	0.0000			
Root MSE	2.8525			

Conclusions and Policy Implications

The empirical findings on the distribution of benefits from the

JFM forests among different households, the descriptive statistics and econometric results of determinants of household use of JFM forests for firewood collection and grazing suggest some interesting policy issues. Although JFM seems to have brought a slight shift in the use of firewood collection from the JFM forests, the overall pressure on the forests remains the same, as people have moved their firewood collection to other non-JFM forests. However, there is an increased use of firewood collection from private land, which is an encouraging sign as far as pressure on the forest is concerned. The econometric results of determinants of firewood collection indicate that number of trees grown on private land has significantly reduced the firewood collection from the forest land. Hence policy to induce firewood substitution should target private lands, aiming to increase number and productivity of trees. The results also point to the fact that substitution to the firewood is a viable solution to reduce pressure on the forests. More efficient cooking technologies such as improved stoves, solar cookers, biogas plants, etc., are potential substitutes for forest firewood and must be considered seriously.

Household use of JFM forests for grazing indicates richer section households use JFM forests more frequently than poorer sections. The problem of grazing in JFM forests has not been addressed adequately, and on average people still depend on JFM forests for grazing for an average of 2 months per year. On-farm production of fodder (grasses), fodder crops and promotion of improved crop technologies could substantially ease the grazing pressure on the JFM forests. Apart from private land the focus should also be on the cultivation of high yielding grass species and trees in the village common land, which should be managed under the rules and regulation of FPCs.

References

Agrawal, A. (2001), 'Common Property Institutions and Sustainable Governance of Resources', *World Development*, Vol. 29, No. 10, October.

Agrawal, A. and E. Ostrom (2002), 'Collective Action, Property Rights, and Decentralization in Resource Use in India and Nepal', *Politics and Society*, 29(4), 485-514.

Ballabh, V., K. Balooni, and S. Dave, (2002), 'Why Local Resources management Institutions Decline: A Comparative Analysis of Van (forest) Panchayats and Forest Protection Committees in India', World *Development*, 30(12), 2153-2167, December.

Behera, B. and S. Engel (2006a). 'Institutional Analysis of Evolution of Joint Forest Management in India: A New Institutional Economics Approach', *Forest Policy and Economics* 8: 350-362.

——(2006b), 'Who Forms Local Institutions? Levels of Household Participation in India's Joint Forest Management Program', ZEF-Discussion Papers on Development Policy, Number 103, University of Bonn, Germany.

Bulte, E. and S. Engel (Accepted for publication.), 'Conservation of Tropical Forests: Addressing Market Failure'. In *Sustainable Development: New Options and Policies*. López, R., Stiglitz, J., and M. Toman (eds.), Oxford University Press, New York.

Damodaran, A. and S. Engel (2003), 'Joint Forest Management in India: Assessment of Performance and Evaluation of Impacts', ZEF-Discussion Papers on Development Policy No. 77, Center for Development Research (ZEF), Bonn, Germany

Edmonds, V. E. (2002), 'Government Initiated Resource Management and Local Resource Extraction from Nepal's Forests', *Journal of Development Economics,* 68(1): 89-115.

Heltberg, R. (2001), 'Determinants and Impacts of Local Institutions for Common Resource Management'. *Environment and Development Economics* 6(2): 183-208.

Kumar, S. (2002), 'Does Participation in Common Pool Resource Management Help the Poor? A Social Cost-Benefit Analysis of Joint Forest Management in Jharkhand, India', *World Development,* 30(5): 763-782.

Joshi, A. (1999), 'Progressive Bureaucracy: an Oxymoron? The Case of Joint Forest Management in India', *Rural Development Forestry Network*, Oversea Development Institute, London.

Khare, A., M. Sarin, N. C. Saxena., S. Palit., S. Bathla., F. Vania and M. Satyanarayana., (2000), *Joint Forest Management: Policy, Practice and Prospects, Policy that works for forest and people series no: 3*, World Wide Fund for Nature-India and IIED London.

Larson, A. M. and J. C. Ribot (2004), 'Democratic Decentralization Through a Natural Resource Lens: An Introduction', *The European Journal of Development Research* 16(1): 1-25.

Mukherjee S. D., Galab, S. and Sunder, B. (2004), From Policy to Practice: A study on Joint Forest Management in Andhra Pradesh, SDC-IC NGO Program, Indo Swiss Natural Resource Management Program Andhra Pradesh, Hyderabad.

Rangachari, C. S. and S. D. Mukherjee (2000), *'Old Roots, New Shoots: A Study of Joint Forest Management in Andhra Pradesh'*, Winrock International and Ford Foundation, India, New Delhi.

Sarin, M. (2002), Devolution as a Threat to Democratic Decision-Making in Forestry? Findings from Three States in India, CIFOR , Indonesia.

Sarin, M. (1999), Policy Goals and JFM practice: An Analysis of Institutional Arrangements and Outcomes, Policy and Joint Forest management Series-3, World Wide Fund for Nature-India.

Sarin, M. (1996), 'From conflict to Collaboration: Institutional Issues in Community Management', In Poffenberger and Betsy McGean (eds), *Village Voices, Forest Choices: Joint Forest Management,* (Oxford University Press, Calcutta).

Saxena, N. C. (1999), 'Forest Policy in India, Policy and Joint Forest Management Series 1', World Wide Fund for Nature, India.

Trossero, M. A. (2002), 'Wood Energy: The way ahead', Unasylva 211(53).

15

Managing Municipal Solid Waste

C. S. Shylajan and Souvik Bhattacharjya

Introduction

Municipal solid waste (MSW) is defined to include refuse from households, non-hazardous solid waste from industrial, commercial and institutional establishments (including hospitals), market waste and street sweepings. It typically consists of paper, plastics, glass, metal, organic wastes etc. Municipal solid waste management (MSWM) encompasses the functions of collection, transfer, treatment, recycling, resource recovery and disposal of municipal solid waste (Schubeler *et al.*, 1996). As part of the non-hazardous waste stream, MSW poses no direct threat to human or environment. However, too much waste entering the environment rather than being recycled or reused puts additional stress on the assimilative capacity of the environment. There are risks to society and the environment if too much waste is generated or if it is improperly managed (Turner, 2000; Callan and Thomas, 2000; World Bank, 1999).

Unmanaged solid waste poses several major problems for the developing world. Health hazards from uncontrolled waste, improper disposal of waste and the economic burden of waste disposal on towns and cities are some of them (Pearce and Turner, 1994). In India, for instance, solid waste management has become a crucial problem in major cities due to the high rates of waste generation by the ever-increasing populace. This is further egged on by the rapid urbanization process. However, so far, waste management has received less attention from the policy makers and academicians than that paid to other environmental problems, such as air pollution, water pollution etc. The issue of improper solid waste management has recently attracted greater attention, after serious health hazards were reported from an urban city [1] in the country.

A Committee constituted by Supreme Court of India to study solid waste problem in Class I cities [2] has reported that lack of financial resources, institutional weaknesses, improper choice of technology and public apathy towards solid waste management have made this service far from satisfactory (Supreme Court, 1999). Due to lack of infrastructure - proper collection, transportation, treatment and disposal of solid waste by most municipalities has become a subject of concern. Realizing the serious environmental hazards due to unscientific management of urban wastes in India, the Ministry of Environment and Forests, Government of India has formulated a set of rules with regard to management and handling of municipal wastes (including bio-medical waste) and recycling and usage of recycled plastics (MOEF, 1998, 1999, 2000 and 2003).

Generally environmental policies related to waste management sector are aimed at reducing waste and to promote safe disposal through recycling and reuse (Turner, 2000). While advanced economies follow a mix of regulatory and economic instruments, less developed economies have been following mostly command and control approaches for achieving waste management goals. This chapter examines various environmental policy instruments for solid waste management in a global perspective, followed by an examination of the existing policy for solid waste management in India. The authors have recommended a waste management strategy, grounded on the use of incentive-based economic instruments and proper institutional mechanisms.

Solid Waste Management: A Global Perspective

Command and Control Regulation Approach: The traditional approach to environmental protection has often relied on command and control (CAC) instruments. These regulatory instruments are institutional measures aimed at directly influencing the environmental performance of polluters/waste generators by the establishment of laws and regulations prescribing objectives, standards, technologies etc, which polluters/waste generators must comply with. There are specific legally established rules for management of municipal solid waste, bio-medical waste, hazardous and non-hazardous waste, regulations for recycling and packaging waste management etc. Sanctions or penalties are applied in the event of any non-compliance. Standards are in fact the most predominant means for direct regulation of environmental quality throughout much of the developed world (Markandya *et al.,* 2002). Some commonly employed standards include, ambient environment quality standards, technology-based standards, performance standards, product standards and process standards. In the waste management sector, standards have been established for waste collection method, collection frequency requirements, waste source segregation requirements, waste storage design standards, waste transportation requirements, water and ambient air quality standards at the landfill site, equipment design standards, waste processing technology standards, waste disposal standards, resource recovery by product quality standards etc (Cointreau and Hornig, 2003; MOEF 1998, 1999, 2000 and 2003).

One of the most frequently reported example of regulatory method related to management of packaging waste is Germany's recycling programme called '*Green Dot Programme*'. This particular recycling policy of 1991 was designed to enforce *"polluter pays"* principle, which in effect stipulates that industry has to be responsible for the collection and recycling of all its packaging waste. The thrust of this policy was to internalize disposal costs and create incentives for designing products for reuse, recycle and waste avoidance. The programme made progress through a system called '*Duals System Deutschland*' (DSD), which led to the collection of a huge amount of plastics. Germany however faced a plastic crisis in 1993, with more plastics collected than could be recycled (Rousso and Shah, 1994). The European Union Commission's Directive on packaging and packaging waste law passed in 1994 is considered as one of the most significant command and control methods to achieve packaging waste management goals by European Union Member States. The Directive has specified the environmental standards (targets) for recovery and recycling of packaging waste to be achieved by the Member States. The targets were specified to recover 50 per cent to 60 per cent of packaging waste and recycle 25 per cent to 45 per cent of packaging by 2001 and achieve a minimum recycling rate of 15 per cent. [3]

Though command and control approach gives the regulator maximum authority to tackle environmental problems, the regulator requires necessary information such as marginal abatement costs, production process etc. which may be difficult to get in the case of non-point source pollution. It has also been criticized for its ineffectiveness in addressing many solid waste management problems, especially with the overall enforcement, penalty system and cost inefficiency (Ilic, 2002; Markandaya *et al.*, 2002). Direct regulation also has limitations due to cost inefficiency, mostly for products that are hazardous and toxic (Mehta et al., 1997). Another major drawback of regulations is that it is static and lacks incentives. In the past few decades, the most recent observable trend in many countries, has been the use of economic instruments and incentives to minimize waste and to encourage reuse and recycle. The subsequent section examines in detail some important incentives/disincentive policy instruments that have been practiced by many countries in the world.

Economic Instruments in Practice: International Experience

Economic instrument approach tries to provide incentives to the consumers, producers and other economic agents to make environmental improvements or reduce adverse environmental consequences due to their activities. Too much waste generation results in environmental degradation if they are not managed properly. There are external costs in terms of loss of human well-being due to unsafe disposal of waste. In principle, economic instruments incorporate ***'polluter-pays principle'*** for environmental management (Turner, 2000). One of the main advantages of economic instruments in the case of solid waste management is that they provide a continuous incentive effect which motivates waste generators and/or waste service providers to find out the least-cost combination of disposal, recycling and re-use that is available to them. These instruments are meant to reduce waste generation; lessen the amount of generated waste that is hazardous; segregate hazardous waste for special handling and disposal; optimize recovery, reuse and recycling of waste; support cost-effective solid waste collection, treatment and disposal systems; minimize adverse environmental impacts related to solid waste collection, transport, treatment and disposal systems and generate revenue to cover costs of waste management (Cointreau and Hornig, 2003).

There has been a growing interest in European Union, OECD and Latin American countries in the application of economic instruments in order to improve the efficiency of the waste management process. A review of available studies shows that various types of revenue generating, revenue providing, fiscal and financial incentive instruments have been implemented in many EU member countries, Central and Eastern European Countries (CEECs), OECD and Latin American countries (Table 15.1). The major economic instruments in use are landfill tax, waste generation charge, waste user charges, waste treatment or disposal tax, waste tipping charges, deposit-refund system, product charges, recycling credits etc. There are also other types of instruments, which have been in practice and include eco-labelling, voluntary agreements, extended producer responsibility etc. It can be seen from Table 15.1 that many countries have applied a mix of economic instruments to achieve their waste management goals.

Charges and Fee System

In most of the countries a fee is charged for providing waste management services either by local government or by private agencies in charge of service delivery. Charges and fee system is a revenue generating instrument aiming at waste reduction by

Table 15.1: Application of Economic Instruments: International Experience

Categories of economic instruments applied to solid waste sector	Countries where use of the economic instruments have been reported
A. Charges and Fees	
Waste Generation Charges (variable rate user charge based on volume of waste generated)	Barbados, Bolivia, Brazil, Chile, Columbia, Ecuador, Jamaica, Mexico, Trinidad and Tobago, Venezuela, Japan, British Columbia, Slovak Republic, United States, The Netherlands, China, Indonesia, Malaysia, Singapore, Thailand.
Waste User Charges (Flat rate charge system)	Belgium, Bosnia, Bulgaria, Herzegovina, Croatia, Czech Republic, Estonia, Hungary, Latvia, Romania, Slovenia, Yugoslavia, Ecuador, Korea, Singapore, Indonesia, Ghana, USA, Canada, Taiwan, Lithuania, Poland, Slovak Republic, Jamaica, Bolivia, New Zealand, Vietnam, Portugal, Ireland, Israel, Japan, Greece, Colombia, Venezuela, Thailand, Canada, Switzerland, The Netherlands, Serbia
Waste Tipping Charges	Czech Republic, Estonia, Hungary, Latvia, Romania, Ecuador, USA, Canada, Slovak Republic, Poland, New Zealand, Barbados, Venezuela, Chile, Australia, Guam, Japan, Greece, France, UK, Turkey, Austria, Italy, Pennsylvannia, Japan, Greece, Colombia, Venezuela, Thailand, Canada, Switzerland, The Netherlands

Contd...

Product Charges	Hungary, Latvia, Korea, USA, Bulgaria, Lithuania, Slovak Republic, Jamaica, Japan, China, OECD, Thailand, Denmark, Bangladesh etc.
Fee reduction for recycling	Argentina
B. Taxes	
Waste Treatment or Disposable Tax	Austria, Denmark, Norway, UK, Italy, Finland
Landfill Tax	Italy, Netherlands, Sweden, UK, Turkey, Latvia, Slovak Republic, France, Scotland, Ghana, Barbados, USA
Taxes to encourage reuse or recycling of problem materials	British Columbia, Norway, Finland
C. Deposit-Refund System	Austria, Denmark, Finland, Netherlands, Sweden, Australia, Canada, Germany, Norway, Portugal, Greece, USA, Serbia, Barbados, Bolivia, Brazil, Chile, Colombia, Ecuador, Jamaica, Mexico, Peru, Trinidad and Tobago, Venezuela, Croatia, Sweden, Denmark, Austria, Netherlands, Switzerland, Ireland, France, Portugal, Spain etc.
D. Product Take-back system	Norway, Germany, British Colombia
E. Fiscal Incentives	Barbados, Brazil, Colombia, Ecuador, Mexico, India, USA, Denmark, Ivory Coast, Ghana, Indonesia
F. Environmental Labelling	OECD countries, India

Source: <www1.oecd.org/scripts/env/ecoInst/index.htm>, [Callen and Thomas (2000), Cointreau and Hornig (2003); Ilic Marina (2002), World Bank (1999) Markandya et al (2002), Speck and Markovic (2001)].

charging a fee either based on a flat rate or unit rate pricing. Waste user charge based on flat rate pricing is a fee charged for delivery of waste service, specifically for collection services, but often designed to cover all service costs, usually based on the ability to pay, size of the property, and level of commercial activity at the property. It is collected alone or tied to water, electricity bills or property tax. Many Central and Eastern European Countries follow user charges for municipal solid waste management (Speck and Markovic, 2001). Bulgaria, for instance, has a user charge system based on value of property instead of amount of waste generated. Many of the Asian countries also follow a flat fee system to cover their cost of waste management (Table 15.2).

Table 15.2: Solid Waste Management Fee System Practised in Various Cities in Asia

City	Household and Commercial Fees
Hanoi	US$ 0.55/person/year
Dhaka	Less than US$ 0.63/person/year. Residents pay a Conservancy Tax for solid waste management
Vientiane	US$ 12-216/Household/year
Chennai	Residents and businesses do not pay any direct waste fees, but pay only property tax. Some households pay NGOs about Rs. 15-20 per month for primary collection service.
Delhi	Proposed system where homeowner has to pay a fixed amount of Rs. 15 to 20 per month for primary collection service.
Beijing	US$ 3-7.20 per household/year
Jakarta	US$ 1.80 to 9.60 per household/year
Denpasar	US$ 6 per household/year
Shanghai	Residents do not pay any direct waste fees
Hong Kong	Private and commercial establishments do not pay any direct waste fees

Source: Adapted from World Bank (1999).

In a flat rate charging system, fee is the same for households regardless of the quantity of waste generated by them. On the other hand, a charge based on unit pricing scheme is calculated based on volume (or weight) of waste generated by the households or commercial establishments. In flat rate system waste generator is charged nothing for additional waste generated, which means that the price does not reflect marginal private cost of providing waste service and hence no incentive to reduce wastes (Callan and Thomas, 2000). While user charges based on flat rate rarely reflect the polluter pays principle, volume-based charges are based on polluter/waste generator-pays principle and gives clear market signal to the waste generators to reduce the waste. Empirical evidence shows that by charging households for the volume of waste they discard, instead of financing waste-management services through property taxes, communities can control the growth of the solid waste, reduce collection and disposal costs, extend the lifetimes of existing landfills, and encourage household recycling while generating the revenues (Jenkins, 1992). The empirical evidence from this study shows that the impact of a *pay-by-the-bag system* on waste reduction is quite significant. A community that replaced a property tax financing system with a $1.50-per-bag waste-collection fee could expect to cut waste by 0.42 pounds per capita per day, from an average of 2.36 pounds. This was about 18 per cent reduction in the volume of solid waste it had to landfill (Jenkins, 1992).

Household solid waste collection charges have been tried and found effective in many large and small communities around USA. Podolsky and Spiegel (1998), through a unique cross sectional data set for 149 municipalities from 5 New Jersey County, estimated the demand elasticity [4] for household municipal waste disposal. Their study shows that the *bag or tag unit pricing programmes*, combined with curb side recycling will improve social welfare and reduce municipal expenditure on waste disposal services. The study also showed that the demand elasticity of waste generation with respect to unit price was very high, almost equal to -0.39. [5] However, one major problem with price per bag system is the problem of illegal dumping (Fullerton and Kinnaman, 1996).

Waste tipping charge is levied as fee for the payment of unloading service, specifically for transfer, treatment, and/or landfill service. Tipping refers to the collection truck unloading at the service facility. Waste generators may pay for these charges in their waste user or waste generation charges. It was reported in the City of Guelph, Canada that waste generation rates were decreased once it increased its landfill tipping fees gradually from no charge in 1985 to Can $ 92 per ton in 1991 (World Bank, 1999). However, Seroa da Motta *et al.* (1999) have reported that landfill charges were found to face implementation barriers in Bolivia and Venezuela, with a lack of institutional capacity for the measurement of waste. Hence the most fundamental requirement for effective implementation of any economic instruments is an integrated regulatory and supporting institutional framework (Seroa da Motta and Sayago, 2001).

Pearce and Turner (1994) have also emphasized that the economic efficiency and environmental effectiveness of any economic instruments is conditioned by the baseline institutional context. They warn that in a poor institutional setting, there is a high probability that any new substantial charging system, for instance, will merely provide waste generators with an increased incentive for avoidance and stimulate more 'illegal' dumping of waste. Hence, creation of proper regulatory framework and supporting institutions are most important prerequisites before introducing any new economic instruments, especially in developing countries. It is recommended that economic instruments need to be imposed along with some other direct regulations, to deal with local specific problems (Markandaya *et al.*, 2002).

Product charges are special fees for handling products with difficult disposal requirements or adverse environmental impacts. Examples are charges on batteries, packaging, tyres, lubricant oils, scrapped cars, fee on imported aluminium cans etc. Generally the revenue generated through these product charges are used for financing collection, treatment, recovery and disposal of problem products such as batteries, tyres etc. Countries such as Hungary, Latvia, Bulgaria, Lithuania, Korea, Japan, China, Thailand and many OECD countries have introduced product charges for safe disposal of problem products.

Taxes

Waste treatment or disposal tax and landfill taxes are important among tax incentive/disincentive schemes. Waste disposal tax is a differentiated tax per ton of waste for final treatment and/or disposal, with lower taxes charged for more environmentally sound treatment or disposal methods. Many EU countries have introduced waste tax as part of their waste management strategy. Denmark, for instance, has introduced a waste tax of 43.9 Euro per tonne on incineration without energy recovery while a tax of 37.2 Euro per tonne has been imposed on incineration with energy recovery (Speck and Markovic, 2001). Other taxes implemented by many European countries are waste disposal levy, duty on carrier bags made of paper and plastics, duty on electric bulbs, NicCd batteries, tyres, surtax on alcoholic beverages, soft drinks surtax, consumption tax on lubricant oil etc.

A tax on business activities or waste weight/volume discharged that is directed towards safe disposal in a landfill site is called a landfill tax. It is aimed at reducing waste to be land filled and takes care of the external costs associated with landfill. Ideally, landfill levy or tax should be equal to the loss of social well-being associated with disposing of an extra tonne of waste in the landfill site. Implementation of landfill tax in Denmark (49.8 Euro per tonne), for instance, resulted in increase in share of reused and recycled waste from 21 per cent to 50 per cent during 1985-93 period (Speck and Markovic, 2001). A differentiated tax is also imposed on refillable versus non-refillable beverage containers to encourage reuse and recycling. Hence, for achieving an efficient outcome, it is important that any waste generation charge or taxes should reflect the external costs associated with waste disposal.

Deposit Refund and Product-Take-Back Systems

Deposit Refund System (DRS) has been practiced in many countries for safe disposal of solid waste. It can be defined as a refundable product charge. A deposit is imposed at the time of purchase of a product and allows the consumer for a refund of the charge at the end of the product cycle. The purpose of DRS is that the consumer must return the product or its container for waste recovery, recycling or safe disposal. Examples include deposit refund system for electric bulbs, beverages and PET (Polyethylene Terephthalate) bottles, lead and accumulators, Nickel-Cadmium batteries, car hulks, soft drink, beer, wine, spirit containers, glass, aluminium cans, pesticide or fertilizer containers etc. Many EU countries have successfully implemented the deposit-refund system as part of their waste management strategy.

In the OCED countries, successful deposit-refund schemes operate in Austria, Belgium, Denmark, Finland, France, Germany, the Netherlands, Norway, Sweden, Turkey and the United States. Studies from USA also show that deposit-refund system is more cost efficient compared to other economic instruments such as recycling subsidies as well as recycled content standards (Palmer and Walls, 1997; Palmer *et al.*, 1997). In many countries producers also take back many products after use for safe disposal. Some examples of the products are electronics, plastics, single-use camera, laser print cartridges, paints, solvents, beverage containers, pharmaceuticals, lubricants and pesticides.

Other Instruments

Apart from the economic instruments identified in the previous sections, there are many other incentives that have been in practice in many countries. The main types are environmental labelling system, fiscal incentives including credit subsidies, tax rebate for energy efficiencies (waste-to-energy systems), long term use of government lands to build solid waste treatment and disposal facilities etc., voluntary approaches and Extended Producer Responsibility (EPR). In the case of environmental or eco-labelling scheme, businesses voluntarily label their products to inform consumers and to promote products determined to be more environmentally friendly than other functionally and competitively similar products. The result is the development of products with lesser environmental impacts, and thus reduced waste, pollution, and waste quantities.

The concept of EPR on the other hand, implies that responsibilities, which were traditionally assigned to consumers and waste management authorities (mostly municipalities and municipal corporations), are to be shifted to the producer of the products. The EPR is defined as "an environmental protection strategy to reach an environmental objective of a decreased total environmental impact from a product, by making the manufacturer of the product responsible for the entire life-cycle of the product and especially for the take-back, recycling and final disposal of the product" (Lindhqvist, 2000). This principle is consistent with the polluter-pays principle and the main objective is to provide incentives for the development of less wasteful products. Japan, Korea and Taiwan have introduced EPR programmes for containers and packaging, among other items. Germany, Netherlands, Sweden, Denmark, Finland and many OECD countries have adopted EPR programmes for many packaging products for safe disposal. It is seen that for most of the countries the success rate has been very high.

Although economic instruments act as one of the most effective environmental policy tools for achieving waste management goals, introduction of any new economic instrument or combination of instruments should be carefully done, especially in the developing country context. Given the very different conditions prevailing in developing countries, the developed country experience in use of economic instruments is not readily transferable to countries like India. The selection of policy instruments should be carefully based on nature of solid waste problem, local conditions, willingness and ability to pay of the people, existing political and institutional context, regulatory framework etc.

Taking these various points under consideration, an overview of solid waste management in the country has been provided with in the section that follows. It includes a discussion on the present urbanization scenario, the waste generation, waste collection efficiency, ensuing costs of managing solid waste and policies available for municipal solid waste management in India.

Management of Municipal Solid Waste in India: An Overview

There has been a significant increase in MSW generation in India in the last few decades. In a report commissioned by the Supreme Court on solid wastes for Class I Cities, total waste generated in 1991 by 217 million people living in urban areas was estimated at 23.86 million tonne per year (Supreme Court, 1999). TERI (2001) has projected that solid waste generation by urban India in 2047 would approximately be 263 million tonne. [6] This enormous increase in solid waste generation is expected to have significant environmental and economic impacts in terms of the land required for waste disposal as well as on methane emissions.

Urban Growth and Solid Waste Problem

In any country, waste generation rates are affected by socioeconomic development, degree of industrialization, urbanization and climate etc. In developing countries like India, population growth is one of the major driving forces behind increase in waste generation. For instance, the solid waste generated by all 299 Class I cities in India (cities with 1 lakh population and above) was estimated at 48,134 tonne per day (CPCB, 2000a). On the other hand, waste generated by 345 Class II towns [7] was estimated at 3,401 tonne per day (CPCB, 2000b). Table 15.3 shows waste generation and generation rates in various cities in India.

It is believed that the management of urban solid wastes will be one of the major challenges faced by the municipal governments in the country given the financial and infrastructural constraints of its urban local bodies.

Table 15.3: Waste Generation Rates in Various Cities in India

State	City	Total waste generated (tonne/day)	Total population (In lakh)	Generation rate (kg/capita/day)
Andhra Pradesh	Hyderabad-Secunderabad	2200	42.31	0.520
Delhi	Delhi	5750	133.63	0.430
Gujarat	Ahmedabad	1272	28.54	0.446
Gujarat	Surat	1000	22.00	0.455
Karnataka	Bangalore	2500	57.00	0.439
Karnataka	Mysore	354	8.79	0.403
Kerala	Cochin	375	7.00	0.536
Madhya Pradesh	Bhopal	600	15.00	0.400
Maharashtra	Mumbai	7025	119.14	0.590
Maharashtra	Pune	1000	25.40	0.394
Maharashtra	Solapur	350	8.73	0.401
Orissa	Puri	35	1.10	0.317
Punjab	Ludhiana	862	19.14	0.450
Rajasthan	Kota	250	7.00	0.357
Tamil Nadu	Chennai	3700	42.16	0.878

Contd...

Tamil Nadu	Coimbatore	800	9.71	0.824
Tamil Nadu	Salem	400	6.95	0.576
Uttar Pradesh	Agra	650	12.71	0.511
Uttaranchal	Dehradun	200	4.47	0.447
West Bengal	Kolkata	2500	44.00	0.568

Source: NSWAI-ENVIS (2003).

Waste Collection Efficiency and Cost of Waste Management

MSW management in urban area is the responsibility of urban local bodies in India. The municipal solid waste is collected by the municipalities/corporations and transported to designated disposal sites (normally a low-lying area) for disposal. Crude open dumping grounds, in general, are the havens for waste disposal in most of the municipal areas. It is shown that the average waste collection efficiency in Indian cities is around 72 per cent. Almost 70 per cent of the Indian cities do not have adequate waste transportation facilities (UNEP, 2001). The Tenth Five Year Plan reports that the major reason for this poor solid waste management in Indian cities is due to organizational inefficiency and lack of financial discipline within municipalities (www.planningcommission.nic.in).

Management of solid waste by urban local bodies in India is faced with a number of challenges. Prime amongst them is the lack of sufficient resources and increase in demand for waste management service coverage due to urban population growth. Urban local bodies have to spend a major part of their expenditure for providing solid waste management service. It is estimated that solid waste management expenditure constitutes 20 to 50 per cent of municipal expenditure (FIRE, 2001). Urban local bodies spend approximately Rs. 700n - Rs. 2,500 per tonne solid waste for collection, transportation, treatment and disposal. Per capita cost per year ranges from Rs. 63 to Rs 531 (Table 15.4). Given the huge financial burden thus, the authors feel that the cost can be partly shifted to generators of waste by adopting some environmental policy tools such as economic and fiscal incentive instruments, producer responsibility initiatives etc.

Environmental Policies for Solid Waste Management in India

Like many developing countries, India follows a command and control (CAC) regulation approach as part of its solid waste management strategy. Generally standards and regulations are used as the most dominant means for direct regulation of environmental quality in India. National policies of solid waste management in India are dominated by standards and regulations (MOEF, 1998; MOEF, 1999 and MOEF, 2000). Most important notifications related to solid waste management issued by the Ministry of Environment and Forests are Bio-Medical Waste (Management and Handling) Rules, Municipal Solid Waste (Management and Handling) Rules and Recycled Plastic Manufacture and Usage Rules (MOEF, 1998; MOEF, 1999; MOEF, 2000 and MOEF, 2003). These rules have specified standards and criteria, which are to be followed by urban local bodies, hospitals and clinics, plastic industries and general public for achieving waste management goals.

Table 15.4: Cost of Solid Waste Management in Select Cities of India

Cities	Cost per tonne of MSW (Rs.)	Cost per capita per year (Rs.)
Hyderabad	954	181
Delhi	1543	242
Aurangabad	577	63
Kolhapur	1303	162
Pune	1068	153
Solapur	746	109
Mumbai	2566	531
Rishikesh	1078	140
Dehradun	891	145
Agra	713	133

Source: NSWAI-ENVIS (2003).

The objective of municipal solid waste management rule is to make every municipal authority responsible for the implementation of the provisions of the rules, and for any infrastructure development for collection, storage, segregation, transportation, processing and disposal of MSW generated in its territory. For environmentally sound management of municipal solid wastes, it needs to be managed and handled in accordance with the compliance criteria and procedure laid down in the rules.

State Pollution Control Boards (SPCBs) are mandated to monitor the compliance of the waste management standards regarding ground water, ambient air, leachate quality in the landfill site and the compost quality including incineration standards as specified under the rules. The Central Pollution Control Board [8] is mandated to co-ordinate with the SPCBs with particular reference to implementation and review of standards and guidelines and compilation of monitoring data. The Ministry of Environment and Forests has also set deadlines for cities to set up waste processing and disposal facilities and to identify landfill sites for future use.

It could be seen that there are only a limited number of economic instruments applied to deal with solid waste problem in India. The government of India has introduced an eco-labelling scheme known as 'Eco-mark' in 1991 for easy identification of environment-friendly products. This scheme helps consumers in prompting manufacturers to adopt clean and eco-friendly technologies and environmentally sound disposal of used products. It provides an incentive for manufacturers and importers to reduce adverse environmental impacts of their products. So far 16 consumer product categories have been awarded the 'Eco-mark' label in India. [9] Some urban local bodies collect flat rate waste user charges, which are usually tied up with property taxes, from the households and commercial establishments for their primary collection service (NIUA, 2002). But this pricing mechanism does not give any incentive for them to reduce waste generation. The key objective of such charge system has been to cover a part of cost of service delivery.

The Government of India's Policy Statement for Abatement of Pollution stated that 'while regulatory measures remain essential for the effectiveness of the policy, economic instruments will be investigated to encourage the shift from curative to preventive measures, internalize the cost of pollution and conserve resources' (GOI, 1992). It also suggested extending the scope of the charge system to solid waste management. The draft new National Environment Policy-2004 prepared by Ministry of Environment and Forests also recognizes the importance of incentive based instruments and states that: 'In future, a judicious mix of incentives based and flat based regulatory instruments would be considered for each specific regulatory situation'. [10]

Financial constraint poses one of the major challenges for the urban local bodies for efficient and safe disposal of municipal solid waste in India (Tewari, 2004). This necessitates the need for implementing some revenue generating instruments such as waste generation charges based on waste volume or weight. These charge system could be gradually experimented in select cities in India. Our country lacks proper waste management policies, which can suitably motivate producers and consumers to follow an integrated solid waste management process aimed at waste minimization, reuse and recycling. Economic instruments, which provide great incentive for taking up recycling activities, need to be actively implemented. The problem of plastic waste for instance, has been a major cause of concern in Indian cities. The share of plastics in waste composition stream has steadily increased in India - though not to the extent observed in most advanced economies (Bhide and Sundaresan, 1983 and EPTRI, 1995).

Plastics carry bags and PET bottles have become a major threat to environment due to their non-biodegradability. Recently Central government has taken plastic waste problem seriously through government rules and regulations; the most relevant being the Recycled Plastics Manufacture and Usage rules, 1999 (amended in 2003) (MOEF, 1999 and MOEF, 2003) for plastic waste management in the country. Standards and guidelines were given in the rules with regard to manufacture and usage of recycled plastics. As per this rule vendors are prohibited using carry bags and containers made of recycled plastics for storing, carrying, dispensing or packaging of foodstuffs. Manufactures of plastics are required to print on each packet of carry bags as to whether they are made of "recycled material" or of "virgin plastic". The minimum thickness of carry bags made of virgin plastics or recycled plastics should not be less than 20 microns. The rule provides the relevant guidelines and standards to be followed while manufacturing the recycled plastics. However, the real problem of reducing plastics waste generation has been neglected.

Hence urban local bodies have to spend a huge amount of money on waste collection and disposal. For an efficient management of plastic waste, some incentive/disincentive instruments such as a tax on plastics or a packaging charge that reflects disposal costs (including collection costs, transportation costs and external costs of waste disposal) associated with packaging waste could be implemented. This would give a market signal to reduce the generation of plastics and also generate revenue (to create an environment protection fund, for instance) for safe disposal of plastics and packaging waste. It is also important to develop required rules for introducing extended producer responsibility (EPR) in the plastic industry to reduce external costs of uncontrolled plastic waste.

Recommendations

Population growth and rapid pace of urbanization in India pose several environmental challenges for large cities. One of these challenges is improper solid waste management. It is evident from the paper that urban local bodies, which are responsible for sustainable and safe management of solid wastes in India face great challenges in fulfilling their responsibilities, either due to paucity of funds or due to infrastructural constraints. Ever-increasing amounts of waste generated, increased demand for service coverage and the scarcity of budgets for waste management impose crucial limitations on their activity. While the cost of effective waste management is quite high, urban local bodies lack adequate financial resources to take proper measures for safe disposal of municipal solid wastes. Hence it is highly important to establish proper financing mechanisms for waste management services including appropriate modes of revenue generation through service charges.

As has been discussed in the paper, economic instruments such as waste generation charges, waste taxes, deposit-refund system, product charges, and fiscal incentives have been applied successfully in many European Union, OECD and Latin American countries as part of their waste management strategy. It is also seen that command and control regulations and standards to be followed by waste service providers and waste generators dominate solid waste management policies in India. It has been realized that these policies and legislations are mostly aimed at taking measures in managing waste generated but not to reduce waste generation.

The study confirms that economic incentive instruments play an important role in outlining the strategy for efficient waste management programme. The authors feel that, it is significant to apply the "polluter pays principle/waste generator pays principle", where appropriate, by setting waste management charges at rates that reflect the costs of providing the services and ensure that those who generate the wastes pay the full cost of waste disposal. In a developing country context, however, the taxes or charges applied to waste management sector should be substantially less so that people will not have an incentive to illegally dump the waste or throwaway, creating negative external costs on the society. Also various incentives such as waste generation charge, waste user charges etc, which generates revenue for service providers should be given preference in India. Proper regulatory and institutional support is however a prime prerequisite before any new economic instruments is introduced.

Additionally, the economic instruments such as charges or taxes should be implemented by conducting proper cost-benefit studies. One important point worth mentioning is that there is a great need for estimation of full external costs of waste disposal (loss of human well-being from health risk, for instance). The public needs to be properly informed about the external costs and benefits of waste disposal and waste reduction programmes.

Creating markets for recyclable and reusable waste material such as plastics, bottles, metals etc is also significantly important for safe disposal of these non-biodegradable wastes. Hence, policy instruments such as deposit-refund system or product take back system need to be promoted by providing the business establishments with adequate financial and fiscal incentives. Though these systems have been practiced for selected products in India, the wide range of product coverage needs to be encouraged. Similarly, a policy of extended producer responsibility has to be promoted especially to deal with packaging and plastics waste management in India. The growth of the Indian plastics industry has been phenomenal during the last few decades. Packaging is the major application of plastics accounting for more than fifty per cent of plastic consumption. The implementation of extended producer responsibility in the growing plastics industry is hoped to shift part of the physical and/or financial responsibility of waste disposal from urban local bodies to the producers of plastics.

The authors strongly feel that a policy is effective in achieving sustainability goals only when it fulfils some basic principles. Following the study done by Cointreau and Hornig (2003), Turner (2000) and Markandaya *et al.* (2002), it is highly recommended to seriously consider the following essential criteria while implementing any new economic instrument or combination of instruments for solid waste management in India.

1. Environmental Effectiveness Principle: The instrument should provide incentive for the desired environmental improvements, such as reduction in waste generation, increased recycling, reduced pollution from waste disposal.

2. Economic Effectiveness Principle: The instrument should create incentives for investment and innovation toward reduction of waste management costs.

3. Administrative Cost Effectiveness Principle: The instrument should involve low administrative and compliance costs.

4. Revenue-raising Principle: The instrument should be able to raise appropriate amounts of finance for given expenditure on waste management.

5. Implementation Principle: The instruments should

possess advantage in terms of implement ability. The administrative and legal requirements, for instance, for introducing a new instrument should be reasonable.

6. Fairness Principle: The instrument should not be significantly regressive, that is, should not impose a disproportionate cost burden on the least well off in society, particularly on lower income households, small businesses, and disadvantaged parties and

7. Acceptance Principle: The instrument should be acceptable to general public and concerned parties as a viable means of cost-effectively achieving environmental improvement without affecting competitiveness, employment, income distribution etc.

Finally, it is also important to realize that waste management is not the sole responsibility of the urban local bodies or Pollution Control Boards. Sustainable waste management with long-term objective of integrated waste management needs the involvement of all the stakeholders viz., NGOs, Community Based Organizations, private sectors, industry associations and the general public. It is expected that given the present ineffective state and high costs of waste management in the country, the various economic instruments as detailed in this study be given due consideration. More such studies are in fact needed for assessing the feasibility and viability of these economic instruments. To sum up, it is advisable that along with the existing command and control approaches and regulatory measures, the policy makers make an attempt to internalize the various economic instruments such that efficient waste management is finally achieved at an optimum cost.

Notes

1. In 1994 the city of Surat witnessed the worst case of epidemic plague. One of the primary reasons for the epidemic was the accumulated filth and garbage, which acted as a breeding ground for rodents.

2. Cities with 1 lakh population and above. There are 391 Class I cities in India as per the 2001 Census of India.

3. Source: http://www.europa.eu.int/scadplus/leg/en/lvb/121207.htm

4. The demand elasticity is measured as a change in the waste per capita of household municipal waste disposal expressed in tonne with a change in the unit price.

5. The negative relationship implies that an increase in the price per ton of municipal waste disposal results in an annual decline in the waste disposal per capita.

6. This estimate is based on 1.33 per cent per capita increase in waste generation per annum.

7. Population with 50,000 and below 1 lakh. There are 401 Class II Cities in India as per Census of India 2001.

8. Central Pollution Control Board along with its counterpart - State Pollution Control Boards, is responsible for implementation of legislations relating to prevention and control of environmental pollution in India.

9. The product categories are Soaps & Detergents, Paper, Food items, Lubricating oils, Packaging materials, Architectural paints and power coatings, Batteries, Electrical/electronic goods, Food additives, Wood substitutes, Cosmetics, Aerosol propellants, Plastic products, Textiles, Fire-extinguisher and Leather.

10. MoEF (2004) http://www.envfor.nic.in/nep/nep.pdf

References

Bhide, A. D and Sundaresan, B. B. (1983), '*Solid Waste Management in Developing Countries*', Indian National Scientific Documentation Centre, New Delhi.

Callan, S. J. and J. M. Thomas (2000), 'Managing Municipal Solid Waste', in *Environmental Economics and Management: Theory, Policy, and Application, The* Dryden Press, USA, pp. 559-90.

Cointreau, S and C. Hornig (2003), 'Global Review of Economic Instruments for Solid Waste Management in Latin America', Inter-American Development Bank, USA.

CPCB (2000a), '*Status of Municipal Solid Waste Generation, Collection, Treatments and Disposal in Class I Cities*', Central Pollution Control Board, New Delhi.

CPCB (2000b), '*Status of Municipal Solid Waste Generation, Collection, Treatments and Disposal in Class II Cities*', Central Pollution Control Board, New Delhi.

'Eco-mark Scheme of India A Scheme on Labeling of Environment-friendly products', courtesy: http://www.envfor.nic.in /cpcb/ cpcb.

html.

Environment Protection, Training, and Research Institute (1995), '*Status of Solid Waste Disposal in Metropilis Hyderabad'*, EPTRI, Hyderabad.

EUROPA: Activities of European Union, *Summaries of legislation: Packaging and packaging waste.*

FIRE (2001), Indo-US Financial Institutions Reform and Expansion Project-FIRE (D) *Project Note* No.26.

Fullerton, D. and T.C. Kinnaman (1996), 'Household Response to Pricing Garbage by the Bag' In *The Economics of Residential Solid Waste Management,* (ed. Kinnaman, T. C., 2003), Ashgate, USA.

Government of India (1992), '*Policy Statement for Abatement of Pollution,* Ministry of Environment and Forests', Government of India, New Delhi.

Ilic, M. (2002), 'Designing Waste Management Strategic Policy Framework. Yugoslavia', Regional Environmental Centre for Central and Eastern Europe.

Jenkins, R. (1992), 'Pay-By-The Bag Household Collection Charges to Manage Municipal Solid Waste', In *The Economics of Residential Solid Waste Management* (ed. Kinnaman, T. C., 2003), Ashgate, USA.

Kinnaman, T. C. (ed.) (2003), '*The Economics of Residential Solid Waste Management',* Ashgate, USA.

Lindhqvist, T. (2000), 'Extended producer responsibility in cleaner production: policy principle to promote environmental improvements of product systems', IIIEE Dissertation 2000:2, Lund: International Institute of Industrial Environmental Economics, Lund University.

Markandya, A., P. Harou., L.G.Bellu and V. Cistulli (2002), *Environmental Economics for Sustainable Growth*, Edward Elgar, UK and USA.

Mehta, S, S. Mundle and U. Sankar (1997), *Controlling Pollution: Incentives and Regulations,* Sage Publications, New Delhi.

MoEF (1998), Bio-Medical *Waste (Management & Handling) Rules 1998*, Ministry of Environment and Forests, New Delhi.

MoEF (1999), *Recycled Plastics Manufacture and Usage Rules 1999*, Ministry of Environment and Forests, New Delhi.

MoEF (2000), *Municipal Solid Waste (Management & Handling) Rules 2000*, Ministry of Environment and Forests, New Delhi.

MoEF (2003), *Recycled Plastics Manufacture and Usage Rules (Amendment) 2003*, Ministry of Environment and Forests, New Delhi.

Ministry of Environment and Forests (2004), '*National Environment Policy-2004*' (Draft for comments) MOEF, Government of India, courtesy:
http://www.envfor.nic.in/nep/nep.pdf

NIUA (2002), 'Management Innovation for Municipal Resource Mobilisation in India', *Urban Finance*, Vol. 5 (2), National Institute of Urban Affairs, New Delhi.

NSWAI-ENVIS (2003), Newsletter on Urban Municipal Solid Waste Management, National Solid Waste Association of India, Mumbai, June.

OECD/EEA Database on Economic Instruments and Voluntary Approaches used in Environmental Policy and Natural Resource Management.

Palmer, K., H. Sigman and M. Walls (1997), 'The Cost of Reducing Municipal Solid Waste' in *The Economics of Residential Solid Waste Management* (ed. Kinnaman, T.C., 2003), Ashgate, USA.

Palmer, K. and M. Walls (1997), 'Optimal Policies for Solid Waste Disposal Taxes, Subsidies, and Standards' in *The Economics of Residential Solid Waste Management* (ed. Kinnaman, T.C., 2003), Ashgate, USA.

Pearce and Turner (1994), '*Economics and Solid Waste Management in the Developing World*', CSERGE Working Paper WM 94-05, Centre for Social and Economic Research on the Global Environment, UK.

Planning Commission,' *The Tenth Five Year Plan (2002-2007)*', Government of India, New Delhi.

Podolsky, M. J. and M. Spiegel (1998), 'Assessing Incentive Based Environmental Policies for Reducing Household Waste Disposal', in *The Economics of Residential Solid Waste Management* (ed. Kinnaman, T.C., 2003), Ashgate, USA.

Rousso, A.S and S.P. Shah (1994), 'Packaging Taxes and Recycling Incentives: The German Green Dot Program', in *The Economics of Residential Solid Waste Management* (ed. Kinnaman, T.C., 2003), Ashgate, USA.

Schubeler, P., K. Wehrle and J. Christen (1996), 'Conceptual Framework for Municipal Solid Waste Management in Low-Income Countries' Urban Management Programme Working Paper

No. 9, World Bank, Washington D C.

Seroa da Motta. R. and D .E. Sayago (2001), 'Economic instruments for waste management in Brazil', in *Environmental Economics and Policy Making in Developing Countries: Current Issues*, (ed. Seroa da Motta. R., 2001), Edward Elgar, UK.

Seroa da Motta. R., R. Huber and H.J. Ruitenbeek (1999) 'Market based instruments for environmental policymaking in Latin America and the Caribbean: lessons from eleven countries', *Environment and Development Economics*, 4 (part 2), pp. 177-202.

Speck, S and M. Markovic (2001), '*Waste Management Policies in Central and Eastern European Countries: Current Policies and Trends*', Final Report, October 2001. Centre for Central and Eastern Europe, Hungary.

Supreme Court of India (1999), '*Solid Waste Management in Class I Cities in India*', Report of the committee constituted by the Hon. Supreme Court of India, New Delhi.

TERI (2001), '*Directions, Innovations, and Strategies for Harnessing Action for Sustainable Development*', The Energy Research Institute, New Delhi.

Tewari, V. (2004), '*Municipal Reforms for Sustainable Urban Infrastructure Development in India*' paper presented at the United Nations Asia Pacific Leadership Forum, Hong Kong, 25-27 February. Turner, R. K. (2000), 'Waste Management' in Folmer H and H. Landis Gobel (eds) *Principles of Environmental and Resource Economics,* Edward Elgar, UK.

UNEP (2001), '*India: State of the Environment 2001*' United Nations Environment Programme, Regional Resource Centre for Asia and the Pacific, Thailand.

World Bank (1999), 'What a Waste: Solid Waste Management in Asia', Urban Development Sector Unit, East Asia and Pacific Region, Washington D C: World Bank.

16

Economic Development and Environmental Degradation in India

Trupti Mishra and Bani Chatterjee

Introduction

There is long standing debate on the relationship between economic development and environmental quality. From a sustainable development viewpoint there has been a growing concern that the economic expansion of the world economy will cause irreparable damage to our planet. That concern stems from two rather intuitive concepts (Grossman, 1995): first, more output requires more inputs resulting in the fact that the earth's natural resources will be quickly depleted; second, more output causes more emission and waste and thus the earth could soon exceed the carrying capacity of the biosphere.

The income-environment relationship specified and tested in literature is a reduced form function that aims to capture the net effect of income on the environment. Islam et al (1999) identified three distinct structural forces that portray income-environment relationship. They are:

- Scale of economic activity
- The composition or structure of economic activity
- The effect of income on the demand and supply of pollution abatement efforts

The activities are known as the scale or level effect, the structure or composition effect and the pure income or abatement effect. The scale effect on pollution, controlling for the other two effects, is expected to be a monotonically increasing function of income since the larger the scale of economic activity per unit area the higher is the level of pollution, all else remaining equal.

The structural change that accompanies economic growth affects environmental quality by changing the composition of economic activity towards sectors of higher and lower pollution intensity. At lower level of income, there is a dominant shift from agriculture to industry with a consequent increase in pollution intensity. At higher incomes, the dominant shift is from industry to service with a consequent decrease in pollution intensity. Hence, the changing share of industry in GDP may represent structural change. The composition is then likely to be a non-monotonic (inverted U) function of GDP, i.e. as the share of industry first rises and then falls with income growth, controlling for other influences is transmitted through income.

Stripped of its scale and composition effects, the income variable represents pure income effects on the demand and supply of environmental quality. On the demand side, at low incomes, increase in income is directed towards food and shelter, and has little effect on the demand for environmental quality, while in a higher income level; increase in income leads to higher demand for environmental quality. On the supply side, higher income makes available the resources needed for increased private and public expenditure on pollution abatement, and induces stricter environmental regulations that internalize pollution externalities. The income variable (stripped of its scale and composition effects) captures the locus of equilibrium abatement levels, where demand and supply, both income-independent, are equal. Hence, abatement effect is expected to be a monotonically decreasing function of income.

Survey of Selected Literature

In early stage of debate, the prevailing view was that economic growth was a threat to the environment. The world will not be able to sustain economic growth indefinitely without running into resource constraint or despoiling the environment beyond repair. The implication was that there is no room for endless economic development; rather we should start thinking in terms of zero growth situations. This was the view primarily of a number of social and physical scientists such as Ehrlich and Holdren (1973) and Meadows and Randers (1992).

At the other end, there was another view that the fastest road to environmental improvement is along the path of economic growth; higher income increases the demand for less material-intensive goods and services and at the same time it brings about an increased demand for environmental protection. Beckerman (1992) strengthens this view by asserting that the strong correlation between incomes and the extent to which environmental protection measures are adopted indicates that in the long run the surest way to improve your environment is to become rich. Furthermore, he argues that there is evidence that although economic growth usually leads to environmental degradation in the early stages of the process, at the end the best - and probably the only- way to attain decent environment in most countries is to become rich.

However, the above debate lacked empirical evidence and remained on a purely theoretical basis for a long time. The main reason may be the unavailability of environmental data for many years. However, the difficulty was also of defining how to measure environmental quality although several indicators of environmental degradation were used to measure the impact of economic growth on the environment. Obviously, the problem is that the use of various indicators leads to the possibility of ambiguous answers as to the impact of growth on environment (Shafik, 1994)

Subsequently, Grossman and Krueger (1991, 1995), Shafik and Bondopadhyaya (1992), Panayotou (1993, 1995), Shafik (1994), Selden and Song (1994) hypothesized that the relationship between economic growth and environmental quality, whether positive or negative, is not fixed along a country's development path, rather it can switch from positive to negative as country reaches a level of income at which people demand and afford more efficient infrastructure and a cleaner environment. The implied inverted-U relationship between environmental degradation and economic growth came to be known as the

"Environmental Kuznet Curve (EKC)".

The basic reason for popularity of EKC hypothesis can also be attributed to the empirical findings on environment-development relationship. The first empirical study in this direction was by Grossman and Kruger (1991). The study estimated EKC for different air pollutants using the panel data of Global Environment Monitoring System. Shafik and Bondopadhyay (1992) fitted EKC to ten different indicators. These two studies used the ambient concentration data, whereas in all subsequent studies, pollution emission data have been used. Panayotou (1993, 1995) estimated EKC between per capita GDP and per capita emission of SO_2, NOx and SPM as well as deforestation. Seldon and Song (1994) considered airborne emissions of SO_2, NOx, SPM and CO using longitudinal data from the world resource institute. From the literature survey of this aspect, it is observed that most of the EKC studies focus on the following two pertinent research questions:

1. Is there an inverted relationship between income and environment degradation?
2. If so, at what income level does environmental degradation start declining?

There are ambiguous answers to both the queries as in the absence of a single environmental indicator, the estimated shape of the environment-income relationship and its possible turning point generally depend on the pollutant considered. However, as an alternative, it is possible to distinguish three main categories of environmental indicators that have been used in literature: air quality, water quality and other environment quality indicators.

In case of air quality indicators, in most of the cases, it shows an inverted U relationship with income. However, earlier studies find that global air pollutants either monotonically increase with income or start declining at income levels well beyond observed range (Grossman, 1995 and Barbier, 1997). For water quality indicators, the empirical evidence on EKC is rather mixed. However, when a bell-shaped curve does exist, the turning point for water pollutants is generally higher than air pollutants (Shafik,

1994). Several authors (Shafik, 1994; Grossman and Kruger, 1995) find evidence of an N-shaped curve for some indicators, as income grows water pollution first increases, then decreases and finally rises again.

Thus, the inverted-U curve might correspond just to the first two portions of this more complex pattern. The existence of N-shaped curve seems to imply that at very high-income levels, the scale of the economic activity becomes so large that its negative impact on the environment cannot be counterbalanced by the positive impact of environment-friendly technological change and a shift towards greener economic activities such as services. Finally, in the absence of single definite measure of environmental quality, many other environmental indicators have been put to test the EKC hypothesis. In general, for most of these indicators, there seems to be little or no evidence of an inverted U-pattern.

Overall, most of the studies discussed above have a number of common features as follows:

1. The typical relationship considered relates per capita emissions or concentrations pollutants to per capita income
2. The analysis is usually conducted on a panel data set of different countries around the world.
3. The considered functional relationship is either linear or log-linear, with a number of studies considering both.
4. Due to the almost complete coverage of world countries, the estimation technique is typically the least square dummy variable method, allowing for both fixed country and time effects.

Need and Objectives of the Study

As discussed earlier, the EKC is a hypothesized relationship between various indicators of environmental degradation and income per capita. In the early stages of economic growth, degradation and pollution increase, but beyond certain level of income per capita, which will vary for different indicators, the trend gets reversed so that at high-income levels, economic growth leads to environmental improvement.

The environmental problems in India are changing with its stages of development, structures of economy, production techniques and environmental policies. Some environmental problems may be associated with the lack of economic development like inadequate sanitation and access to safe drinking water, whereas others are heightened by the growth of economic activity such as different types of pollution. On the other hand, the steady growth of human as well as livestock population, the widespread incidence of poverty, and the current phase of economic and trade liberalization are exerting heavy pressure on India's limited resources for competing uses like forestry, agriculture, pastures, human settlement and industries.

In this backdrop, the present chapter attempts to examine the relationship between economic development and environmental degradation based on environmental kuznet hypothesis for Indian economy. Accordingly, the paper is organized as follows: Section I briefly analyses the theoretical framework of the linkage between economic growth and environmental quality. Section II gives some selective literature on this linkage, section III discusses the database and methodology for the study and section IV presents the results and discussion of the study.

Methodology and Database

Most of the studies have studied the income-environment relationship by specifying and estimating flexible functional forms with linear and log linear terms, which relate ambient emission or concentration level to income per capita and to other specific variables. In this study we have used cubic functional form to estimate the relationship.

$$LED_{it} = \alpha_1 + \alpha_2 LY_{it} + \alpha_3 LY_{it}^2 + \alpha_4 LY_{it}^3 + \alpha_5 t + \varepsilon_{it}$$

where LED_{it}: Natural Logarithm of the measure of ambient emission level in the state in the year t, LY_{it}: Natural logarithm of State domestic Product (SDP) at constant price, ε_{it}: Error Term and α: Parameters to be estimated. Here we have taken the measure of ambient emission by considering three major water pollutants BOD, COD and TSS at both residential and industrial location and treated them as dependent variables of the study, whereas Per Capita State Domestic Product at constant price is treated as independent variable. Linear time trend is included to capture exogenous advances in technology and/or increases in environmental awareness.

Following the literature, two different versions of equation viz. fixed and random effects have been estimated. The fixed effect version treats differences in the intercepts as due to deterministic factors. The random effect version treats those differences as being due to stochastic factors. The Hausman test is used to determine the preferred version. "Unidirectional causality from the economy to environment" is assumed. Goldfeld-Quandt test has been used to check the Heteroscedasticity and partial correlation coefficients has been used to check the multicolinearity.

The study is based on secondary data. The major sources of data are Central Pollution Control Board, State Pollution Control Boards, and Indian Economic surveys of different years and Economic Survey of Different States. Basically, balanced panel data is used for the study. The sample size is 20 Indian states for the period 1995-2005.

Results and Discussion

The results for both the industrial and residential locations and also for both fixed effect and random effect are presented in Table 16.1 and Table 16.2.

In order to estimate, logarithmic form of all the variables have been taken. The value of R^2 for all the measures of environmental degradation reveals that the reduced form of model explains much of the variations in the measure of environmental degradation. The null hypothesis ($\alpha2= \alpha3= \alpha4= \alpha5=0$) is rejected at 5 per cent level of significance and also the overall significance is rejected through f-test.

The regression result of industrial location is presented in Table 16.1 for both fixed effect and random effect models. From

Table 16.1: Results of Reduced Form Model for Environmental Quality in Industrial Locations

	BOD		COD		TSS	
	FE	RE	FE	RE	FE	RE
Constant	81.92	103.21	-106.56	-109.28	-34.02	-19.36
LSDP	3.25 (1.069)	-34.86 (-0.654)	68.45 (2.539)	32.85 (1.833)	21.64 (1.774)	1.92 (0.973)
LSDP2	-0.28 (-1.03)	3.89 (0.666)	-6.98 (-2.47)	-3.91 (-1.79)	-2.54 (-2.688)	-0.39 (-1.012)
LSDP3	0.067 (1.028)	-0.1553 (-0.678)	0.027 (2.429)	0.141 (1.752)	0.086 (2.628)	0.0006 (1.816)
Trend	-0.11 (-4.86)	-0.001 (-0.013)	-0.1 (-2.32)	0.001 (0.439)	-0.082 (-2.34)	-0.001 (-0.81)
R2	0.69	0.71	0.72	0.68	0.78	0.71
Hausman's X2 Probability		24.72 (0.012)		34.21 (0.381)		40.86 (0.348)

Table 16.2: Results of Reduced Form Model for Environmental Quality in Residential Locations

	BOD		COD		TSS	
	FE	RE	FE	RE	FE	RE
Constant	142.87	158.42	101.85	108.63	118.36	138.62
LSDP	-24.52 (-0.58)	-53.75 (-1.113)	-42.85 (-1.11)	-34.57 (-0.94)	-36.25 (1.774)	-40.92 (-1.23)
LSDP2	3.21 (0.62)	5.92 (1.14)	4.62 (1.11)	3.95 (0.63)	4.02 (1.07)	4.21 (1.16)
LSDP3	-0.09 (-0.64)	-0.18 (-1.16)	-0.24 (-1.10)	-0.12 (-0.91)	-0.14 (-1.004)	-0.18 (-1.09)
Trend	-0.06 (-3.76)	-0.003 (-1.106)	0.005 (0.25)	-0.0006 (-0.37)	-0.029 (-1.62)	0.0006 (-0.28)
R2	0.72	0.68	0.71	0.69	0.76	0.71
Hausman's X2 Probability		16.89 (0.013)		3.98 (0.381)		4.23 (0.348)

the results of BOD, it is found that none of the coefficients is significant except time trend. The time trend is significantly different from zero implying that a reduced form model is inappropriate for BOD in industrial location. It implies that reduced form model cannot be used to establish the beneficial relationship between income growth and environmental degradation. However, for COD and TSS, all the coefficients are significantly different from zero which implies that cubic functional form rather than quadratic is appropriate. The estimated coefficients for both COD and TSS validate $\alpha 2 > 0$, $\alpha 3 < 0$ and $\alpha 4 = 0$. It indicates that an inverted U-shape curve exists for these two indicators in industrial locations.

The result of the reduced form model for all three environmental degradation indicators for residential data is presented in Table 16.2. Here also, the time trend coefficient of BOD is different from zero and is significant which entails time related exogenous shift in technology unrelated to income level or any other induced variable which might be responsible for deterioration in environment. The estimated coefficients for residential location validate $\alpha 2 < 0$, $\alpha 3 > 0$ and $\alpha 4 < 0$, which lead us to find an inverted N-shape between economic development and environmental quality for the study period. This suggests that environmental degradation will first decrease as income per capita rises, then increase and finally decrease with income per capita after the second turning point has been surpassed. However, since the value of estimated coefficients is not significantly different from zero, a definite curvature may not be found between income and environmental indicators of these pollutants.

Concluding Remarks

To sum up, it may be stated that the reduced form models for environmental water quality in both industrial and residential locations suggest a mixed evidence of the relationship between economic growth and environmental quality. Even if there is existence of beneficial relationship in some environmental quality, the values of the coefficients are not very much significant.

As a whole, the findings of the study give a modest evidence of favourable relationship between per capita income and selected measures of environmental degradation in selected states for the study period. And from this, it emerges that Indian economy does not have the luxury of being able to grow out of its environmental problems. Thus, if it wishes to prevent further environmental degradation, it would seem that concerted policies and incentives are required to reduce pollution intensity per unit of output across sectors, a shift in production pattern to less polluting sectors and to lower environmental damage associated with aggregate consumption plan. Finally, there should be implementation of some active environmental policies to mitigate emission and resource depletion in early stage of development, which will also support the inverted U shape relationship for important pollutants.

References

Barbier, E.B. (1997), "Introduction to Environmental Kuznet Curve Special Issue", *Environment and Development Economics*, Vol. 2, No. 4, pp. 369-382.

Beckerman, W. (1992), 'Economic Growth and the Environment: whose growth? Whose Environment?', *World Development*, 20, pp. 481-496.

Ehrlich, P. R. and J. P Holdren (1973), *Human Ecology: Problems and Solutions*, W. H. Freeman, San Francisco.

Grossman, G. and A. B. Kruger (1991), 'Environmental Impacts of a North American Free Trade Agreement', National Bureau of Economics Research, Working Paper No. 3914.

Grossman, G. (1995), 'Pollution and Growth', in I. Goldin and L.A Winters (eds.), *The Economics of Sustainable Development*, Paris: OECD, pp. 19-46.

Grossman, G. and A. B Kruger (1995), 'Economic Growth and Environment', *Quarterly Journal of Economics*, 112, pp. 353-377.

Islam, N., J. Vincent and T. Panayotou (1999)," Unveiling the Income-Environment Relationship: An Exploration into the Determinant of Environmental Quality", HIID Development Discussion Paper No.701.

Meadows, D. H., D. L Medaows, and J. Randers (1992), 'Beyond the Limits Global Collapse or a Sustainable Future', Earthscan, London.

Meadows, *et. al.* (1972), 'The Limits to Growth', Universe Books, New York.

Panayotou, T. (1995), 'Environmental Degradation at Different Stage of Economic Development', in I. Ahmed and J.A Doeleman (eds.), *Beyond Rio: The Environmental Crisis and Sustainable Livelihoods in Third World*, Macmillan, London.

Panayotou, T. (1993), 'Empirical Tests and Policy Analysis of Environmental Degradation at Different Stage of Economic Development', in *Technology, Environment, and Employment*, International Labour office, Geneva.

Selden, T. M and D. Song (1994), 'Environmental Quality and Development: Is There a Kuznet Curve for Air Pollution Emission', *Journal of Environmental Economics and Management,* 27, pp. 147-162.

Shafik, N. (1994), 'Economic Growth and Environmental Quality: An Econometric Analysis', *Oxford Economic Papers*, 46, pp. 757-773.

Shafik, N. and S. Bandyopadhyay (1992), 'Economic Growth and Environmental Quality', *Background Paper for the World Development Report*, Washington D. C., The World Bank.

Index

Index